THE NEW DEPORTATIONS DELIRIUM

CITIZENSHIP AND MIGRATION IN THE AMERICAS
General Editor: Ediberto Román

Tierra y Libertad: Land, Liberty, and Latino Housing
Steven W. Bender

No Undocumented Child Left Behind: Plyler v. Doe and the Education of Undocumented Schoolchildren
Michael A. Olivas

Marginal Workers: How Legal Fault Lines Divide Workers and Leave Them without Protection
Ruben J. Garcia

Run for the Border: Vice and Virtue in U.S.-Mexico Border Crossings
Steven W. Bender

Those Damned Immigrants: America's Hysteria over Undocumented Immigration
Ediberto Román

Strange Neighbors: The Role of States in Immigration Policy
Carissa Hessick and Gabriel G. Chin

Revoking Citizenship: Expatriation Policies in America from the Colonial Era to the War on Terror
Ben Herzog

Beyond Deportation: The Role of Prosecutorial Discretion in Immigration Cases
Shoba Sivaprasad Wadhia

The New Deportations Delirium: Interdisciplinary Responses
Daniel Kanstroom and M. Brinton Lykes

The New Deportations Delirium

Interdisciplinary Responses

Edited by Daniel Kanstroom and M. Brinton Lykes

NEW YORK UNIVERSITY PRESS
New York and London

NEW YORK UNIVERSITY PRESS
New York and London
www.nyupress.org

© 2015 by New York University
All rights reserved

References to Internet websites (URLs) were accurate at the time of writing. Neither the author nor New York University Press is responsible for URLs that may have expired or changed since the manuscript was prepared.

Library of Congress Cataloging-in-Publication Data
The new deportations delirium : interdisciplinary responses /
Edited by Daniel Kanstroom and M. Brinton Lykes.
pages cm. — (Citizenship and migration in the Americas)
Includes bibliographical references and index.
ISBN 978-1-4798-6867-4 (cl : alk. paper)
1. Deportation—United States. 2. Detention of persons—United States. 3. Illegal aliens—United States. 4. Emigration and immigration law—United States. I. Kanstroom, Dan, editor. II. Lykes, M. Brinton, 1949– editor.
KF4842. N49   2015
364.6'8—dc23   2015027831

New York University Press books are printed on acid-free paper, and their binding materials are chosen for strength and durability. We strive to use environmentally responsible suppliers and materials to the greatest extent possible in publishing our books.

Manufactured in the United States of America

10 9 8 7 6 5 4 3 2 1

Also available as an ebook

For my mother, who still lives in my memory and in my heart. And for Julie, Emily, Hannah, and Harper, who remind me every day how lucky I am.

—D.K.

For the migrants forced to "leave home" with whom I have been privileged to walk and talk as they struggle for a better life for themselves and their families both here and in their countries of origin. And for Cathy, whose life journey continues to challenge, inspire, and nurture me.

—M.B.L.

CONTENTS

Acknowledgments   ix

Foreword: Mayan Migrants Speak Out   xi
   Luis Argueta

Introduction: Migration, Detention, and Deportation: Dilemmas and Responses   1
   Daniel Kanstroom and M. Brinton Lykes

PART I: THE LEGAL, ADMINISTRATIVE, AND POLITICAL RESPONSES

1. Unhappy Families: The Failings of Immigration Law for Families That Are Not All Alike   33
   David B. Thronson

2. Improving Conditions of Confinement for Immigrant Detainees: Guideposts Toward a Civil System of Civil Detention   57
   Dora B. Schriro

3. You Be the Judge: Who Should Preside Over Immigration Cases, Where, and How?   89
   Denise Noonan Slavin and Dana Leigh Marks

4. Immigration Reform: Will New Political Calculations and New Actors Overcome Enforcement Inertia?   113
   Ali Noorani, Brittney Nystrom, and Maurice Belanger

PART II. INTERDISCIPLINARY RESEARCH, ADVOCACY, AND ACTIONS FOR AND WITH MIGRANTS AFFECTED BY DETENTION AND DEPORTATION

5. Legal and Social Work Responses to the Detained and Deported: Interdisciplinary Reflections and Actions   147
   Jessica Chicco and Elaine P. Congress

6. Immigrants Facing Detention and Deportation: Psychosocial and Mental Health Issues, Assessment, and Intervention for Individuals and Families 167
   Kalina M. Brabeck, Katherine Porterfield, and Maryanne Loughry

7. Participatory Action Research with Transnational and Mixed-Status Families: Understanding and Responding to Post–9/11 Threats in Guatemala and the United States 193
   M. Brinton Lykes, Erin Sibley, Kalina M. Brabeck, Cristina Hunter, and Yliana Johansen-Méndez

8. Unwelcome Returns: The Alienation of the New American Diaspora in Salvadoran Society 227
   Katie Dingeman-Cerda and Rubén G. Rumbaut

   About the Editors 251

   About the Contributors 253

   Index 259

ACKNOWLEDGMENTS

This book has been a labor of love that has required a lot of both. We have shared equally in the editorial task and in developing the interdisciplinary framework for this volume. A work of this breadth and scope—years in the making against an ever-shifting backdrop of political, legal, and cultural changes—also inevitably demands help from many sources. We have been extremely fortunate to have had such help from too many people to name, especially all those who attended the interdisciplinary conference at Boston College in 2010 that first spawned the idea for such a work. Still, we wish to thank a few stalwarts, even as we apologize to others for not naming them specifically. We hope that they know how much we have appreciated their help and support. For collegiality, logistical support, and various types of assistance and inspiration, we particularly wish to thank David Hollenbach, SJ, Donald Hafner, Anjani Datla, Timothy Karcz, Jessica Chicco, and Rachel Rosenbloom, as well as our Guatemala-based colleagues: Ana Maria Alvarez López, Ricardo Falla, SJ, José Daniel Chich González, Luisa Hernández Simaj, and Megan Thomas. We thank the Boston College graduate and undergraduate students who contributed to this volume in multiple ways, including especially Erzulie Coquillon, Kristin Gordon, Rachel Hershberg, and Jacqueline Sims. We also thank Deans George Brown, Vincent Rougeau, and Maureen Kenny for financial and other forms of support.

We are very grateful to Ediberto Román and Debbie Gershenowitz for early support, guidance, and ideas. We also very much appreciate the assistance of Clara Platter, our current editor at NYU Press, for staying with the project and seeing it through to completion with us. Our reviewers were particularly helpful and thorough in bringing various complexities to our attention. Their careful reading improved the book tremendously. Special thanks, too, to Constance Grady for helping with uncountable details.

Finally, we are deeply grateful to all of the contributors to this volume for their patience, thoughtfulness, enthusiasm, generosity of spirit, and willingness to take the leap into interdisciplinary collaboration. We hope they agree that their efforts have been synergistic and have improved our collective understanding of the nature of the deportation system. As the book goes to press we (along with millions of noncitizens) seek to decipher President Obama's executive action while the U.S. Congress remains unable—or unwilling—to compromise on long-overdue comprehensive immigration reform. We hope that this volume helps policymakers to envision more imaginative and more humane responses to the excesses and unnecessary cruelties that have been visited upon millions of people during what we believe history will view as a tragically flawed deportation experiment.

FOREWORD: MAYAN MIGRANTS SPEAK OUT

From abUSed: The Postville Raid *to Education and Advocacy: One Individual's Journey*

LUIS ARGUETA

When approximately 900 heavily armed agents of Immigration and Customs Enforcement (ICE) entered Agriprocessors, Inc., the largest kosher slaughterhouse and meatpacking plant in the country, on May 12, 2008, and arrested 389 undocumented workers, I was in a different place, in a different time. I was living in New York City directing four episodes for *We Are New York*, a TV series geared toward recently arrived immigrants in the city. I didn't pay much attention to the event then. However, about a month later, on July 11, I read Julia Preston's article on the front page of the *New York Times*, in which she discussed Erik Camayd-Freixas's essay about his work as an interpreter in the post-raid Postville context. Camayd-Freixas and 12 other interpreters were hired by the federal government to assist in the legal proceedings following the raid. After reading Preston's article, I went to the link and read Camayd-Freixas's personal account of his experiences interpreting after what he called "the largest ICE raid in US history" and I said: Everybody who believes in democracy, everybody in this country, should read this essay. I immediately contacted Camayd-Freixas and asked him about the rights to publish his essay in Spanish. I then contacted my friend and colleague, Raul Figueroa Sarti, founder and editor-in-chief of F&G Editores, and asked him: "If I get the rights to this essay will you publish it?" Both Camayd-Freixas and Figueroa Sarti agreed and that essay became book #8 in F&G's series, *Cuadernos del Presente Imperfecto* (Camayd-Frexias 2009).

My next move was to call Saint Bridget's Catholic Church, the site widely reported to have been the refuge to thousands of family members of the primarily Mexican and Guatemalan detainees from the raid. I asked them if they could help me set up some interviews with people in Postville affected by the raid. They also said yes.

On the morning of July 23, 2008, my friend and co-producer, Vivian Rivas, and I left for Postville. Our plan was to spend four days there, tape a few interviews with the immigrants who remained in town, return to New York, and edit these interviews into short segments for a web series titled *And there I am: Documenting Silent Voices* that I had begun a couple of years earlier. I undertook the web series project as a result of several visits I had made to the Guatemalan Mobile Consulate[1] during the time when Rosa Maria Mérida de Mora was Guatemala's General Consul in New York. I traveled with her to New Bedford in the wake of the March 6, 2007, ICE raid on the Bianco factory where mostly Guatemalan and Mayan undocumented workers were employed to make U.S. military uniforms. These people would tell me their stories on camera; I would then excerpt them and post them online. Another time I interviewed a gentleman at the Guatemalan consulate in New York City who had been brought there by ICE to secure a one-way travel document so he could be deported. Today, the process is done by videoconference. I posted his interview under the title *Deportee* (http://www.youtube.com/watch?v=ovQ22X8sJGc).[2] He was the first future deportee that I met. I was developing an interest in the subject; but I was very ignorant of immigration policies and enforcement practices.

My real immigration education began the day I arrived in Postville. My initial interviews included women whose husbands had been sent to jail while they had been sent home with ankle bracelets to wait for a court order that took months to arrive; children whose mothers were detained and who—afraid that ICE would also detain and deport their children—denied being mothers, and local members of the Postville community who had formed a first response team to support those detained and the families left behind. Those were my first immigration enforcement lessons.

My first visit to Postville included the weekend of July 26 and 27, 2008. On Saturday, Congressman Luis V. Gutiérrez (U-IL) led a Congressional Hispanic Caucus (CHC) delegation which included Chairman Joe Baca (D-CA) and Congressman Albio Sires (D-NJ) in a visit to Postville to meet with those most affected by the raid of May 12. On the following

Figure 1. Fermin Loyes was sent to prison for five months and then deported to Guatemala. Photo by Luis Argueta.

Figure 2. Ilvana Loyes Zamora (three years old), Rosa Zamora de Loyes, and Merlin Loyes Zamora (eight years old). Rosa Zamora—Fermin's wife—was sent home with an electronic ankle bracelet to care for her two underage daughters. Ilvana is a U.S. citizen while Merlin is a Guatemalan citizen. Photo by Ezequiel Sarudiansky.

Figure 3. Pedro Arturo Lopez Vega (12 years old). Pedro Arturo's mother, Consuelo, was arrested and—afraid that ICE would take her children to jail and deport them with her—said she was alone, without any family. Photo by Ezequiel Sarudiansky.

day, Sunday, July 27, activists from across the country gathered in Postville for an interfaith service, march, and rally calling for comprehensive immigration reform, family unification, and just labor practices.

I met local residents and people from Des Moines, Minneapolis, Chicago, Madison, and even Boston; nuns, parish priests, Lutheran and protestant ministers, Jewish rabbis, labor organizers, and lay people. This display of solidarity and the stories that I had been hearing, both in Spanish and in English, energized me and made me decide to stay for an extra week.

By the end of my first trip to Postville, I realized how this complex story was a paradigm of twenty-first-century U.S. immigration. After that week I returned again, and again, and again. It took 29 trips to Postville to gather the material that later would be edited to become my documentary film, *abUSed: The Postville Raid*.[3] I realized that through the intersection of these immigrant stories, the stories of the responses of U.S. businesses that employed and sometimes abused migrants, and the stories of people who accompanied and supported the immigrants—or those that protested their presence in the "heart of America"—I was learning—and could teach—about immigration. Through telling the story of Postville I could give the context of the political, historical, and social forces that brought Mexicans and Central Americans north. The interviews I was doing helped me to better understand that context, the raid itself, its aftermath, and the human and workers' rights issues involved. For me, Postville was a small laboratory, a crash course on immigration. By producing a film that recreated my findings, I hoped to provide a similar opportunity for a wider public.

I realized that to get a complete picture of the situation of the migrants in Postville, I needed more information about the families "left behind" in Guatemala. That is why I offered to accompany a group of five migrant families from Postville who had decided not to fight their case and requested "voluntary departure." Many migrants in Iowa asked me if I would take photos and letters to family members in Calderas, Guatemala. I recorded people reading the letters and looking at the photos and brought back video-letters to the families in Iowa. This small act of solidarity gave me more credibility with them and with their relatives in Guatemala. However, I realized that, while I was getting some information in these initial interviews in Guatemala, I was just scratching the surface. To obtain in-depth accounts that would lead me to understand why their husbands, brothers, sons, and daughters had headed north would require multiple conversations and deeper trust. Therefore, I

Figure 4. Postville Solidarity march on July 27, 2008. Photo by Vivian Rivas.

Figure 5. From left to right: Beatriz Gallardo, field producer in Guatemala, and Vicente Ordoñez, Rosa Zamora's brother-in-law (holding photos sent from Iowa). Photo by Luis Argueta.

went back to Guatemala a second, and a third, and a fourth time. I traveled to Guatemala 17 times before I completed the film. Because I was born there, and had lived there for the first 20 years of my life, and by now have lived in the United States for four decades, I was able to bridge the cultural and language barriers, that is, the Anglo-Guatemalan gap. There was a joke among many that I didn't speak Spanish, but Guatemalan! This made a big difference. (You know how *desconfiados* [distrustful] we Guatemalans are!).

Once I had the migrants' trust, I explained to them that I needed detailed information about their situations to better understand the implications of the raid in Postville and other U.S. policies and practices for their families and communities on both sides of the border. Through multiple interviews in Postville and Guatemala I sought to better understand why people risk their lives in the journey north, why they mortgage their homes and land, go into debt, and take out loans that have interest rates of 5–20 percent monthly. At the beginning, these decisions were beyond my capacity to grasp. Finally speaking with a woman who had experienced horrific abuse crossing the borders and the desert, I got the answer. I asked her why she had decided to take the risk, knowing the dangers she might encounter. She answered using an expression that I had heard 30 years earlier in the cotton fields of Guatemala from a man who had just finished a day's labor. I had asked him how much he made for a day's hard labor picking cotton. He responded: "Dos o tres chocas." (Two or three quarters.) "You're kidding me!" I said. "No, es verdad. Pero de algo a nada hay mucha diferencia." (No, it's true. But between nothing and a little bit there is a big difference), he said. The woman in Iowa answered me the same way: "Es que de algo a nada hay mucha diferencia." In Guatemala she was raising a family on approximately $150 a month that she earned working six days a week. "When I came to Postville, it only took me a day and a half to make the same amount of money," she said.

Some people told me they had to leave home because their kids needed medicine and they could not afford it. A woman from Mexico who had a couple of years of college education could not find a job where she earned enough to afford her son's asthma medicine. A woman from Guatemala, whose mother had Alzheimer's, worked as a supervisor at a plant packing flowers for export. However she did not earn enough to support her family and help her mother, despite the fact that her husband was also working. Their low wages and dire conditions made them risk it all and try to come to the United States. The lack of opportunity to get ahead in Mexico, Guatemala, and the other "sending countries" is immense. Deciding to head north in hope of a better life for themselves, their children, and their aging parents is often the last recourse for the poor.[4]

These stories have led me to conclude that it is not so much that we need to revise the American dream, but rather that we need to find ways of giving people greater opportunities in their countries of origin so they won't have to keep risking everything—including their lives—to get to the United States. The challenges facing unauthorized migrants in the United States begin long before they get here. In Guatemala I interviewed several of those who had been deported after the Postville raid. They described having gone through the process of applying for a visa to the United States. They had incurred the costs and gone through the multiple procedures involved only to be denied a visa because they didn't have a job that paid a living wage or the assets needed to convince the U.S. Consular officer that they would return to Guatemala. They lacked a bank account, a job offer in the United States, or other forms of collateral required by immigration authorities prior to the granting of a visa. It was a vicious circle. To get out of poverty you need a job and to get a job you need a visa. But you cannot get a visa if you are poor and in need of work.

One of the greatest challenges facing undocumented migrants in the United States is the lack of education about their labor rights. They need to know that as workers, independent of their immigration status, they have labor rights. They need programs that allow them to work in this country and they need to have their labor rights protected. However, temporary work programs are only a partial solution. Unless well supervised and administered, they can result in labor abuses and be a dead end road where workers have no protections and lack educational opportunities which can provide them with upward mobility and a sense of belonging to their community. I also think that the sending countries must do a better job of educating people about what it means to come to the United States without proper documentation.

The federal immigration policies and practices in the United States are complex. In the absence of comprehensive immigration reform, states and cities—although not unanimously—have initiated and passed legislation that makes a big difference in the lives of immigrants. While on the one hand, 13 states have passed legislation making it possible for all age-eligible immigrants who can pass state driving tests to obtain a driver's license; on the other hand, Arizona and Nevada deny driver's licenses to youth granted deferred action under the Deferred Action for Childhood Arrivals (DACA) program.

There are immigration "remedies" that are not well known and often confusing to understand. For example, the U visa, created as part of the Violence Against Women Act (VAWA), gives victims of some violent crimes temporary legal status and work eligibility for up to four years. But it is complex, and applies in only certain situations.[5] The technical and legal questions are difficult to grasp, even by a person with a master's degree. For immigrants who in the great majority have not finished the sixth grade, the task is daunting. In addition, immigrants who

Figure 6. From left to right: Thomas H. Miller, Iowa Deputy Attorney General; Agustín Obispo, Tom Miller, Iowa Attorney General, Jimmy Gomez, Luis Argueta, and Adam Burke. Agustín Obispo and Jimmy Gomez, underage workers at Agriprocessors at the time of the raid, were granted Community Benefit Parole by ICE, in the summer of 2010, in order for them to be material witnesses at the state trial for Child Labor violations against Agriprocessors's former general manager. As a result they were able to apply for a U visa. Agustín Obispo's U Visa was approved in July 2011. Jimmy was granted a U visa a year later. They and their families are currently working in Iowa. Photo by Robert Brammer.

are victims of violent crimes need to collaborate with law enforcement in order to apply for this relief. However, unauthorized immigrants are afraid to contact police for fear of deportation. Iowa Work Force Development had a hard time interviewing some of the minors working at the plant as part of an investigation into child labor violations; these youth responded by running out the back door when investigators would come in the front door.

When I learned that even immigration rights advocates and law enforcement agents are not always aware of how the U visa works, I decided to begin the production of another documentary, *The U-Turn*. This film features the U visa and focuses on the changes in the lives of women who overcame their fear and told their story about the violence they had experienced at the plant in Postville and the changes in the lives of the minors who were victims of child labor violations. The film recounts how they collaborated with authorities in the prosecution of the plant's general manager and some of the changes in the lives of the people who supported them in their quest for justice.

Enforcement-only immigration policies affect not only undocumented migrants but also U.S. citizens. U.S.-born citizen children who have been returned to Guatemala with their deported parents, whom I call *de facto deportees*, are now living in extreme poverty with limited access to education, without access to healthcare, and subsisting on very deficient diets. I have seen several of these children age over these past few years, but they are not growing. They are now about one-third the size that they would be had they remained in the United States. These kids are showing signs of stunting. Hearing their mothers report that they had to stop giving them milk because they had no money and that the children survive on a diet of diluted coffee, beans, and tortillas outraged me. It presents a moral and legal issue for all, Guatemalan and U.S. citizens alike. U.S. citizen children are growing up malnourished alongside Guatemalan children, many of whom are their siblings. One answer is a nutrition program for all children now living in those communities.

I had planned to do a follow-up documentary focusing on these children, to follow them over time, and, with academic support and collaboration, record and study some of the short-, medium-, and long-term consequences of having been deported from their country of birth alongside parents who had been criminalized by the U.S. government. Unfortunately, I was unable to secure funding for the project. However, I was able to find support to produce *ABRAZOS*, a film documenting the transformational journey of a group of U.S. citizen children from Minnesota who travel to Guatemala to visit their grandparents for the first time.

I call on educators and psychologists in the United States and in Guatemala to help me design a study guide to use this film (a) in conversations about child migration across borders in the context of rights, family, and identity; and (b) in providing a contextual, practical, on-the-ground example of the way a community can respond creatively—within the limits of existing law—to the challenges U.S. communities are facing around migration. Interdisciplinary work can strengthen what I can do as an artist and filmmaker by creating a forum through which to reach wider audiences and, over time, help shift U.S. policy toward these mixed-status, transnational families.

Raising awareness through collaborations with educators. Film creates immediacy, a vehicle for voices often silenced or not heard by the majority population and realities not seen. It is not the same thing to read a testimony by someone who works on human rights and deportation issues, as it is to hear the voices of those directly affected, to see their faces, even if it is only for a few minutes. In order to situate those voices within their wider historical and social contexts, I have benefited from the advice of many in the academic community. And now that the first film has been completed, by showing the film in academic circles, both at conferences as well as in classrooms at high schools and universities, I have been able to move people's hearts and minds. Students have said to me that they have begun to question some of the preconceived ideas they held about undocumented migrants. I've had conversations with university professors who have said that students have either written papers or made comments that seeing the film and discussing it has radically affected their outlooks.

A very productive collaboration with Professor Jennifer Cooley, and two Master's degree candidates, Ashley Bloch and Erin Hilmar, at the University of Northern Iowa, led to the production of a bilingual study guide that follows the 21-chapter structure of the new bilingual version of *abUSed: The Postville Raid*. Questions for each chapter are divided into three levels to accommodate students from elementary/middle schools, high schools, and universities. The questions are focused on four categories: background information, comprehension, discussion, and connection. They are designed to help students understand the context and what is reported in the film; to encourage them to share their opinions and ideas about what is presented in the film; and to help them relate their personal experiences to those of the people in the film. The study guide can be downloaded for free in the Educational Sources section at http://www.abusedthepostvilleraid.com/.

I think that there is still more to do in these collaborations between academics and artists. Multidisciplinary groups in the academy can contribute importantly to better understanding immigration today, as it is a multidisciplinary phenomenon. You cannot separate the historical and political forces from economic and social issues. Academics develop the "thick" descriptions and analyses of these realities, but I think film can synthesize these complex issues and present them in ways that a wider public can grasp quickly.

Using film to educate beyond the classroom. I have also done a lot of faith-based community organizing through church group presentations. Unitarians, Catholics, even Baptists, have showed the film. Some are more pro-immigration and some are less well informed or even unsure of the benefits that immigrants bring to the United States. The Baptists have just started putting immigration on their agenda.[6] I've shown them the film and most responded with disbelief, acknowledging that they had not known that the situation was as it was experienced in Postville. Through the presentation of the film they get a global view of the transnational and historical realities that lead many to migrate—as well as of some of the consequences for many who come to the United States without documents. Churchgoers and others who seek to support migrants are particularly touched by the section in the film that shows the priest talking about staying through the night with those who came to the church in Postville for solace and comfort. Faith-based groups can show the entire film or use selected scenes from the film, like the one described above, and adapt the questions in the guide to include scripture passages about immigrant stories.

Some screenings of the film in Iowa have included discussions with a small panel of immigration experts and migrants from Postville. In those cases, audiences have been deeply affected by seeing the ways ICE agents, and other enforcement agencies, acted in Postville, and by listening to live testimonies from migrants who were present on the day of the raid. For many people, to see migrants up close and realize that they are hard-working, family-oriented people, is eye-opening and can be immensely valuable in changing attitudes. Audiences that are less sympathetic, or even unsympathetic, to migrants, are still affected by the testimonies of the teacher/EMT volunteer, the attorney who refused to participate in the arraignments, and the federal judge who confesses to being "ashamed of being a federal judge that day."

Using the film to educate—on both sides of the border. In December 2012, *abUSed: The Postville Raid* had its national premiere on PBS as part of the World Channel's America Reframed Program. On May 12, 2013, the fifth anniversary of the raid in Postville, a second national broadcast took place and included IPTV, the Iowa Public TV station, which had not aired the film the first time.

The film can also be used in work with the undocumented migrants living in the United States, to educate them about their rights and possible paths toward legalization. Some migrant women had never heard of the U visa until they saw the film and learned the story of 22 women who obtained U visas because of violence they had experienced in their homes or in their workplaces and their collaboration with law enforcement. Undocumented minors learn about their rights when they watch the story of the underage workers who were given U visas because Agriprocessors, Inc. had violated their labor rights as minors. Distributing and discussing resources, such as the *Know Your Rights* pamphlets produced by Casa de Maryland, at film screenings can help those living "in the shadows" here in the United States gain access to more important information (CASA de Maryland 2008).

Spanish-language versions. I have now produced a subtitled version and a dubbed version of the film. The Spanish subtitled version premiered in Guatemala at the national theater, on May 11, 2011, the eve of the third anniversary of the Postville raid. The support of the Soros Foundation in Guatemala helped pay for a large advertising campaign, press coverage, and a full house of 2,000 people, plus a two-week run in five movie theaters in the capital and in Quetzaltenango and Escuintla, two other large cities in Guatemala. The DVD is available at several bookstores and from the most popular video distributor in Guatemala. Through these screenings more members of the Guatemalan community have taken notice of issues that previously they had ignored. These filmgoers don't typically get close to migrants. Many consider that migrants are heading north simply "para buscarle tres pies al gato" (to look for trouble) and that that is why they get arrested and deported. Through the film they come to realize that the reality of their own countrymen and women is that they are heading north in search of opportunities for a better life that they don't have at home. The film thus becomes a very good educational tool, exposing those with limited knowledge and/or many stereotypes to the lived experiences of many Guatemalans who migrate north.

Figures 7 and 8. May 11, 2011 Premiere in Guatemala at the National Theatre.

In order to reach audiences in the counties and cities that send so many of their population north, and where literacy is low, I produced a Spanish-dubbed version of the film. With the support of the municipal governments, we had a screening in the city of Patzún, department of Chimaltenango, and in Dueñas, department of Sacatepéquez. In both cases we had full houses and overwhelmingly positive reactions.

Some people in Guatemala would like the film to be a deterrent to immigration, while others see it as a tool to educate people about their rights and about possible resources or remedies for confronting their detention and/or deportation. I cannot control how different communities and constituencies will use the film. My main goal in making the film has always been to educate.

Those who seek to use it as a deterrent are perhaps naïve—or misled. You cannot think that by educating people about the risks of migration, you will deter them. You need to provide them with alternatives to migration. I have been trying to identify possible development models through which people can achieve lives of dignity and hope; models that have worked or are currently working in the kinds of communities from which many Guatemalans are migrating. To date I have found three examples: (1) San Lucas Tolimán mission, which has a coffee production cooperative, a women's center, a radio station program, and a clinic with a staff doctor, and a school (http://www.sanlucasmission.org); (2) CAFÉ R.E.D. in Quetzaltenango, "a *social entrepreneurship venture* seeking to address the difficulty of returned migrant reintegration; support the local economy by buying and marketing local furniture, food and fair trade crafts; provide a space for people to trade their experience with local economic experts; and work to build and strengthen a local sustainable economy" (http://desgua.org/initiatives/cafe-r-e-d/); and (3) GRUPO CAJOLÁ in Quetzaltenango where nearly 40% of the people from the town of Cajolá have migrated to the United States. Some have returned and "are working there to organize the community to develop opportunities for a better life so that no one has to leave his family and community behind in order to survive" (http://www.grupocajola.org/Home.html). Their ongoing projects include a preschool center, a weavers' cooperative, an egg farm cooperative, an Internet center, a library, and a carpentry center. Despite such efforts, in communities like these some people will continue to think about leaving. However, if they have a viable alternative at home, watching the film and seeing the suffering experienced by their fellow countrymen and women in the United States may lead them to think twice about their decision.

Concluding reflections. It is amazing to me that one *New York Times* article would lead me down a path that has been so life-changing. Creating the film about Postville allowed me to develop deep and lasting relationships with those most directly affected by the raid and with those who came to the aid of the migrants on the day of the raid. The reality of the migrants in Iowa taught me about "the pull factors." The

Figure 9. From left to right: Merlin Loyes Zamora (nine years old), Fermin Loyes, Attorney Sonia Parras-Konrad, Rosa Zamora de Loyes, and Ilvana Loyes Zamora (four years old). After Rosa received a U visa for the abuses suffered at the plant, she petitioned for Fermin as her derivative. On May 13, 2011, 3 years and one day after the raid separated them, Fermin flew to Des Moines, Iowa with Sonia Parras to be reunited with his family. As of September 5, 2011, he was still waiting for his work permit, which is part of the U visa. Photo by Violeta Aleman.

commitment of the first responders inspired me. Getting to know the Guatemalan families of the migrants and their communities helped me understand "the push factors."

But it was not only learning about the gross injustices and violations of the rights of the undocumented that changed me. What truly changed me was the sum of all the personal moments spent visiting the immigrants at their homes; sharing meals with them; attending the children's classes and school activities; accompanying the women with ankle bracelets to their ICE appointments; being with a father and his three children the day that their mother, his wife, called from Mexico where she had landed as a deportee after five months in jail; visiting the cemetery with a diabetic mother who had lost her baby when pregnant because she had not been allowed enough rest at work; and listening to parents in Guatemala recount the moment when they learned that their sons had been arrested in Postville on May 12, 2008.

I think the deep-seated fear of unauthorized migrants is based primarily on ignorance—ignorance of them as human beings and ignorance of their economic and cultural contributions to U.S. society. My purpose in making *abUSed: The Postville Raid* is to help bridge that gap and to contribute to a new narrative about immigrants that depicts them not as the "other" but as us, not as an enemy to be feared but as a neighbor to be welcomed. The film allows us to discover immigrants' aspirations and their contributions to society and the economy. We are better able to understand why migrants leave their countries of birth. They come here because they have no prospects at home and because here they do. We need the type of labor they are willing to provide. To combat fear and ignorance about immigrants we need a national educational campaign about immigration. Once we become knowledgeable of what is behind this reality of immigration, everybody will be better off. Not just the undocumented migrants, but all of us.

I have now completed the English version of *ABRAZOS*, the second documentary film of my immigration trilogy, the Spanish-subtitled and Spanish-dubbed versions, and a study guide. The third film of my immigration trilogy, *The U-Turn*, is now in post-production.

NOTES

1 The Mobile Consulate is an outreach initiative of Guatemala's Foreign Ministry and consists of the consulate officers traveling to immigrant communities to provide services on-site, thus saving the immigrants the costs and risks of the trip to the New York office.

2 In an ironic twist, in that interview, the gentleman in deportation proceedings says, "US authorities should deport those who have problems with the law, not those working honestly." This commonsense wisdom from a person who, when asked by a consular officer to sign his name, states that he is illiterate and instead has to put down his fingerprint, seems to finally have seeped into the policies of the Department of Homeland Security (DHS). On August 18, 2008, DHS announced that they would focus on removing only those undocumented persons who pose a threat to security and safety instead of low-priority individuals.

3 *abUSed: The Postville Raid*. Directed by Luis Argueta and co-produced by Vivan Rivas. See http://www.abusedthepostvilleraid.com/

4 Immigration studies do not take into account a factor present in many migrants' decisions to leave home in spite of knowing the risks the trip entails. That factor is faith and the conviction that their life is in the hands of G-d. Many believe that if something bad happens, it is G-d's will. At the same time, they strongly believe G-d will protect them and see their journey through.

5 See http://www.usimmigrationsupport.org/visa-u.html for a description of the U visa.
6 In 2011 in Arizona, the Southern Baptist Convention resolved: "That we affirm that while Southern Baptists, like other Americans, might disagree on how to achieve just and humane public policy objectives related to immigration, we agree that, when it comes to the gospel of Jesus Christ and to His church, the message, in every language and to every person, is 'Whosoever will, may come.'"

REFERENCES

Camayd-Freixas, Erik 2008. *Interpreting after the Largest ICE Raid in US History: A Personal Account*. PhD diss. Miami: Florida International University. June 13, 2008. Accessed October 8, 2014. http://graphics8.nytimes.com/images/2008/07/14/opinion/14ed-camayd.pdf.

Camayd-Freixas, Erik. 2009. *Postville: La criminalización de los migrantes*. Cuadernos del Presente Imperfecto, 8. Spanish translation by Omaira Hernández Fernández y Luz María Ramírez Hernández-Ede. Guatemala: F&G Editores.

CASA de Maryland. 2008. "Know Your Rights." Accessed October 23, 2014. http://casademaryland.org/wp-content/uploads/2014/03/KYR-booklet_English.pdf.

Preston, Julia. 2008. "An interpreter speaking up for migrants." *New York Times*, p. A1. July 11, 2008. Accessed October 8, 2014. http://www.nytimes.com/2008/07/11/us/11immig.html?pagewanted=all&_r=0.

Introduction

Migration, Detention, and Deportation: Dilemmas and Responses

DANIEL KANSTROOM AND M. BRINTON LYKES

The structure of the present immigration system is predicated on the assumption that the physical removal of an alien from the United States is a transformative event that fundamentally alters the alien's posture under the law . . . Removed aliens have, by virtue of their departure, literally passed beyond our aid.
—Board of Immigration Appeals
(Matter of *Andres Armendarez-Mendez* 2008)

This book explores the workings of an apparent deep contradiction. How can a massive, harsh deportation system operate within (and increasingly beyond) the borders of a nation-state that prides itself on being an open society, supportive of immigration as national policy, and generally protective of the rights of noncitizens? Obviously, this question raises many theoretical and applied issues. One might, for example, ask:

- Can the United States legitimately claim to be a "nation of immigrants" when its massive deportation machinery continues to negatively affect many millions of people? (Kanstroom 2007, 2012);
- What is the best understanding of the "rule of law" in the immigration context? Are those who enter without proper documents or who overstay visas outside of the rule of law? Are they criminals?
- Does physical deportation from U.S. national territory mark the end of legal rights to challenge deportation practices?
- Have globalization and transnational realities led to a decline in the legitimacy and power of the nation-state? If so, does this imply that greater attention must be paid to international human rights norms for migrants?

- What are the psychological and social consequences of policies and practices that force hundreds of thousands of migrants living within U.S. borders—many of whom are members of transnational families—"into the shadows"?

This book derives from and engages these questions and many similar ones. But it is not our primary purpose to answer them as problems of theory. Many other works have sought to do that, though, unsurprisingly, their conclusions vary widely. Our aim is to approach such questions inductively and empirically. We examine how deportation, detention, Immigration Courts, and social service agencies actually work and how they affect real people (though we concede that the verb, work, is sometimes descriptive and sometimes euphemistic). We consider legal norms and real-world effects. We explore how those who actually toil in these systems think they might be improved. We include important empirical research that examines the effects of deportation on individuals, children, families, and communities.

The authors come from a wide range of professional backgrounds and disciplines, including psychologists, sociologists, social workers, lawyers, judges, policy advocates, and government administrators. In previous work, Kanstroom unearthed the historical roots of the U.S. deportation system to suggest that it implicates powerful underlying normative debates, concerns about legal legitimacy, and deep, inherent tensions in the very self-definition of the "nation of immigrants" (Kanstroom 2007). But this was just the beginning of the theoretical and empirical issues that call for study. This edited volume therefore addresses important new questions, including:

- What are the effects of deportation on individuals, families, and communities, both in the United States and in the countries of origin of our deportees to which they are returned?
- What are the best practices for responding to the legal, psychological, health, educational, and survival challenges facing undocumented migrants living in Northern shadows?

Though such diversity of inquiry creates substantial challenges, our shared background assumptions start with the proposition that the

United States has proudly considered itself to be a nation of immigrants. There is surely truth within this vague and complex self-assessment. Rhetorically derived from John F. Kennedy's 1958 formulation (and earlier antecedents), it implies important demographic realities as well as sociopolitical and cultural aspirations. Indeed, though their forms have evolved substantially over time, both aspects—the demographic and the aspirational—predate the founding of the Republic (Kennedy 1958; Kanstroom 2007).

The nation of immigrants is clearly a current demographic reality. Many millions of visitors, students, and workers travel to the United States today. More than a million new immigrants arrive each year, in addition to the tens of thousands of refugees, asylum-seekers, trafficking victims, and others who receive legal status (US Department of Homeland Security 2013; Martin 2005). The benefits of such policies are well-known and largely respected across the political spectrum. Indeed, many polls confirm that most citizens, albeit in varying degrees, support a wide range of related ideals, including racial, ethnic, and religious diversity; demographic rejuvenation; and social dynamism. Most U.S. citizens still support Emma Lazarus's evocative double-entendre of the "golden door" beside which the Statue of Liberty lifts her lamp to welcome:

> Your tired, your poor,
> Your huddled masses yearning to breathe free,
> The wretched refuse of your teeming shore. (Lazarus 1883; see also
>   Higham 1984; Neuman 1996; Gibney 1989)

The reality of U.S. immigration, however, has been much more complex and often more troubling than this. Recurrent waves of nativism and restrictionist sentiment have bedeviled the nation of immigrants from its founding to the present (Higham 1955, 1983; Kanstroom 2007). Today, a largely dysfunctional immigration system and the lack of comprehensive immigration reform, combined with harsh, wide-ranging deportation policies has, for many, turned the United States into a "deportation nation" in which many millions live in a tenuous state of fear (Kanstroom 2007; Rosenblum and Meissner 2014). The tension between the open immigration ideal and systems of exclusion and removal is hardly new. Indeed, George Washington qualified the ideal as early as 1783, when he reminded a group of Irish immigrants that the "bosom of America is open to receive . . . the oppressed and persecuted of all Nations and Religions." He cautioned, however, that such welcome was contingent: "*[I]f, by decency and propriety of conduct, they appear to merit the enjoyment* (Fitzpatrick 1938: vol. 27, 254) [emphasis added]).

The combination of an aspiration of humanitarian openness with certain restrictions is neither necessarily irrational nor even contradictory. Indeed, such combinations may be inevitable. Consider, for example, whether Nazi war criminals or terrorists should receive asylum if they face persecution in their countries of residence. But the combination demands careful balancing and is always a work in progress. Who decides what is decency, propriety of conduct, and merit? And what do we do with those who fail to meet such tests? What mechanisms are prohibited (or required) by adherence to a regime that also respects basic human and constitutional rights? At what point does exclusion or removal begin to dominate and call into question the viability of the open ideal itself? When is it fair to speak, as we do herein, of a "deportations delirium"?

Here is one way to answer the last question: We might compare admissions and expulsions to see how the balance has been struck in various historical periods. Clearly, this is an imprecise measure; but it provides a framework into which other facts may be added. Louis Post, who was once in charge of (what was then called) the Bureau of Immigration, wrote a book about harsh deportation actions led by Attorney General Mitchell Palmer and the young J. Edgar Hoover in 1919–20 against alleged anarchists such as Emma Goldman. Post (1923) evocatively called the episode (known as "the Palmer raids") a "deportations delirium." There were certainly severe violations of rights in that period and many civil libertarians rallied against government abuses of power (Kanstroom 2007; Kanstroom and Ozolins 2014). Comparisons between eras are difficult for many reasons. But, as a rough metric, consider this: According to government statistics, in 1920, the total number of U.S. deportations was 14,577. Immigrant admissions totaled 430,000. The ratio of deportees to immigrants was thus about 3:100. From 1997 (the year in which deportation laws changed dramatically) to 2012, however, the United States admitted about 15.5 million legal permanent residents, an achievement of which we should be proud. However, total removals and returns exceeded 19.7 million, for a ratio of 127:100 (127 ordered to leave to 100 admitted as permanent residents), more than a 40-fold increase in the removal/return ratio since 1920 (U.S. Department of Homeland Security 2013, table 1, table 39).[1] Even if we just calculate formal removals (over 4.2 million) we still achieve a ratio of about 27:100, a ninefold increase from 1920. A recent report coauthored by a former U.S. Commission of Immigration notes that the pace of formal removals has increased from some 70,000 in 1996 to 420,000 in 2012. There can be no doubt that the Obama administration has "inherited—and further expanded upon—unprecedented capacity to identify, apprehend, and deport unauthorized immigrants" (Rosenblum and Meissner 2014, p. 1). If 1920 warranted the epithet of delirium, the years since 1997 have been at least that, if not an extended terrifying nightmare for many noncitizens and their families.

The lives of many millions of people have been affected by this huge expansion of deportation. Large-scale systems of arrest, removal, and detention have now run for a quarter century like a menacing underground river beneath the nation of immigrants ideal (Kanstroom 2007). Since 1996, when U.S. deportation laws were toughened, millions of migrants in the United States—including tens of thousands of long-term legal permanent residents (i.e., people with "green cards")—have experienced summary arrest, incarceration without bail, transfer to remote detention facilities, family separation, deportation without counsel, and life-time banishment from what is, in many cases, the only country they have ever known as home (Rosenblum and McCabe 2014). Their families (often comprised of U.S. citizens) and communities must cope with the devastating loss of a spouse, parent, or child.

Further, in recent years, many have discovered that they were *wrongly* deported. This can arise in various ways. Perhaps the most common errors are forensic mistakes (e.g., a court may misread a criminal record or other documents). Indeed, even some U.S. citizens have found themselves wrongly deported in recent years (Kanstroom 2012).

Other cases involve late recognition by courts of legal errors. For example, in 2010 the Supreme Court considered whether the "ineffective assistance" of criminal defense counsel could be raised as a defense by a person facing deportation (*Padilla v. Kentucky* 2010). Mr. Padilla, a long-term lawful permanent resident of the United States, apparently had been advised to plead guilty to a drug-related charge. Unbeknownst to him (and apparently also to his lawyer), this virtually guaranteed his deportation and lifetime banishment from the United States and his family (Kanstroom 2011). The Supreme Court, in a path-breaking doctrinal decision, upheld Mr. Padilla's claim that his criminal defense counsel was "ineffective" due to this incorrect advice concerning deportation. He was thus allowed to withdraw his guilty plea and perhaps save himself from deportation. The Court recognized that deportation now often has a very close connection to the criminal process. The two systems have become inextricably linked. Further, the Court recognized that the deportation regime has limited the authority of Immigration Judges "to alleviate the harsh consequences of deportation" (*Padilla v. Kentucky* 2010: 357). As a result of these changes, noted the Court, the "drastic measure" of deportation or removal ". . . is now *virtually inevitable* for a vast number of noncitizens convicted of crimes." Deportation has become "*an integral part*—indeed, sometimes the most important part—of the penalty that may be imposed on noncitizen defendants who plead guilty to specified crimes" (*Padilla v. Kentucky* 2010: 362; emphasis added). Although the Court's *Padilla* decision was limited to certain process rights, its logic shows why substantial due process protections, and also some of the more specific protections normally tied to the criminal justice system, are warranted (Kanstroom 2011: 2000). However, the Court has not applied the *Padilla* case retroactively, thus insulating many similar past deportations from meaningful scrutiny.[2]

Those who do not regularly engage with the U.S. deportation system are often stunned not only by its harshness, but also by how complex it is, as the brief preceding discussion of retroactivity shows. Consider a rather typical scenario, a composite that is based on cases with which the authors have been involved:

> Dith arrived in the United States at the age of 4 in 1980, with his aunt, Arunny, as a refugee from Cambodia. He lived with Arunny, and later, also with her second husband, as his parents were both killed in Cambodia by the Khmer Rouge. Dith had difficulty adjusting to life in the United States. He was depressed about the loss of his parents, had problems in school, lived in tough neighborhoods in Lowell, Massachusetts, and eventually joined a local gang of other Cambodian boys formed for

self-protection (Cahn and Stansell 2005). In 1998, Dith was convicted of possession of cocaine. He had become a lawful permanent resident in the United States, but was never naturalized as a citizen. He never understood the difference.

Dith left the gang after serving a prison sentence for the cocaine conviction. In the following year he married Melissa, a U.S. citizen. Dith and Melissa had a child, Chris, born in the United States in 2001. Dith was arrested by immigration authorities in 2004, and he learned that a "repatriation agreement" had been signed between the United States and Cambodia in 2002. The agreement removed obstacles to the deportation of Cambodians from the United States. Dith was soon transferred to immigration detention in South Texas and was deported in 2005. He knew no one in Cambodia, speaks only English, and had no idea how he would live there. In 2006, the U.S. Supreme Court ruled that a drug possession crime such as Dith's should not have been considered drug trafficking and should not have been considered an "aggravated felony" under immigration law. Dith should have been able to ask an Immigration Judge for a "waiver" of deportation. But now, he was told, it was too late. Deportation cases such as his could not be re-opened after a deportee is taken from U.S. soil. He was barred from the United States for life.

Dith's aunt was terrified and confused by his removal. She could not understand why the country that had granted them refuge after they had survived the atrocities of the Khmer Rouge would send Dith back to Cambodia. She was also uncertain about what would happen to Dith when he returned, as most of their family had either been killed in the 1970s or had left Cambodia many years earlier. Melissa and Chris were also distraught over Dith's removal. Beyond the emotional toll of losing a beloved spouse and father, Melissa had relied upon Dith's full-time income to help support the family and to allow her to stay at home part-time with Chris. Since Dith's deportation, Melissa has had to return to full-time work and to rely on government assistance to keep herself and Chris fed and housed (Wessler 2009).

In early 2009, Melissa was killed when the car she was driving home from an evening work shift was struck by a drunk driver. Dith was unable to return for her funeral. After Melissa's death, Chris went to live with Arunny and her husband, both of whom are now of advanced age.[3] Since Melissa's death, Chris has exhibited increasingly severe socio-emotional problems. He is afraid to fall asleep at night, is defiant and depressed, and recently has begun saying that he would rather die than live without his parents. Dith's aunt and uncle are having difficulty caring for Chris due to the severity of his symptoms. The cumulative effects of the losses Arunny experienced in Cambodia, her advanced age, the loss of Dith to deportation, and Melissa's death are also taking a toll on her. A social worker is working with the family to try to help Chris and to maintain stability in the home. She thinks that it is in Chris's best interest to be with his father, but neither Melissa's parents nor Dith's aunt and uncle want Chris to be sent to Cambodia.

This case obviously raises deep questions about the nature and limits of deportation law. But its implications extend far beyond technical legal analysis. The family's situation compels inquiry into the multiple legal and policy decisions that affect access to health, educational, and human services necessary to live a life of dignity, or to obtain the most basic rights guaranteed by such instruments as the Universal Declaration of Human Rights and the International Covenant on Civil and Political Rights (Capps et al. 2004; Ku and Matani 2001; Simich, Wu, and Nerad 2007). As a practical matter, the professionals involved with the family bring differing expertise, which may lead to conflicting and sometimes contradictory recommendations. For example, the deep-seated psychological effects of multiple losses for Arunny as well as the generational and cultural gaps between her and Chris suggest the need for psychosocial services from culturally and linguistically competent counselors. Arunny's sadness may yield to depression, making it more difficult for her to care for Chris, while the recommendation that Chris be with his father has apparently been made with minimum family engagement and has exacerbated rather than relieved Arunny's situation. Thus, those who respond to this family's needs must consider a complex array of legal, psychological, educational, social, health, and human services issues. This demands an integrated approach by an interdisciplinary professional team with legal, cultural, and linguistic expertise and resources. Of course, this would be difficult enough to secure in the United States for intact, functional families. But it is nearly impossible for Arunny to access such services in the country to which Dith has been deported (Yoshikawa 2011).

Consider, too, the legal problem of the border. Reasonable minds may well differ about how this case and others like it ought to be resolved. But a more basic question arises: can Dith's case be considered at all? May judges even hear it? At present, for those who are still within U.S. borders, adequate judicial consideration is possible, though the systems are difficult to navigate and options are limited. For those beyond U.S. borders (i.e., the deported), however, the answer in many situations has been a simple and emphatic "no." Much of the rule of law, in particular the possibility of re-opening or re-considering a wrongly decided deportation case, ends at the border for deportees. This has begun to change, due to extensive federal litigation efforts in which the editors of this volume have been participants.[4] Still, after deportation from the United States, there often is no law; there is only—at most—executive discretion; and even that is severely limited.

Given the scope of current detention and deportation systems, we must also consider the significant challenges facing the approximately 11 million immigrants living out of status in the United States today, the so-called illegal aliens. For some members of this group, recent administration initiatives such as DACA (Deferred Action for Childhood Arrivals) have provided at least temporary relief (Menjívar and Kanstroom 2013). But the millions who have been deported over the past two decades, many of whom had legal status of one form or another (U.S. Department of Homeland Security 2013; Rosenblum and McCabe 2014), have suffered a harsh and in many cases irremediable fate. And as of this writing, the future prospects for the undocumented remain poignantly unclear.

Still, migrants and their families surely have powerful rights claims, including rights to human dignity, proportionality, fair processes, and family unity. The question is how such rights can be instantiated in U.S. practice. What this book seeks to support and develop is thus both a systemic critique and a holistic professional model. Our work draws on international human rights discourse and practice to press for and exemplify fairer policies and practices that will allow migrants to move out of the shadows and to participate more fully in life within the United States. In this way, we may better comprehend *and respond to* the current rather grim multifaceted realities of U.S. migration and deportation.

The authors in this volume, as noted, are lawyers, judges, social workers, academic researchers, clinical and community psychologists, educators, community activists, and a filmmaker. Drawing on decades of experience working within and across our respective areas of expertise and engagement with immigrant communities within the United States and in immigrants' countries of origin, our major goal has been to reflect critically upon the multiple challenges facing migrants, their advocates, and their advisors today. We are particularly concerned about how U.S. policies and practices of the Immigration and Customs Enforcement (ICE) and Customs and Border Enforcement (CBP) agencies affect children (many of whom are U.S. citizens) whose parents may lack proper documents or who face deportation for other reasons. We suggest that an interdisciplinary perspective that brings together scholars from diverse fields, practitioners, community activists, and migrants in collaborations that embrace a participatory and action research paradigm responds best to the realities facing migrants and the wider society of which they are an integral part.

A Brief Overview of Deportation

What is deportation? How large a system is it? What are its goals and its effects? Deportation (also known under U.S. law as "removal") may be most simply defined as the physical expulsion of a noncitizen or "alien."[5] More generally, though, it can be better understood as a major, complex law enforcement system that governs the lives of the many millions of migrants who live, study, travel, and work in a country that is not their birthplace (Kanstroom 2007). In the United States, deportation has two basic forms which reflect two somewhat different, if inter-related, functions: *extended border control*, which seeks to remove those noncitizens who have evaded the myriad of rules that govern legal entry into the United States; and *post-entry social control*, which regulates the conduct of those who have legally entered but who then engage in a wide variety of prohibited behaviors, some quite serious, others surprisingly minor (Kanstroom 2007). These forms implicate related but different theories of nation-state control over the entry and lives of noncitizens. Most simply put, *extended border control* seeks to buttress failed border control with interior enforcement. The goals of *post-entry social control* are much more complex, overlapping with such other enforcement systems as criminal law (Kanstroom 2012). Within the Obama administration, as noted above, there has been some movement to ameliorate the harshness of *extended border control* deportations of certain young people. There has been little, if any Obama administration impetus, however, to reform *post-entry social control* deportations. Indeed, so-called smart enforcement has focused on "criminal aliens," including many long-term legal residents convicted of very minor offenses (Kanstroom 2012; Rosenblum and McCabe 2014) Courts have played a more important role regarding protection of rights in this realm.

In some of its guises, deportation is a relatively formal legal process, in which certain basic procedural rights are well accepted. In many settings, however, it can be a very informal administrative mechanism with little in common with trials. For example, a process known as *expedited removal* has been designed as a fast-track mechanism for illegal entrants who have not been in the United States for long periods of time. Similarly, those who reenter illegally after removal face a very informal, fast-track regime known as *reinstatement of removal* in which most rights claims are unavailing (Kanstroom 2012). Indeed, much of the late twentieth and early twenty-first century story of deportation is a story of de-formalization in which even certain very basic procedural rights recognized by courts—such as the right to be heard by a judge—have been severely restricted.

In all of its forms, however, deportation has long been an anomalous legal system, largely exempt from many of the most important protections of the U.S. rule of law. Specifically, people facing deportation do not have:

- the right to jury trial (cases are decided by Immigration Judges who are employed by the U.S. Department of Justice; see chapter by Judges Slavin and Marks in this volume);
- the right to counsel (if a deportee cannot afford a lawyer she generally has no right to one);[6]
- the right to bail (many thousands face mandatory detention every day) (*Demore v. Kim* 2003);
- the right to have illegally seized evidence suppressed (unless the police conduct was "widespread" or "egregious") (*INS v. Lopez-Mendoza* 1984);
- the right against *ex post facto* laws (a person can be deported for conduct that was not a deportable offense when it was done) (Kanstroom 2007); or
- the right against selective prosecution (one may be selected for deportation due to nationality, political opinion, etc.) (*Reno v. AADC* 1999).

Much of the system is highly discretionary. For example, decisions about whom to arrest and place in removal proceedings are virtually immune from review. Discretion of the ameliorative type has long been a major part of deportation law. However, another aspect of the 1996 changes to the law was the limitation of the powers of Immigration Judges to grant such relief. This was one of the reasons why the Supreme Court in the *Padilla* case highlighted the importance of proper legal representation in criminal court. Once a noncitizen pleads guilty to or is convicted of a crime, the possibilities for discretionary relief are highly constrained. Moreover, judicial review of the exercise of discretion is limited and varies widely in practice (Kanstroom 2012). Finally, as noted above, for many deportees, physical removal has essentially ended their ability to access the U.S. legal system. This has undoubtedly shielded from judicial scrutiny innumerable government errors (especially cases based upon legal theories later found to be incorrect) and many disproportionately harsh actions.

What are the goals of the deportation system? It is surprisingly hard to answer this basic question. Clearly, much of it was designed to help with border control, national security (broadly defined), and to some degree with crime control within the United States. Put simply, though, deportation has no independent goals, nor should it. It is typically described as "an instrument of immigration policy, not a policy in itself."[7] Although this book does not explore in detail whether the deportation system has achieved its own goals, there is considerable doubt about this among scholars and policy analysts (Kanstroom 2012). The border has obviously not been controlled, notwithstanding massive walls, fences, billions of dollars spent, and the *extended border control* deportations of millions of migrant workers (Rosenblum and Meissner 2014). The widespread, harsh use of deportation as part of a post–9/11 security frenzy yielded little, if any, positive results (Kanstroom 2007). And much recent research has shown that deportation is remarkably inefficient as a crime control strategy. Indeed, the vast majority of criminal deportees have long been relatively minor offenders. A 2009 report by Human Rights Watch, for example, found that more than 70 percent of those deported for criminal conduct were deported for a nonviolent offense (Human Rights Watch 2009).[8] Moreover, programs such as Secure Communities, an element of *post-entry social control*, have generated enhanced fear of authorities among migrants, weakening rather than strengthening local law enforcement.

Many deportees are not newcomers to the United States. A 2006 study found that some 70 percent of those charged had lived in the United States for more than a decade. The median length of residence was fourteen years (TRAC 2006; Rosenblum and McCabe 2014). Such data prompt hard questions: If the system is not removing serious or violent criminals in large numbers, what justifies it? Should a long-term lawful permanent resident with U.S. family ties be deported for possession of a marijuana cigarette (Bernstein 2010)? Or for drunk driving? Is the *post-entry social control* system working in a fair and just way?

Social science researchers have highlighted a paradox that warrants serious thought (Rumbaut and Ewing 2007). Assimilation, as traditionally understood, involves the acquisition by immigrants and their descendants of language proficiency, higher levels of education, job skills, and other attributes that improve their chances of success. However, in contrast to what this theory would predict, the life situations of immigrants—and that of their children—often *worsen* the longer they live in the United States, as they become more acculturated (Garcia Coll and Marks 2012). The children and grandchildren of many immigrants—as well as some immigrants themselves—become subject to economic and social forces, such as higher rates of family disintegration and drug and alcohol addiction. This exposure has been found to increase the likelihood of criminal behavior. The conclusion is disturbing for the proponents of deportation: "If there was an 'immigrant crime problem' it was not found among the immigrants, *but among their US-born [US citizen] sons*" (Rumbaut and Ewing 2007). It is difficult to see how the best solution to such a problem could be deportation of noncitizens for minor offenses.

Deportation looms over the heads of some 40 million foreign-born people who live in the United States along with their families (Pew Research Center: Hispanic Trends 2013). Many still think that only the so-called illegal aliens need be concerned with deportation; but, as noted above, this is clearly not correct. There are some 20 million lawful permanent residents within the foreign-born population. About a million new legal immigrants arrive each year as permanent residents. Millions more live in a variety of complex tenuous, quasi-legal statuses with arcane names like "VAWA applicants"; "U and T visa holders"; "Temporary Protected Status," etc. Also, some 170 million "non-immigrants" enter the United States legally each year as tourists, students, workers, etc. (U.S. Department of Homeland Security 2012, table 25).

Moreover, nearly 9 million immigrants are part of "mixed-status" families (Passel and Cohn 2009), a number that has increased significantly over the last several decades, and includes some 4.5 million children (Passel and Cohn 2011). Best estimates suggest that children born to undocumented migrants have made up 6.8 percent of youth in U.S. schools (Passel and Cohn 2009). Of these children, approximately 82 percent are U.S. citizens (Passel and Cohn 2009). In addition to these children of migrant parents, there are over 2 million migrant youth in the United States who traveled with parents during childhood or by themselves (Gonzalez 2009; Chavez and Menjívar 2010). Large numbers of migrants who are deported are separated from their U.S.-born citizen children. Estimates are that between July 2010 and September 2012, 205,000 deportees reported having at least one U.S.-citizen child, resulting in an estimated annual average of approximately 90,000 parental deportations (Wessler 2012). The Immigrant Rights Clinic at the New York University School of Law found that between 2005 and 2010, 87 percent of processed immigration cases of noncitizens with citizen children resulted in deportation (NYU School of Law Immigrant Rights Clinic 2012).

The most basic fact is that for all of these millions of people and for their families, many of whom are U.S. citizens, deportation law is the primary part of the "rule of law" with which they must be concerned. If they run afoul of its often highly complicated, technical, and obscure commandments, they may well be subject to arrest, detention, and lifetime banishment from this country and separation of family members, including young children from their parents.

Some may suggest that this fear is overstated. However, the numbers are daunting: In the past quarter century, the number of times an individual noncitizen has been caught somewhere on U.S. soil, and determined to be subject to deportation (i.e., removal or return), has exceeded 25 *million*. Actual removals and returns have regularly exceeded one million per year (U.S. Department of Homeland Security 2013, table 39), though the numbers were down a bit in 2013–14. Still, DHS has, for many years, annually detained over 280,000 people for at least 24 hours, in over 400 facilities, at an annual cost exceeding $1.2 billion. The current number of "funded beds" for immigration detainees exceeds 30,000 (Rosenblum and Meissner 2014; Siskin 2012; Gavett 2011; Special Rapporteur on the Human Rights of Migrants 2008; Dougherty, Wilson, and Wu 2005). The deportation system has grown steadily since the late 1990s (Kanstroom 2007, 2012). Indeed, the number of deportations during the Obama administration increased substantially from that of the George W. Bush administration (Slevin 2010).

Contemporary deportation law changed dramatically during the Clinton administration, when new laws amplified the authority of the federal government to arrest, detain, and deport noncitizens. These laws included the Illegal Immigrant Reform and Responsibility Act (1996) and the Anti-terrorism Effective Death Penalty Act (1996). The 1996 laws expanded the offenses for which a noncitizen could be deported, allowed for retroactive deportation, increased the categories of persons subject to removal, and eliminated the range of judicial review and due process rights formerly available to immigrants. In 2001, following the attacks on the World Trade Center, the Bush administration signed into law the *Uniting and Strengthening America by Providing Appropriate Tools Required to Intercept and Obstruct Terrorism* (PATRIOT) Act. By expanding the ability of the government to deport persons deemed "threats to national security" and allowing for use of secret evidence in such cases, the Act further marginalized migrants, increasingly labeling them as dangerous threats to the newly denominated "homeland" (Kanstroom 2007). As significantly, for many mixed-status families, the federal welfare reform legislation of 1996, the *Personal Responsibility and Work Opportunity Reconciliation Act* (PRWORA), sharply restricted eligibility for federal means-tested programs for legal immigrants arriving that year or thereafter. Federally funded benefits for migrants were restricted to Medicaid emergency funds, although citizen children were eligible for all federal benefits as well as those supplemented by the states (Yoshikawa 2011). Despite this, as research has demonstrated, many legal immigrants as well as migrant parents hesitate to avail themselves of the resources to which their children are entitled (Xu and Brabeck 2012; Yoshikawa 2011). They fear contact with the legal system, and rightly so.

Put simply, since major, harsh changes were implemented to the deportation system and in welfare policies, tens of millions of people—most undocumented migrants, but also many hundreds of thousands with legal immigration statuses, asylum claims, and the like—have suffered repeated indignities. These include hunger, lack of adequate housing, healthcare, higher education, and a livable wage, or being ordered to leave the United States. Many of those ordered out are barred by law from ever returning. Indeed, the last two decades have witnessed the creation of what amounts to a large, new American diaspora peopled by deportees, many of whom have been here since early childhood (Kanstroom 2012). As significantly, a growing number of U.S. citizen children have become "*de facto* deportees" (Argueta 2011), having been returned to their parents' country of origin and consigned to rural poverty. And yet, many of those who are not citizens are surely "Americans" by virtually any measure beyond the formalistic legal one (Motomura 2007).

The challenges these migrants and deportees face require inter- and cross-disciplinary dialogue, research, and practice as well as university-community partnerships. For example, the Migration and Human Rights Project (MHRP) at Boston College[9] has been engaged collaboratively with immigrant organizations in New England—Centro Presente, Organización Maya K'iche', English for Action, Casa El Salvador, and Women Encouraging Empowerment. These collaborations have been facilitated by participatory and action research initiatives, legal representation of individual clients, participatory educational activities (e.g., Know Your Rights workshops, Domestic Violence Training workshops, and an English for Speakers of Other Languages Tool Kit), community organizing, and media outreach, including press conferences, newsletter publications, and professional journal articles.

This approach draws on earlier models of interdisciplinary work among service providers and academic researchers. Klein's (1996, 2005) "knowledge integration model," for example, emphasizes an iterative triangulation of knowledge depth (disciplinary and professional practice approaches), breadth (multiple theoretical perspectives), and synthesis (achieving interdisciplinary outcomes through collaborative actions). Similarly, Amey and Brown (2000) focus on the development of discipline orientation, knowledge engagement, and working relationships within each stage of collaboration and partnership development, culminating in "energetic teamwork." Both models assume that interdisciplinary collaboration can yield important new ideas that rely simultaneously or iteratively on theories from multiple disciplines and reflections on applied work (see Chicco and Congress, this volume).

Participatory Action Research with Migrants and Deportees

Some of the contributors to this volume apply interdisciplinary theories and participatory action research (PAR) to the problems migrants and deportees face. PAR offers a set of strategies and reflexive practices to build partnerships across university-community borders and for all involved to think critically and reflexively about themselves and those with whom they work. Such reflection is especially important as university-based scholars seek to connect with local communities. PAR is a resource through which individuals—migrants or deportees and their families—self-consciously empower themselves to take effective, collective action toward improving conditions in their own lives and to bring about a more just and equitable society (Reason and Bradbury 2001; Park 1993). Thus, PAR facilitates alliances among researchers and immigrant rights advocates and migrants themselves who are all too often afraid to advocate for their rights. It facilitates processes through which some of these migrants have emerged from the shadows, affirming their stories and struggles, as well as their rights to a better future.

Although PAR is often described as a qualitative research method or approach, it is also conceptualized as a worldview, a "philosophy of life" (Rahman and Fals Borda 1991:29) or a "life project" (Fals Borda 2001). PAR posits a distinctive conception of knowledge co-constructed through collaborative actions and reflection on those actions. Hence, knowledge is neither universal nor objective, but is situated, local, and socially constructed, a perspective deeply resonant with many of the challenges facing migrant communities. Further, PAR assumes that knowledge is inextricably linked with power; knowledge mechanisms including socialization, education, and the media have defined and legitimized both what counts as useful knowledge and whose interest (the educated, white middle class) this knowledge serves (Gaventa and Cornwall 2001; Rahman 1991). Thus, the goals of collaborations and the

PAR methodology situate researchers alongside migrants as knowledge co-producers and advocates, affirming their dignity and human rights.

Participatory and action research is, thus, a means of recognizing the research capabilities of marginalized and disenfranchised people and facilitating processes through which they acquire tools with which they can create knowledge "from the bottom up" and transform their lives and their communities (Park 1993). The outsider—often a university-based researcher or human service professional—plays a catalytic and supportive role, seeking to generate opportunities for co-research. She joins migrants in pragmatic solidarity, coming together within local communities to (1) challenge oppressive structural features that silence them or force them "into the shadows"; and (2) affirm their rights to a more just and humane immigration policy. PAR thus contributes to real and material changes in what people do, what they value, how they interact with others, and how they interpret their world (Park 1993; Kemmis and McTaggart 2005). These are the overall goals—and challenges—that inform the participatory and action research model that animates this work. (See, e.g., Brabeck, Lykes, and Hershberg 2011; Brabeck and Xu 2010; Lykes, Brabeck, and Hunter 2013.)

It is especially important to listen to the voices of "deportable" migrants. These people—whose voices are too often unheard—speak about workers headed north in search of a better future for their children, seeking to escape structural poverty resulting from decades of war and state-sponsored violence. They have been met by what they call a "second war": the U.S. Immigration and Customs Enforcement (ICE) response to what one mother whom the editors of this volume interviewed described as a "heart divided." This Mayan woman was referring to the painful decision to separate from her children in order to be a "responsible parent" (Brabeck, Lykes, and Hershberg 2011). Such heart-wrenching decisions are made by more and more parents from the Southern Hemisphere in order to ensure that their children will escape the systemic marginalization, poverty, and violence that have deeply constrained their lives.

This book thus reflects knowledge generated through action-reflection processes in ever-widening circles of participants. We began with a preface from migrants themselves, as reflected in the recent films of Guatemalan filmmaker, Luis Argueta. We then engage with these realities from the perspective of lawyers, judges, and activists seeking to manage the legal conundrums generated by contemporary laws and administrative practices. We present several suggested interdisciplinary approaches that animate our collaborative work, followed by ethnographic and participatory action research projects through which activist scholars and migrants engage material and socio-emotional complexities of sustaining family and/or community transnationally.

The chapter by law professor David Thronson examines the profound tensions between the aspirations and real practices of immigration and family law, noting in particular how the best interests of the child fare remarkably poorly in the immigration system. As summarized above, deportation laws have devastated families in the United States as they separate U.S. citizen children from their parents, spouses from each other, and disrupt the fabric of American communities. Some 33 million native-born citizens have at least one foreign-born parent (U.S. Census Bureau 2010). Further, among the estimated 11 million undocumented people in the United States, more than 1.5 million are children (ibid.). The family may lose a breadwinner; those left behind may face eviction; and the family suffers emotionally from having a loved one in detention, often thousands of miles away (Morawetz 2000). In many cases, deported parents are separated from their U.S.-born children. Baum, Jones, and Barry (2010), for example, found that between 1997 and 2007, 88,000 U.S. citizen children (44,000 of whom were under the age of 5) lost a legal permanent resident parent to deportation. Furthermore, recent research by Wessler (2012) from the Applied Research Center (ARC) reported that at least 5,100 children whose parents were detained or deported currently live in U.S. foster care and face significant barriers to reunification with parents. Exemplifying the challenges "within disciplines," Thronson highlights the stark contradictions between the best practices of family law and children's rights versus deportation law. There is mounting evidence about the negative effects of deportation on U.S. families and communities, especially the children of the undocumented, millions of whom are U.S. citizens. Tens of thousands of such children have seen their families split; some have experienced the effective deportation of the entire family to what, for them, are foreign countries (Kremer, Moccio, and Hammell et al. 2009). As Thronson explains, we need a better, more holistic theory of interpretation to account for human rights to dignity and family and a better trained group of attorneys who can counsel and represent their clients on the basis of both family and immigration law.

Many of the most specific and difficult immigration policy challenges in the last few years have involved the immigration detention system. The 1996 changes to U.S. deportation law have led to a massive and unprecedented increase in the detention of noncitizens for deportation. Detention, which had been largely abolished by INS in 1954, except for those who were likely to abscond or who were deemed dangerous to national security or public safety, has gradually come to be a defining characteristic of the immigration enforcement system (Kanstroom 2007, 2012). As Mark Dow noted in his 2004 book, *American Gulag*, enforcement procedures that had long "tended to be casual," became increasingly "brutal." The majority of detainees are held in facilities near where they were arrested. However, large numbers of people have been summarily transferred to remote locations, causing innumerable hardships. To examine this phenomenon, the book's second chapter is written by Dora Schriro. Dr. Schriro was the former director of the Office of Detention Policy and Planning for the Department of Homeland Security, where she led an overhaul of the nation's immigration detention system. She describes the size and scope of the system, the resources dedicated to detention, and the challenges of developing "best practices" at the intersection of increasing need and limited resources. Most importantly, she offers a sensible and humane reform agenda for detention systems.

Immigration Judges Denise Noonan Slavin and Dana Leigh Marks next focus on the multiple roles, responsibilities, and challenges facing judges in the current regime. The judges examine the deeply dysfunctional nature of our immigration adjudication system, which must process hundreds of thousands of deportation cases annually. The judges' candor and incisive perspectives offer a unique window into some of the most difficult systemic legal and policy contradictions facing those who adjudicate removal cases. As significantly, they engage the delicate balance in their roles as defenders of the administration's policies while seeking to respond humanely to the concrete dilemmas facing migrants who have risked all to secure access to life within U.S. borders and are now being "sentenced home."

This section of the book concludes with a chapter co-authored by Ali Noorani, executive director of the National Immigration Forum and long-time activist and community organizer, and Brittney Nystrom and Maurice Belanger, organizers, immigration experts, and former Forum colleagues. They address the state of immigration law and policy in the United States today and describe a national community organizer's agenda for building responses. These four chapters highlight the challenges of comprehensive immigration reform in a context of ongoing detentions and deportations despite a change in executive and legislative leadership in Washington. The descriptions of experiences "inside the beltway" and in courtrooms throughout the nation frame more detailed discussion about specific approaches to the problems faced by those affected by current policies and practices.

Part II of this book examines the lives of migrants and how those working directly with migrants assist them as they respond to severe challenges. It includes chapters that consider deep tensions within and across multiple disciplines, all of which contribute importantly to work with migrants. Building on the integration of theory and practice through direct work with migrants and deportees, the first chapter in Part II is a multidisciplinary discussion from the perspectives of law and social work, that is, legal and community-based work with migrants in New England and beyond. Attorneys and social workers act as advocates for their clients. They also have common goals, albeit from different professional perspectives and with different codes of professional ethics and responsibility. The authors discuss interdisciplinary and multidisciplinary scholarship and practice, exploring their respective approaches to advocacy and practice. Jessica Chicco, an immigration attorney who has worked extensively with deportees, and Professor Elaine Congress, an academic researcher and advocate for immigrants, co-authored a discussion of such complexities of advocacy. Situating migrants within an ecological framework, social workers emphasize the forces affecting the migrant and her or his family at various levels. As importantly, they see the migrants' journey in terms of its multiple stages, that is, beginning in their countries of origin wherein the focus is on the push and pull factors that contributed to decisions to "leave home." This more personal decision is situated within the political, economic, social, and personal factors that constrain and facilitate the migrant's choice. Stage 2 examines the journey or transition experiences, while the third and final stage involves assessing migrants in their current environments, including socioeconomic issues, migration status, and their physical and socio-emotional well-being. Chicco demonstrates how this framework can usefully serve the immigration attorney who must situate the immediate demand for relief within the wider migration story, seeking to locate a wider range of needs which can contribute to an attorney's ability to determine whether or not the client has personal equities that may be taken into consideration in the increasingly narrow circumstances available for a legal case seeking relief. Thus the attorney brings knowledge of the law into dialog with the client and draws not only on the framework offered by a social worker but on the listening skills typically engaged by the psychologist. This chapter uses vignettes developed from individual cases on which the editors have worked to show how professionals can collaborate in defending undocumented migrants while also exploring tensions that arise due to differing professional ethics and standards of practice. The authors conclude with several suggestions of how to build bridges across these potential contradictions in search of stronger and more effective advocacy for migrants.

In the second chapter of this section, psychologists Kalina Brabeck, Katherine Porterfield, and Maryanne Loughry offer a set of highly textured analyses of psychosocial interventions and clinical assessments of migrants and their families. They draw on the same cases referenced by Chicco and Congress, vignettes built from composite stories of migrants from a variety of countries that exemplify the challenges facing clinicians who are often asked to render judgments about the psychological effects of forced migration, detention, and deportation and/or about the lives to which migrants would be forced to return should they be deported. They must also weigh the stories of violence and extreme poverty that those with whom they work faced prior to risking all to head north. Thus, they bridge the broad policy concerns raised by Professor Thronson and the practical adjudication issues raised by the judges with real-world insights into the needs of undocumented migrants and their families on both sides of the border who are caught up in these systems. These authors write from within the subfields of counseling, clinical and social psychology in dialogue with the lived experiences of immigrants, detainees, and deportees and their families.

The next two chapters in Part II address the transnational dimensions of this work. The first chapter, co-authored by the volume's co-editor, community and cultural psychologist M. Brinton Lykes and her colleagues, examines transnational and mixed-status families within the context of interdisciplinary community-university partnerships. They document interdisciplinary participatory and action research processes through which lawyers, social workers, psychologists, educators, community organizers, and activist scholars have collaborated with local migrants and their families within New England and in the southern Quiché region of Guatemala. The chapter describes the findings from interviews with parents and children in mixed-status and transnational families in New England and transnational families in New England and Guatemala. This chapter focuses on Central American families' experiences and the meanings they make of migration, detention, and deportation from within and beyond the U.S. border. Such experiences and meanings are situated within their histories and current realities, including state-sponsored violence and armed conflict in their countries of origin; ongoing extreme violence in migrants' countries of origin (e.g., femicide, drug and human trafficking, gang violence) (Internal Displacement 2011; Stone 2011); recent iterations and intensification of U.S. immigration policies and practices; and other global social structural factors (e.g., extreme poverty in countries of origin as well as NAFTA, CAFTA, and other IMF and World Bank policies) (Cohen 2006; Washington Office on Latin America 2003). The chapter then examines the psychosocial effects of migration, detention, and deportation on children of migrants living in the United States and in the country of origin. Stories of children "left behind," of young fathers and mothers "deported home," and of grandparents and school teachers seeking to sustain and support families represent the complexities of life for those living in the shadows of the policies and practices described in the earlier chapters of this volume. As importantly, it explores migrants' experiences of discrimination, racism, and poverty on both sides of the border—despite the widely reported importance of remittances to countries of origin—and analyzes how migrants' children incorporate and resist the criminalization of their parents by law enforcement within the United States and how activist scholars collaborate in teaching-learning processes through which these migrants *Know Your Rights*. The activist scholarship described herein suggests how partnerships across disciplines can generate audiences to hear the voices of migrants out of the shadows and into actions that can influence policies within and across borders. In the final chapter of Part II, sociologists Katie Dingeman-Cerda and Rubén G. Rumbaut examine the grim realities of deportation in El Salvador and the poignant contradictions and unintended consequences of U.S. policy there. The U.S. government's long-term support of the Salvadoran civil war (1980–1992) and subsequent natural disasters as well as the repatriation of Salvadoran youth who had established gangs in the United States frame the challenges facing thousands of Salvadorans who have been "sentenced home." Drawing on the lived experiences of many of these youth, Dingeman-Cerda and Rumbaut document how those within this "new American diaspora" negotiate their identities and the multiple material challenges they face when forcibly returned to their parents' country of origin, a country that is often tepid to hostile to their return. These two chapters demonstrate the transnational nature of detention and deportation, as well as the deeply entwined political, economic, and social histories of the United States and Central America.

In sum, this book examines a range of theoretical and practical problems that often elude analysis within single disciplines. As importantly, this work has been developed at the *interface* of theory and practice. It presses for theory based on lived experiences and applications that engage theory. Its basic goals are to marshal the experiences and critical reflections of those working alongside migrants to develop better frameworks for policy recommendations for the U.S. Congress and the president and to provide guidance for ourselves and others who collaborate with migrants, detainees, deportees, and their families, during what the authors anticipate will continue to be heated debates about immigration reform in years to come.

NOTES

1 According to DHS, "[r]emovals are the compulsory and confirmed movement of an inadmissible or deportable alien out of the United States. . . . Returns are the confirmed movement of an inadmissible or deportable alien out of the United States not based on an order of removal." Returns, however, also invariably involve coercive government action.

2 See *Chaidez v. United States*, 568 U.S. ___ , 133 S. Ct. 1103 (2013) (*Padilla* does not apply retroactively to cases already final on direct review). Some state courts, however, have held that *Padilla* should be retroactively applied. The Supreme Judicial Court of Massachusetts (SJC), for example, has held that *Padilla* is retroactive, at

least as to state convictions that became final after April 1, 1997 (the effective date of relevant changes to deportation law). *Commonwealth v. Sylvain*, 466 Mass. 422 (2013). The effects are profound for many deportees with *state* (as opposed to federal) convictions, though the practical difficulties involved in bringing such claims on behalf of deportees are significant.
3 Melissa's parents are alive, but she had been out of contact with them in recent years and was in foster care for much of her childhood. Melissa and Chris maintained a relationship with Dith's aunt and uncle after his deportation, however.
4 The *Post-Deportation Human Rights Project* at Boston College was founded by the editors in order to conceptualize this emerging body of law, to study the effects of deportation, and to aid deportees, their families, and attorneys who wish to take on such cases. *See* http://www.bc.edu/centers/humanrights/projects/deportation.html.
5 The word, "alien," though pejorative in common discourse (especially if preceded by the adjective "illegal"), is a legal term of art, defined as "any person not a citizen or national of the United States"; 8 USC § 1101(a)(3).
6 But see the previous discussion of *Padilla v. Kentucky*. Also, there have been important recent inroads made to provide counsel in New York City, a model that may soon be followed elsewhere.
7 In other words, it is "a means of implementing a policy of selecting those allowed to become and remain residents of the United States" (Hutchinson 1981:443).
8 70.5 percent were deported for a nonviolent offense and 29.5 percent were deported for a violent or potentially violent offense.
9 A project supported by the Center for Human Rights and International Justice at Boston College.

REFERENCES

Amey, Marilyn J. and Dennis F. Brown. 2000. *Interdisciplinary Collaboration and Academic Work*. Paper presented in Seattle, Washington at the annual meeting of the Association for the Study of Higher Education.
Antiterrorism and Effective Death Penalty Act of 1996, § 440(e), 110 Stat. 1277 (1996).
Argueta, Luis. (Producer). 2011. *abUSed: The Postville Raid*. USA/Guatemala: New Day Films.
Baum, Jonathan, Rosha Jones, and Catherine Barry. 2010. *In the Child's Best Interest?: The Consequences of Losing a Lawful Immigrant Parent to Deportation*. Accessed May 29, 2015. Berkeley: University of California. http://files.eric.ed.gov/fulltext/ED536693.pdf
Benhabib, Seyla. 2004. *The Rights of Others*. Cambridge, UK: Cambridge University Press.
Bernstein, Nina. 2010. "How One Marijuana Cigarette May Lead to Deportation." *New York Times*. March 30, 2010. Accessed October 22, 2014. http://www.nytimes.com/2010/03/31/nyregion/31drug.html?pagewanted=all&_r=0.
Brabeck, Kalina M., M. Brinton Lykes, and Rachel Hershberg. 2011. "Framing Immigration to and Deportation from the United States: Guatemalan and Salvadoran

Families Make Meaning of Their Experience." *Community, Work, and Family* 14:1–22. doi:10.1080/13668803.2010.520840

Brabeck, Kalina and Qingwen Xu. 2010. "The Impact of Detention and Deportation on Latino Children and Families: A Quantitative Exploration." *Hispanic Journal of Behavioral Sciences* 32:341–361. doi: 10.1177/0739986310374053

Cahn, Dori and Jay Stansell. 2005. "From Refugee to Deportee: How US Immigration Law Failed the Cambodian Community." In Kimberly Hold Barrett and William H. George, eds., *Race, Culture, Psychology & Law* (pp. 237–254). Thousand Oaks, CA: Sage.

Capps, Randy, Michael Fix, Jason Ost, Jane Reardon-Anderson, and Jeffrey S. Passel. 2004. *The Health and Well-Being of Young Children of Immigrants*. Washington, DC: Urban Institute. Accessed October 22, 2014. http://www.urban.org/uploaded-pdf/311139_childrenimmigrants.pdf.

Chavez, Lilian and Cecilia Menjívar. 2010. "Children Without Borders: A Mapping of the Literature on Unaccompanied Migrant Children to the United States." *Migraciones Internacionales* 5:71–111. Accessed October 22, 2014. http://www2.colef.mx/migracionesinternacionales/ revistas/MI18/n18-071-111.pdf.

Cohen, Salomon. 2006. "CAFTA: What Could It Mean for Migration?" Accessed December 11, 2011. http://www.migrationinformation.org/USfocus/print.cfm?ID=388.

Dougherty, Mary, Denise Wilson, and Amy Wu. 2005. *Immigration Enforcement Actions 2005*. U.S. Department of Homeland Security, Office of Immigration Statistics. Accessed October 22, 2014. http://www.dhs.gov/xlibrary/assets/statistics/yearbook/2005/Enforcement_AR_05.pdf.

Fals Borda, Orlando. 2001. "Participatory (Action) Research in Social Theory: Origins and Challenges." In Peter Reason and Hilary Bradbury, eds., *Handbook of Action Research: Participative Inquiry and Practice* (pp. 27–37). Thousand Oaks, CA: Sage.

Fitzpatrick, John C., ed. 1938. *The Writings of George Washington from the Original Manuscript Sources, 1745–1799*. Washington, DC: U.S. Government Printing Office.

García Coll, Cynthia and Amy Kerivan Marks, eds. 2012. *The Immigrant Paradox in Children and Adolescents: Is Becoming American a Developmental Risk?* Washington, DC: American Psychological Association.

Gaventa, John C. and Andrea Cornwall. 2001. "Power and Knowledge." In Peter Reason and Hilary Bradbury, eds., *Handbook of Action Research: Participative Inquiry and Practice* (pp. 172–189). Thousand Oaks, CA: Sage.

Gavett, Gretchen. 2011. Map: the U.S. Immigration Detention Boom. *PBS Frontline*. Accessed October 22, 2014. http://www.pbs.org/wgbh/pages/frontline/race-multicultural/lost-in-detention/map-the-u-s-immigration-detention-boom/.

Gibney, Mark. 1989. "United States Immigration Policy and the Huddled Masses Myth." *Georgetown Immigration Law Journal* 3:361–389.

Gonzalez, David. 2009. "A Family Divided by 2 Words, Legal and Illegal." *New York Times*, April 29, 2009. Accessed October 22, 2014. http://www.nytimes.com/2009/04/26/nyregion/26immig.html.

Higham, John, 1955. *Strangers in the Land: Patterns of American Nativism 1860–1925*. New Brunswick, NJ: Rutgers University Press (copyright renewed 1983).

Higham, John. 1984. *Send These to Me: Immigrants in Urban America*. Baltimore, MD: Johns Hopkins University Press.

Human Rights Watch. 2009. *Forced Apart (By the Numbers)*. Accessed November 4, 2014. http://www.hrw.org/reports/2009/04/15/forced-apart-numbers-0.

Hutchinson, Edward P. 1981. *Legislative History of American Immigration Policy 1798–1965*. Philadelphia: University of Pennsylvania Press.

Internal Displacement Monitoring Centre and Norwegian Refugee Council. 2011. *Internal Displacement: Global Overview of Trends and Developments in 2010*. Accessed May 4, 2014. http://www.internal-displacement.org/assets/publications/2011/2011-global-overview-2010-global-en.pdf.

Kanstroom, Daniel. 2007. *Deportation Nation: Outsiders in American History*. Cambridge, MA: Harvard University Press.

Kanstroom, Daniel. 2011. The Right to Deportation Counsel in Padilla v. Kentucky: The Challenging Construction of the Fifth-And-A-Half Amendment. 58 *UCLA L. REV.* 1461. Accessed October 22, 2014. http://www.uclalawreview.org/pdf/58-6-4.pdf.

Kanstroom, Daniel. 2012. *Aftermath: Deportation Law and the New American Diaspora*. New York: Oxford University Press.

Kanstroom, Daniel and Marija Ozolins. 2014. "Doesn't Love a Wall." In Lois Lorentzen, ed., *Hidden Lives and Human Rights in the United States: Understanding the Controversies and Tragedies of Undocumented Immigration*, Vol. 2 (pp. 41–72). Santa Barbara, CA: ABC/CLIO.

Kemmis, Stephen and Robin McTaggart. 2005. "Participatory Action Research." In Norman K. Denzin and Yvonne S. Lincoln, eds., *Handbook of Qualitative Research*, 3rd ed. (pp. 559–604). Thousand Oaks, CA: Sage.

Kennedy, John F. 1958. *A Nation of Immigrants*. New York: Anti-Defamation League of B'Nai B'rith.

Klein, Julie Thompson 1996. *Crossing Boundaries: Knowledge, Disciplinarities, and Interdisciplinarities*. Charlottesville: University Press of Virginia.

Klein, Julie Thompson 2005. "Interdisciplinary Teamwork: The Dynamics of Collaboration and Integration." In Sharon J. Derry, Christian D. Schunn, and Morton A. Gernsbacher, eds., *Interdisciplinary Collaboration: An Emerging Cognitive Science* (pp. 23–50). Mahwah, NJ: Lawrence Erlbaum Associates.

Kremer, James D., Kathleen A. Moccio, Joseph W. Hammel, et al. 2009. "Severing a Lifeline: The Neglect of Citizen Children in America's Immigration Enforcement Policy." Report for the Urban Institute. www.dorsey.com/files/upload/DorseyProBono_SeveringLifeline_ReportOnly_web.pdf.

Ku, Leighton and Sheetal Matani. 2001. "Left Out: Immigrants' Access to Health Care and Insurance." *Health Affairs: The Policy Journal of the Health Sphere* 20(1):247–256.

Lazarus, Emma. 1883. *The New Colossus*. Accessed November 3, 2014. http://xroads.virginia.edu/~cap/liberty/lazaruspoem.html.

Lykes, M. Brinton, Kalina M. Brabeck, and Cristina Hunter. 2013. "Exploring Parent-Child Communication in the Context of Threat: Mixed-Status Families Facing Detention and Deportation in Post 9/11 USA." *Community, Work and Family* 16(2):123–146. doi: 10.1080/13668803.2012.752997.

Martin, David A. 2005. *Twilight Statuses: A Closer Examination of the Unauthorized Population.* Migration Policy Institute. Accessed October 22, 2014. http://www.migrationpolicy.org/pubs/MPI_PB_6.05.pdf.

Menjívar, Cecilia and Daniel Kanstroom. 2013. *Constructing Immigrant "Illegality": Experiences, Critiques, and Resistance.* Cambridge, UK: Cambridge University Press.

Morawetz, Nancy. "Understanding the Impact of the 1996 Deportation Laws and the Limited Scope of Proposed Reforms," *Harvard Law Review* 113:1936 (2000).

Motomura, Hiroshi. 2007. *Americans in Waiting: The Lost Story of Immigration and Citizenship in the United States.* New York: Oxford University Press.

Motomura, Hiroshi. 2014. *Immigration Outside the Law.* New York: Oxford University Press.

Neuman, Gerald L. 1996. *Strangers to the Constitution: Immigrants, Borders, and Fundamental Law.* Princeton, NJ: Princeton University Press.

New York University School of Law Immigrant Rights Clinic. 2012. *Insecure Communities, Devastated Families: New Data on Immigrant Detention and Deportation Practices in New York City.* Accessed May 4, 2014. http://www.familiesforfreedom.org/sites/default/files/resources/NYC%20FOIA%20Report%202012%20FINAL_1.pdf.

Park, Peter 1993. "What Is Participatory Research? A Theoretical and Methodological Perspective." In M. Brydon-Miller, Peter Park, Budd Hall, and Ted Jackson, eds., *Voices of Change: Participatory Research in the United States and Canada* (pp. 1–29). Ontario: OISE Press.

Passel, Jeffrey S. and D'Vera Cohn. 2009. *A Portrait of Unauthorized Immigrants in the United States.* Accessed October 22, 2014. Washington, DC: Pew Research Center. http://pewhispanic.org/files/reports/107.pdf.

Passel, Jeffrey S. and D'Vera Cohn. 2011. *Unauthorized Immigrant Population: National and State Trends.* Accessed October 8, 2014. Washington, DC: Pew Research Center. http://www.pewhispanic.org/2011/02/01/unauthorized-immigrant-population-brnational-and-state-trends-2010/.

Pew Research Center. 2013. *A Nation of Immigrants.* Accessed October 22, 2014. http://www.pewhispanic.org/2013/01/29/a-nation-of-immigrants/.

Post, Louis F. (1923) *The Deportations Delirium of Nineteen-Twenty: A Personal Narrative of an Historic Official Experience.* Chicago: C.H. Kerr.

Rahman, Mohammad Anisur. 1991. "The Theoretical Standpoint of PAR." In Orlando Fals Borda and Mohammad Anisur Rahman, eds., *Action and Knowledge: Breaking the Monopoly with Participatory Action Research* (pp. 13–23). New York: Apex Press.

Rahman, Mohammad Anisur and Orlando Fals Borda. 1991. "A Self-Review of PAR." In Orlando Fals Borda and Mohammad Anisur Rahman, eds., *Action and Knowledge: Breaking the Monopoly with Participatory Action Research* (pp. 24–34). New York: Apex Press.

Reason, Peter and Hilary Bradbury. 2001 "Introduction: Inquiry and Participation in Search of a World Worthy of Human Aspiration." In Peter Reason and Hilary Bradbury, eds., *Handbook of Action Research* (pp. 1–10). Thousand Oaks, CA: Sage.

Rosenblum, Marc C. and Kristen McCabe. 2014. *Deportation and Discretion: Reviewing the Record and Options for Change.* Accessed November 6, 2014. Migration Policy Institute. http://www.migrationpolicy.org/research/deportation-and-discretion-reviewing-record-and-options-change.

Rosenblum, Marc C. and Doris Meissner. 2014. *The Deportation Dilemma: Reconciling Tough and Humane Enforcement.* Accessed October 22, 2014. Migration Policy Institute. http://www.migrationpolicy.org/research/deportation-dilemma-reconciling-tough-humane-enforcement.

Rumbaut, Rubén G. and Walter A. Ewing. 2007. *The Myth of Immigrant Criminality and the Paradox of Assimilation: Incarceration Rates Among Native and Foreign-Born Men.* Accessed October 22, 2014. Washington, DC: Social Science Resource Council. http://borderbattles.ssrc.org/Rumbault_Ewing/printable.html.

Simich, Laura, Fei Wu, and Sonya Nerad. 2007. "Status and Health Security: An Exploratory Study of Irregular Immigrants in Toronto." *Canadian Journal of Public Health* 98(5):369–373. http://www.jstor.org/stable/41994958.

Siskin, Alison 2012. *Immigration-Related Detention: Current Legislative Issues.* Accessed October 22, 2014. Washington, DC: Congressional Research Service. http://fas.org/irp/crs/RL32369.pdf.

Slevin, Peter. 2010. "Deportation of Illegal Immigrants Increases Under the Obama Administration." *Washington Post*, July 26, 2010. Accessed October 22, 2014. http://www.washingtonpost.com/wp-dyn/content/article/2010/07/25/AR2010072501790.html.

Special Rapporteur on the Human Rights of Migrants. 2008. *Promotion and Protection of all Human Rights, Civil, Political, Economic, Social and Cultural Rights, Including the Right to Development* (report A/HRC/7/CRP.3). Accessed November 5, 2014. Office of the United Nations High Commissioner for Human Rights.

Stone, Hannah. 2011. "Guatemala Anti-Drug Operations Force Refugees into Mexico." *InSight Organized Crime in the Americas.* Accessed December 10, 2011. http://www.insightcrime.org/news-briefs/guatemala-anti-drug-operations-force-refugees-into-mexico.

Transactional Records Access Clearinghouse (TRAC). 2006. *How Often Is the Aggravated Felony Statute Used?* Accessed October 22, 2014. http://trac.syr.edu/immigration/reports/158.

U.S. Census Bureau. 2010. "Nation's Foreign-Born Population Nears 37 Million, More Than One in Five People in the U.S. Are First or Second Generation." U.S. Census Bureau. Accessed October 19, 2014. http://www.census.gov/newsroom/releases/archives/foreignborn_population/cb10-159.html.

U.S. Department of Homeland Security, Office of Immigration Statistics. 2012. *2012 Yearbook of Immigration Statistics, Department of Homeland Security.* Accessed October 22, 2014. http://www.dhs.gov/publication/yearbook-2012.

U.S. Department of Homeland Security, Office of Immigration Statistics. 2013. *2013 Yearbook of Immigration Statistics, Department of Homeland Security.* Accessed November 4, 2014. http://www.dhs.gov/yearbook-immigration-statistics.

U.S. Department of Justice, Executive Office for Immigration Review, Office of Planning Analysis and Technology, 2008. *FY 2007 Statistical Year Book.* Accessed October 22, 2014. http://www.justice.gov/eoir/statspub/fy07syb.pdf.

Washington Office on Latin American (WOLA). 2003. *What Is CAFTA and Why Is It Important?* Accessed December 11, 2011. http://www.wola.org/publications/what_is_cafta_and_why_is_it_important.

Wessler, Seth Freed. 2009. "Double Punishment." *ColorLines News for Action.* October 22, 2009. Accessed October 22, 2014. http://colorlines.com/archives/2009/10/double_punishment.html.

Wessler, Seth Freed. 2012. "Nearly 250K Deportations of Parents of U.S. Citizens in Just Over Two Years." *Color Lines News for Action.* Accessed October 4, 2014. http://www.colorlines.com/archives/2012/12/us_deports_more_than_200k_parents.html.

Xu, Qingwen and Kalina M. Brabeck. 2012. "Service Utilization Among Unauthorized Latino Immigrant Families." *Social Work Research* 32(3):341–361. doi: 10.1093/swr/svs015.

Yoshikawa, Hirokazu. 2011. *Immigrants Raising Citizens: Undocumented Parents and Their Young Children.* New York: Russell Sage Foundation.

CASE CITATIONS

Chaidez v. United States, 568 U.S. __ , 113 S. Ct. 1103 (2013).
Commonwealth v. Sylvain, 466 Mass. 422 (2013).
Demore v. Kim, 538 U.S. 510 (2003).
Fong Yue Ting v. United States, 149 US at 759 (Field, J. dissenting) (1893).
INS v. Lopez-Mendoza, 468 U.S. 1032 (1984).
Matter of Andres Armendarez-Mendez, Int. Dec. 3626; 24 I. & N. Dec. 646 (BIA 2008).
Padilla v. Kentucky, 559 U.S. 356 (2010).
Reno v. AADC, 525 U.S. 471 (1999).

PART I

The Legal, Administrative, and Political Responses

1

Unhappy Families

The Failings of Immigration Law for Families That Are Not All Alike

DAVID B. THRONSON

Happy families are all alike; every unhappy family is unhappy in its own way.
—Leo Tolstoy, *Anna Karenina*

Immigration law privileges certain families, those "happy families" whose individual and group characteristics align with the narrow parameters that immigration law makes vital to successfully navigate the maze of immigration law. The central role of family ties in assisting such families move smoothly toward lawful immigration status creates a ubiquitous yet inaccurate impression that the promotion of family unity is a key value underlying immigration law. By focusing only on the happy families that benefit from immigration law, it is easy to ignore the disdain for family unity that is evident in the failure of immigration law, by acts and omissions, to keep families together. Family can play a significant role in immigration law, but in a much more narrow and less benign way than is generally contemplated.

For families that do not meet the exacting templates of immigration law, the story is not of family unity but rather of separation and hardship. By failing to value basic notions of family independence and decision-making, immigration law fails these "unhappy families," those that do not conform to the model family recognized and rewarded by immigration law. These families find themselves at odds with the harsh mandates of immigration law and demonstrate that the law is not always, or even usually, a family-friendly endeavor.

As immigration law intrudes upon and shapes family decisions about who will live where and with whom, it stands out for the starkness of its demands and the frequency with which its dictates conflict with the values and narratives that are foundational to ideas of family in broader society and other areas of law. A closer inspection of the role of family in immigration law reveals that for families outside the exacting mold that immigration values, family is of little use in slowing robust deportation efforts and, even more broadly, in providing avenues that would allow families to achieve lawful immigration status and protect themselves from fear of deportation.

The failings of immigration law for families that do not conform to particular characteristics result in family separation, hardship and suffering for families, and predictably prevalent patterns of poverty that impact many immigrant families. These failings also lead to confusing interactions with other societal institutions and legal systems, such as family courts, that attempt to effectuate family unity and work in the best interests of children. As an outlier in its treatment of children and families, immigration law is out of step with broader values and efforts to preserve families.

Privileged Narratives—Narrowing What Matters

In general society, the importance of family is rarely questioned. Yet in the confidence of this presumed importance it is all too common to overlook the ways in which public policy choices and the law fail to support and protect families. Nowhere is the gap wider between rhetoric touting the importance of family and the reality of the law's impact than in the area of immigration. A review of the role of family in immigration law reveals the extent to which immigration law strays from the values and views of family that we espouse in other public policy arenas and in other legal realms, such as family law.

Outside immigration, family and notions of family unity play a central and privileged role in the U.S. legal system. Despite the absence of the word "family" anywhere in the U.S. Constitution,[1] the Supreme Court consistently has acknowledged that "the Constitution protects the sanctity of the family precisely because the institution of the family is deeply rooted in this Nation's history and tradition. It is through the family that we inculcate and pass down many of our most cherished values, moral and cultural" (*Moore v. City of East Cleveland* 1977). In family law, an important means to protect family integrity has been emphasis on the parent-child relationship, as "the interest of parents in the care, custody, and control of their children is perhaps the oldest of the fundamental liberty interests recognized by the Court"[2] (*Troxel v. Granville* 2000). While elevating the parent-child relationship, however, the Court also has recognized that families may decide they are best served by living in some arrangement other than the traditional nuclear family and that the Constitution prohibits the government "from standardizing its children and its adults by forcing all to live in certain narrowly defined family patterns" (*Moore v. City of East Cleveland* 1977). Although uneven in their success, legal frameworks in the United States generally strive to effectuate the vitality and independence of the family that the centrality of family demands.

Immigration law stands in stark contrast to soaring rhetoric about the family's fundamental importance and independent diversity. As a result, there is tremendous potential for deep conflict as immigration law and family law intersect. The vindication of immigration law often compromises family integrity, and family integrity often can be accomplished only in violation of immigration laws. Through the operation of immigration law, parent-child relationships routinely are strained and broken. And even when immigration law provides benefits or relief on the basis of family for some, rigid and standardized notions of family limit options for many families that do not exhibit a narrow range of characteristics.

Through stilted statutory frameworks, narrow notions of family, and harsh provisions that anticipate and accept infliction of family suffering, immigration law renders compelling narratives and facts about families largely irrelevant to immigration analysis. The veneer of family friendliness that often is attributed to immigration law fades under closer observation.

Enforcement and Deportation—Things That Matter Made Irrelevant

U.S immigration law at first blush appears oriented toward advancing family unity through an elaborate system of family-sponsored immigration and provisions for derivative immigration of the family members of certain immigrants who qualify for immigration benefits. *See* Immigration and Nationality Act (INA) § 201(b)(2)(A)(i), 8 U.S.C. § 1151(b)

(2)(A)(i) (Supp. 2011), (excluding "immediate relatives" of U.S. citizens from direct numerical limitations on immigrant visas); § 1151(c) (2006) (setting levels of family-sponsored immigrants); 1153(a) (2006) (creating preference categories for family-sponsored immigrants); § 1153(d) (2006) (permitting some family members to accompany or follow to join family members with immigrant visas). Indeed, reports of U.S immigration law often attribute to it the goal of keeping families intact (see also Sanger 1987). The conflict between this perception and the reality of immigration law is most obviously apparent in situations where a family member faces deportation from the United States, but deeper tensions in the basic family immigration framework occur less openly but quite effectively to keep families from living together in conformity with immigration law.

First, when a person faces removal from the United States it is as an individual, not as a family unit (*But see* 8 U.S.C. § 1227(a)(4)(B) (2006) and 8 U.S.C. § 1182(a)(3)(B) (2006), making spouses and children deportable based on their relationship to a noncitizen involved in terrorist activity; see also Nessel 2005). For example, removal proceedings may result in an order of deportation against a parent that does absolutely nothing to affect directly the immigration status of a child or other family members. This hardly means, however, that family members are not affected.

Family can play a limited role in mounting a defense to removal from the United States, but the legal framework that permits this is narrow and eliminates consideration of most facts that obviously come to mind when thinking about the reality of a family facing the prospect of losing the presence of a family member. The compelling narratives of loss and separation that accompany the enforcement of immigration law are rendered largely irrelevant.

For example, persons without lawful immigration status who are placed in removal proceedings may apply for cancellation of the removal if they meet a number of criteria, including having been physically present in the United States for ten years and being of good moral character (INA § 240A, 8 U.S.C. § 1229b (2006 and Supp. 2011)).[3] To qualify, they also must prove that removal would cause "exceptional and extremely unusual hardship" to a legal permanent resident or U.S. citizen spouse, parent, or child (INA § 240A, 8 U.S.C. § 1229b (2006 and Supp. 2011)). The standard here is high and has proven difficult to satisfy. Cancellation applicants not only must have qualifying family members but also must demonstrate hardship "substantially different from, or beyond that which would normally be expected from the deportation of an alien with close family members here" (*In re Monreal-Aguinaga* 2001).

In other words, the expected or normal hardship that the deportation of a family member entails is made irrelevant as an expected result of the enforcement of immigration laws. Under this reasoning, for example, separation between parents and children left behind in the United States is unlikely to rise to "exceptional and extremely unusual hardship" because such separation is not unusual and "[d]eportation rarely occurs without personal distress and emotional hurt" (*Sullivan v. INS* 1985). Family separation is "simply one of the common results of deportation or exclusion [that] are insufficient to prove extreme hardship" (*Jimenez v. INS* 1997). Anticipating suffering, immigration law renders it irrelevant and insufficient to warrant relief from deportation.

Arguments that the requisite hardship will result if families choose not to separate by having members accompany the deported person abroad are an equally difficult path to immigration relief. For example, diminished access to education, healthcare, and economic opportunities for U.S. citizen children who are raised in other countries similarly are viewed simply as the anticipated results of deportation and thus do not meet the "exceptional and extremely unusual hardship" standard (*Jimenez v. INS* 1997).[4] So high is the standard to establish extreme hardship that one circuit court of appeals described its role as reviewing the record for hardship that is "uniquely extreme, at or closely approaching the outer limits of the most severe hardship the alien could suffer and so severe that any reasonable person would necessarily conclude that the hardship is extreme" (*Hernandez-Cordero v. INS* 1987).

The meager and dwindling set of narratives that can lead to relief in the cancellation of removal context is contrary to mainstream values and approaches in other areas of law, such as family law, where the importance of considering children's interests in legal decisions regarding family is well established: "The custody law in every state in the United States ... embraces the 'best interests' standard" (Blair and Weiner 2005). Over the last several decades, however, immigration law has moved away from considering such narratives. Immigration law demands no more than mere avoidance of exceptional and extremely unusual hardship to certain family members, while anticipating that significant hardship is inevitable. Immigration law dismisses narratives of family suffering that accompany deportation for not matching the extremes it requires. The unique and deeply felt experiences of families facing the loss of loved ones are gathered together as expected, and disregarded. Immigration law ignores the uniqueness of each family by requiring a particular and demanding form.

Second, even where exceptional and extreme hardship exists, immigration law limits relief by restricting its application to a short list of relationships based on the traditional nuclear family. By failing to acknowledge the importance of nontraditional arrangements for caretaking and support of children, immigration law again limits the relevance of compelling family narratives that result from the application of immigration law. Immigration law's restrictive use of a narrow construct of family effectively "negates other prevalent family configurations which make up functional families, such as single-parent households, grandparent-grandchild households, same-sex couples, polygamous marriages, and extended family configurations (King 2010, p. 515)."[5] This approach fails to consider that millions of children in the United States "grow up in families in which care is not provided exclusively by two heterosexual opposite-sex parents. Instead, caregivers increasingly include gay and lesbian families, single parent or 'cohabiting' parent families, families with grandparents (either as primary caregivers or in addition to primary caregivers), and various other formations" (Kavanagh 2004, p. 91).

The failure to recognize nontraditional families in immigration law creates disparate impacts across racial and ethnic lines. For example, ignoring the reality of grandparents who care for their grandchildren in immigration law has a particular impact on Latino populations because "Hispanic grandparents are the largest population of noncitizen caregiver grandparents" (Zug 2009, p. 242). By insisting on an outdated and restrictive construction of family, immigration law advances "a false construct of human society, cultural constructions, and racial and ethnic prejudices" (King 2010, p. 515).

Beyond the context of immigration law, families routinely function in ways that diverge from the traditional notion of the nuclear family. Family decisions about who lives with whom often take into account who cares for or provides for whom. Indeed, these decisions, which create networks of interdependency and support, are hallmarks of the notion of family. By removing many of the basic realities of families from consideration when family members face deportation, immigration law proceeds on a faulty premise and fails to respond to the realities it creates.

Third, beyond the substance of immigration law, the manner in which immigration law is enforced has tremendous impact on families. Shifts in immigration enforcement strategies to emphasize interior enforcement significantly affect immigrant families. First, the past decade saw raids targeted at workplaces, often large-scale, dramatic events that impacted hundreds of immigrants and their families and disrupted entire communities (Capps et al. 2007). The more recent shift to raids targeted at homes results in events that are of smaller scale and less likely to generate widespread media coverage, but this makes them no less dramatic in nature for the individual families involved.[6] Immigration enforcement activities are traumatic for those arrested and for witnesses alike, especially children who witness the arrests of parents or other relatives (Hendricks 2007).

The increase in interior enforcement contributes to a climate of fear among immigrants who often are settled into communities and previously might not have felt targeted by immigration law enforcement. The larger workplace raids in particular result in "crisis scenarios in terms of the care arrangements for the hundreds of children who temporarily los[e] their parents . . . [and lead] 'to a general sense of chaos and fear" (Capps et al. 2007, p. 34). Reports of one major raid indicate that at times the "situation deteriorated further toward outright panic" and families hid "in their basements or closets for days" (ibid.). Living with family members who lack authorized immigration status means living with the constant fear that a family member will face deportation. Kevin Johnson writes: "The fear of deportation haunts many immigrants. They know that they can be torn away from established lives, family, friends, and community in an instant for lacking the proper immigration papers or for even something as minor as failing to file a change of address form with the U.S. government within ten days of moving" (Johnson 2007, p. 46).

Immigration raids have a particular impact on children in immigrant families because "many children face [] traumatic circumstances and insecure care . . . in the period after the raids" (Capps et al. 2007, p. 37). The Department of Homeland Security's Office of Inspector General notes that it does not require the collection of data on the status of children of persons who are deported (USDHS 2009). Still, recent data from US Immigration and Customs Enforcement suggest that about 90,000 parents of US-born citizen children have been deported each year for the past several years. (Wessler 2012).

According to "[c]hild psychology experts . . . children suffer most from the disruption of armed agents coming into their homes and taking away their parents—and sometimes themselves. Children can experience stress, depression and anxiety disorders" (Hendricks 2007). "The most destabilizing impact on the children of arrestees following worksite enforcement actions came from the separation and fragmentation of families" (Capps et al. 2007, p. 42). For children, "emotional trauma . . . followed separation from one or both parents" (ibid., p. 50). Younger children cannot understand the concept of immigration law and any "sudden separation [is] considered personal abandonment" (ibid., p. 51). Moreover, "children who witness their parents being taken into custody lose trust in their parents' ability to keep them safe and begin to see danger everywhere" (Hendricks 2007).[7]

Aside from the initial trauma, a parent's detention or deportation removes that parent's earnings from the household, creating "a more unstable home environment and remov[ing] one of the main strengths in immigrant families—the presence of two parents" (Capps et al. 2007, p. 41). Furthermore, when the parent who is arrested is a working parent, he or she often is the person in the family who is most integrated into U.S. society, so that the connection with broader society is diminished (Capps et al. 2007).

In the wake of mass immigration enforcement raids, children have exhibited increased absenteeism in schools (WCCO 2007). Often, enforcement actions that are widely known in the community cause "some degree of polarization between Latino immigrants and other community residents" (Capps et al. 2007, p. 51). Children experience social isolation when they are "harassed by other children or branded as criminals because their parents were arrested" (ibid., p. 52). Following one large raid, at school "[m]any children exhibited outward signs of stress . . . [and] lost their appetites, ate less, and lost weight" (ibid.; see Brabeck et al., this volume).

The enforcement of immigration law creates searing family narratives of separation, hardship, and trauma, yet immigration law ignores these compelling stories and renders them legally irrelevant. Removal proceedings provide no opportunity or framework to hear the voices of those most directly and deeply affected by the enforcement of immigration law. By narrowing what is relevant, deportation is accomplished without having to confront the reality evidenced by the voices and narratives of immigrant families. Things that matter deeply—family separation, hardship and trauma—are swept aside.

Failing Families before Deportation

Deportation and post-deportation consequences do not happen in a vacuum. The frameworks for lawful immigration create the pool of persons and families that will be subject to deportation through the allocation of lawful immigration status to some and the withholding of this from others. As in the context of deportation, the restricted role of family in determining who will obtain lawful status, and thus exemption from some of the harshest provisions of immigration law, is often misapprehended.

On a practical level, many choices about who is permitted to immigrate to the United States lawfully are personal. It is commonly understood that immigration law addresses the ability of persons to immigrate or remain in the United States, but it is often overlooked that immigration law in large part is about determining when U.S. citizens, legal permanent residents, may create immigration rights in others. By specifying who is empowered to generate immigration rights in certain family members, immigration law privileges some families and relationships, while devaluing others. A narrow set of personal choices are empowered while others are rejected.

The Immigration and Nationality Act's family-sponsored immigration framework permits legal permanent residents and citizens to petition for immigrant visas only for certain family members (*see* 8 U.S.C. § 1151(b)(2)(A)(i) (2006); 8 U.S.C. § 1153(a) (2006)). Under this scheme, a "petitioner," a person having legal immigration status, files for a "beneficiary," a person wishing to immigrate and who the law presumes is waiting outside the country. If the principal beneficiary has a spouse or children, in some instances the spouse or children may acquire immigration status as derivatives (*see* 8 U.S.C. § 1153(d) (2006)). Through this framework, petitioners with lawful immigration status regulate the flow of immigration status from themselves to qualifying relatives and their dependents.

Immigration law assigns various levels of priority to such family-sponsored immigration petitions based upon the immigration status of the petitioner and the relationship between the beneficiary and the petitioner (see 8 U.S.C. § 1153(a)). Citizens of the United States can petition for their spouses, children, siblings, and parents (*see* 8 U.S.C. § 1153(a); 8 U.S.C. § 1151(b)(2)(A)(i)). Lawful permanent residents may petition only for spouses and unmarried children (see 8 U.S.C. § 1153(a)).

In this framework, petitions filed by citizens receive priority over those filed by lawful permanent residents. Similarly, petitions based on what are considered close familial relationships are privileged over those based on less favored family relationships (Demleitner 2003; Kelly 2001; Motomura 1995; Romero 2005; Zug 2009). Because petitions of citizens for their spouses and unmarried minor children are not subject to numerical limits, they face no backlogs and are immediately available (*see* 8 U.S.C. § 1151(b) (2006 and Supp. 2011).[8] Relationships that are less favored, such as those between a legal permanent resident parent and a child, are subject to numerical limitations and are subject to extensive backlogs.[9] Immigration petitions receiving the lowest priority, based on the relationship between adult citizens and their siblings, can be backlogged for periods extending decades (USDS 2011). When immigration laws that recognize "certain family ties but not others, and then rank those ties in order of importance ... indicate which relationships matter the most in the eyes of the state. In short, laws relating to the family inherently embody normative ideals" (Huntington 2009, p. 413).

In addition to privileging some families over others, this framework has a particular impact on children. First, it adopts a restrictive definition of the word "child," guaranteeing that not all children are recognized as "children" for immigration purposes. Children can be recognized as a "child" only if they meet the criteria of a "particularly exhaustive" statutory definition (*INS v. Hector* 1986; *see also* Immigration and Nationality Act § 101(b)(1), 8 U.S.C. § 1101(b)(1) (2006 and Supp. 2011)). With clear intent not to include all children, a "child" is defined as one who meets other qualifying conditions, such as being born in wedlock or having a father who has taken specified steps to "legitimate" his child (*see* 8 U.S.C. § 1101(b)(1)). By basing the qualifications of who becomes a "child" on the actions and decisions of parents, this definition empowers parents as "rights holders who may take action to recognize a 'child' for immigration purposes. Children, in contrast, are by definition passive objects subject to parental control" (Thronson 2002, p. 992).

As in the deportation context, functional relationships outside formal statutory confines are ignored.[10] For example, even when a woman's "relationship with her nieces closely resembles a parent-child relationship, [the courts] are constrained to hold that Congress, through the plain language of the statute, precluded this functional approach to defining the word 'child'" (*INS v. Hector* 1986, pp. 90–91).[11] Although courts have noted that with regard to "the technical definition of 'child' contained within this statute . . . it could be argued that the line should have been drawn at a different point . . . these are policy questions entrusted exclusively to the political branches of our Government" (*INS v. Hector* 1986, p. 89, citing *Fiallo v. Bell* 1977). Immigration law's formalistic approach fails to account for choices outside the child's control about who can and will provide care for her, and contrasts with the treatment of children in other areas of law. "To be sure, the [Immigration and Nationality Act's] definition of 'child' may be far out of step with the times, and may have particularly deleterious effects on aliens whose culture's definition of 'family' is legitimately broader than the traditional definition of those related by blood or adoption" (*Dorado v. Gonzalez* 2006, p. 902).[12]

Even where adults have acted in such a way that children may be recognized as children under immigration law, the result is not that children are empowered under immigration law, but rather that immigration law allows parents to decide if their children may benefit from the exercise of the parents' rights (*see* 8 U.S.C. § 1151(b)(2)(A)(i) (2006) (allowing petitions for children by U.S. citizen parents); 8 U.S.C. § 1153(a)(2) (2006) (allowing petitions for children by permanent residence parents.)) An "unfortunately common problem with the family-based immigration regime . . . [is that] [d]erivative beneficiaries are just that—derivative—meaning that they have few rights of their own and instead depend on the competence and cooperation of the principal immigrant" (*Fornalik v. Perryman* 2000, pp. 527–528).[13] Not all parents are cooperative, and others are not able to competently avoid actions or decisions that preclude their attainment of lawful immigration status.

By effectively limiting family-sponsored immigration access to lawful permanent resident status for children to their status as dependents, immigration law subordinates children to their parents' rights and abilities.

Family-sponsored immigration provides no benefits to children because they are children. The "right" parent who advances successfully through the maze of immigration law is rewarded, and the child may benefit. But other than as a dependent of the "right" parent, the major paths to acquiring lawful immigration provide no special recognition or rights to children as individuals or based on their status as children.[14] Immigration law values families in which a family member has status, but not all such families. Those in which an adult holds status are privileged, and those in which children hold status are excluded.

By focusing on the adults in children's lives rather than children themselves, U.S. immigration law fails to recognize children as individuals. Arbitrarily limiting the pool of adults in children's lives who matter for purposes of immigration law further devalues the perspective of the child in immigration law. This rejection of the perspectives and realities of children reinforces the conception of children as dependents, not as individuals. This has negative consequences for the child lacking the "right" parent, and the pervasive influence of this limiting conception of children further impedes children who immigrate on their own or outside legal pathways.

Immigration law's asymmetric treatment of adults and children is in evidence in other aspects of immigration law where family relationships are granted significance by immigration law. For example, in situations where a person is eligible for an immigration visa, grounds for inadmissibility still may preclude a beneficiary from being able to immigrate to the United States (*see* 8 U.S.C. § 1182 (2006 and Supp. 2011)). For example, immigration law includes provisions that bar for three years the reentry of people who leave the United States after remaining here unlawfully for more than 180 days (*see* 8 U.S.C. § 1182(a)(9)(B)(i)(I) (2006)). A person who remains in the United States unlawfully for a year or more, then leaves, is barred from reentry for ten years (see 8 U.S.C. § 1182(a)(9)(B)(i)(II) (2006)). As a result, people who have been in the country unlawfully for more than a year cannot initiate the consular process to obtain lawful permanent resident status for which they are eligible without facing a ten-year wait outside the country. This is critical for persons who entered the country without inspection and on that basis are barred from processing their immigration petition in the United States through a process known as adjustment of status (*see* 8 U.S.C. § 1255(a)–(c) (2006)). The disconnect created by these statutory provisions between eligibility for lawful status and the realistic ability to obtain that status has particular impact on families with members from Mexico and Central America, as persons from these regions are overrepresented among those who entered without inspection.[15]

Acknowledging the hardship that a bar to admission for three or ten years can impose, immigration law does provide for a waiver of these grounds of inadmissibility by establishing that inadmissibility would result in hardship to family members (see 8 U.S.C. § 1182(a)(9)(B)(v) (2006)). Under the terms of the waiver provision, however, only hardships faced by adult family members, i.e., spouses and parents, are relevant (see 8 U.S.C. § 1182(a)(9)(B)(v) (2006)). Hardships that will affect children are excluded from relevance under the statute, so children's interests are excluded from the waiver process (see 8 U.S.C. § 1182(a)(9)(B)(v) (2006)). Here again, immigration law silences the voices of those most directly impacted by its application and renders everyday narratives of hardship irrelevant to the operation of immigration law.

By writing the reality of immigrant families and children out of immigration law frameworks, immigration law restricts families from successfully navigating the immigration system to regularize immigration status for all family members. This, in turn, creates the pool of persons and families that will be impacted most directly and deeply by deportation. The reality is that post-deportation consequences for families must account for the skewed immigration law framework that effectively protects some families by providing avenues for obtaining lawful status while simultaneously blocking such results for others. The balance struck by immigration law must be questioned when, for example, the relatively minor fact of an entry without inspection decades earlier can overcome a lifetime of hard work and nurture on behalf of a family that will suffer immensely from the application of immigration law. Immigration law punishes decisions to pursue better opportunities for families, yet these are precisely the type of aspirations and decisions that are expected and rewarded in other contexts.

Ongoing Impacts

Restrictions on the relevance of family in immigration matters contribute greatly to the resulting demographics of the nation's immigrant population. In particular, it results in a large and rising number of mixed-status families, that is, families in which all family members do not share the same immigration or citizenship status (Fix and Zimmermann 1999, p. 2). A mixed-family status can include families in which all family members have some form of lawful immigration status, but many are comprised of family members who are authorized to remain in the United States together with others who are not.

Children in immigrant families now account for nearly one-fourth of all children in the United States (Hernandez and Cervantes 2011, p. 6). The majority of children in immigrant families, 59 percent, have at least one parent who is a U.S. citizen (Hernandez 2009). Still, 5.5 million children have at least one parent who lacks lawful immigration status (Passel and Cohn 2011). In 2008, "of the 5.5 million children of unauthorized immigrants, 4 million, or 73%, were born in the United States" (ibid.).

In addition to differences in status between parents and children, there are also divides within families among siblings. Adolescent children in families with unauthorized parents are more likely to be unauthorized themselves than their younger siblings (Capps et al. 2007). Because more "younger children were born here, there are many mixed-status families in which the younger children are citizens but the older children—like their parents—are noncitizens" (Urban Institute 2006, p. 2; *see* Lykes et al., this volume).

Including adults along with children, almost 9 million people live in families with at least one unauthorized immigrant (Passel and Cohn 2009). Included in the population of unauthorized immigrants are 3.8 million parents of U.S. citizen children (Passel and Cohn 2009). Parents of U.S. citizen children, therefore, make up 37 percent of the adult population of unauthorized immigrants (ibid.). By any measure, the population of mixed-status families is significant. The realities that they face are deeply affected by issues of immigration status.

Harsh Realities for Immigrant Families

The immigration status of family members is not without consequence, especially for citizen children of unauthorized immigrants who often fail to benefit from the full promise of their citizenship. These children often find themselves effectively stateless because they face barriers not encountered by children in non-immigrant families as many "policies that advantage or disadvantage noncitizens are likely to have broad spillover effects on the citizen children who live in the great majority of immigrant families" (Fix and Zimmermann 1999, p. 2).

Unsurprisingly, immigration status has an effect on the economic status of children and families, and nearly half of all immigrant families live below 200 percent of the poverty line (Hernandez 2009). In fact, "children of immigrants [are] 1.5 times more likely than children in native-born families to live in a family with an income below the official federal poverty threshold, at 27.8 percent versus 18.6 percent" (Hernandez and Cervantes 2011, p. 9). When parents are unauthorized the figure is slightly higher, and a third of the children of unauthorized migrants live in poverty (Passel and Cohn 2009). Unauthorized migrants and their U.S. citizen children together account for 11 percent of people below poverty level, twice their percentage of the total population (Passel and Cohn 2009). Nearly half of all unauthorized migrant children and a quarter of U.S. citizen children of unauthorized migrants are uninsured (ibid.). Overall, "children of immigrants are substantially more likely than children with U.S.-born parents to be poor, have food-related problems, live in crowded housing, lack health insurance, and be in fair or poor health" (Capps et al. 2005, p. 5).

Even though citizen children are often eligible for benefits without regard to their parents' status, citizen children of immigrant parents access public benefits at a lower rate than children born to citizen parents (Fix and Passel 2002). This fact alone undermines myths that immigrants are drawn to the United States by the availability of public assistance (Fix and Passel 2002). Since the passage of welfare reform legislation in 1996, many social benefits laws differentiate between citizens and noncitizens, including those noncitizens with legal immigration status, reducing the overall availability of benefits to immigrant families.[16] When citizenship status limits eligibility and only some family members are eligible for benefits, citizen children who live "in households with noncitizens . . . suffer[ ] the disadvantage of . . . reduced overall household resources" (Fix and Zimmermann 1999, p. 2).

This means that citizen children in immigrant families commonly do not receive the needed benefits for which they are eligible as individuals. Benefits for children often are obtained only through a parent's initiative, and parents who are themselves ineligible may be inhibited in seeking benefits for which their children qualify (Fix and Zimmermann 1999). When parents are deterred from seeking benefits for their children, "inequalities in access within families have been created informally through the actions of parents and public program staff... resulting in a hierarchy of citizen children's access to social benefits, which is ordered by their parent's citizenship and immigration status" (Leiter, McDonald, and Jacobson 2006, p. 18). In such instances, children's formal rights to social benefits are trumped by parents and program personnel who act upon misguided beliefs that the parents' immigration status makes children ineligible. While "citizen children of immigrant parents are formally 'insiders' and therefore are fully eligible for social benefits, their parents' non-citizen, 'outsider' status may eclipse their children's citizenship, resulting in citizen children informally taking on their parent's citizenship status" (ibid.). Citizen children in mixed-status families thus often take on the status of undocumented children, with all the economic disadvantages that entails.

Tensions with Other Legal Institutions and Systems

The looming possibility of deportation and the inability to regularize the presence of large numbers of persons in mixed-status families not only impact the economic realities of families, they also create tensions as immigrant families interact with other societal institutions and legal systems. For example, when a parent is deported or when parents in immigrant families divorce, family courts routinely are called upon to make custody determinations that are challenged by the context of immigration laws and enforcement. As detailed above, immigration status is a potent force that shapes the life experiences of many immigrants and immigrant families. As such, the immigration status of parents and children forms an understandably tempting, though questionable, area of inquiry for family judges struggling to make difficult determinations about the interests of children on the basis of family law's vague and indeterminate criteria.

The handful of appellate courts that have directly discussed whether immigration status per se should affect child custody have rejected the notion outright. One court, for example, ruled that without regard to their immigration status, parents stand "on equal footing ... when asserting their right to custody of their children" (*Rico v. Rodriguez* 2005).

In rejecting the argument that a father "should be denied custody solely because of his immigration status," a court in Washington observed that the "due process and equal protection provisions prevent denying an illegal immigrant custody based on that ground" (*In re Parentage of Florentino* 2002).[17] The commonly advanced notion that parents without authorized immigration status have diminished rights in the parent-child relationship is without basis.

This constitutional, and commonsense, conclusion does not make the operation of family law easy in the face of immigration law realities. For example, if immigration law blocks the preferred family law outcome of a child staying with a parent in the United States, analysis of alternatives can create new challenges to the expertise and resources of family courts. Social workers and courts cannot assume that U.S. citizen children of parents facing deportation must remain in the United States, because there is no inherent reason that parents forced by immigration law to leave the country can no longer care for their children.[18]

Still, in such instances a parent's "location abroad presents many challenges for any child welfare agency assigned by the state to oversee the welfare of the child" (Boye 2004, p. 1517). There are "many unavoidable obstacles, including information disadvantages, financial limitations, cultural differences, communication barriers, and the involvement of multiple judicial systems" (ibid.). When immigration law prohibits a parent from returning to the United States, these cross-border difficulties are compounded. Yet these barriers are not insurmountable, and certainly the imperative to preserve the parent-child relationship requires efforts to overcome them. In this context, the impact of immigration law is felt throughout family court and child welfare systems that must deal with the aftermath of immigration law's disruption of living arrangements that often were serving the interests of families and children quite well.

Even when no family member faces imminent deportation, family courts struggle to accommodate the collateral consequences of a party's immigration status in their daily decisions. For example, family courts struggle to implement child support obligations in matters involving persons not authorized to work in the United States.[19] Workers paid in cash, as their immigration status generally prevented them from having documentary proof of their incomes to establish the appropriate levels of child support (*Gomez v. Fernandez* 2004). And income records may be wildly inaccurate due to immigration-related fraud. In such instances, when support obligations are not met, garnishing wages proves difficult at best.

The limitations of immigration law that put families outside the law result in untold complications in applying the law and legal regimes to which they remain subject. These have deep and lasting repercussions not only for immigrants and immigrant families, but also for institutions and legal systems that are built to serve and preserve families. With immigration law working at odds with the basic goals and values of these systems, resources are wasted and important goals for the well-being of families and children are undermined. Given the frequency of these forced interactions, vigilance is required to ensure that the values of systems designed to preserve families are not similarly warped and undermined.

Conclusion

The privileges that immigration law bestows on those "happy" families whose characteristics align with its narrow requirements cannot entirely mask the failure of immigration law to value families that differ from the ideal. Devaluing basic notions of family independence and decision-making, immigration law fails these unhappy families that do not conform. The result is family separation, hardship, and suffering for immigrant families and barriers to full participation in society. In the wake of immigration enforcement, it is not the immigration system but families and other legal systems that are left to sort through the complications and problems left behind.

The contradictions and inhumanity inherent in the current immigration law and its enforcement are enabled by a legal framework that strips compelling facts and narratives of relevance and sweeps them away. The force of family narratives that accompany immigration law must be restored, in immigration law and in society. Sweeping away the pain of families impacted by immigration law hides reality and warps efforts at meaningful reform.

NOTES

1 In contrast, international human rights instruments expressly address the central importance of family. The Universal Declaration of Human Rights (UDHR) art. 16(3) declares that the "family is the natural and fundamental group unit of society and is entitled to protection by society and the State." G.A. Res. 217 (III) A, U.N. Doc. A/RES/217(III), (Dec. 10, 1948) *See also* 1966 International Covenant on Civil and Political Rights (ICCPR) art. 23(1), "The family is the natural and fundamental group unit of society and is entitled to protection by society and the State." International Covenant on Civil and Political Rights, Oct. 5, 1977, 1966 U.S.T. 521, 999 U.N.T.S. 171; International Covenant on Economic, Social and Cultural Rights (ICESCR) art. 10(1), Dec.16, 1966, 993 U.N.T.S. 3 ("The widest possible protection and assistance should be accorded to the family, which is the natural and fundamental group unit of society"); 1969 American Convention on Human Rights, art.17(1), Nov. 22, 1969, O.A.S.T.S. No. 36, 1144 U.N.T.S. 123 ("the family is the natural and fundamental group unit of society and is entitled to protection by society and the state"); African [Banjul] Charter on Human and Peoples' Rights art. 18(1), June 27, 1981, O.A.U. Doc. CAB/LEG/67/3 rev. 5, 1520 U.N.T.S. 217 ("The family shall be the natural unit and basis of society. It shall be protected by the State which shall take care of its physical health and moral"); European Convention for the Protection of Human Rights and Fundamental Freedoms art. 8, Nov. 4, 1950, 213 U.N.T.S. 222 ("Everyone has the right to respect for his private and family life").

2 See also *Meyer v. Nebraska* (1923); *Pierce v. Soc'y of Sisters* (1925), affirming that parents have the right, and duty, "to direct the upbringing . . . of children under their control"; *Flores v. Reno* (1993), noting that by "our society and this Court's jurisprudence [parents] have always presumed to be the preferred and primary custodians of their minor children."

3 Variations of cancellation of removal also apply to persons already granted legal permanent resident status (Immigration and Nationality Act § 240A, 8 U.S.C. § 1229b(a)(1) (2006)), and children and spouses who have been battered or subjected to extreme cruelty by U.S. citizens or legal permanent residents (Immigration and Nationality Act § 240A, 8 U.S.C. § 1229b(b)(2) (2006)).

4 "Congress has never accepted the theory that minor American-born children of deportable aliens must, or even should, remain in the United States, and that living with their deportable parents in their home country would result in 'extreme hardship' to them." *In re Piggot* (1974).

5 Regarding recent developments for same-sex couples, see Benjamin P. Edwards (2013).

6 See Julia Preston (2007) for a discussion of issuance of government guidelines following a raid in which a nursing mother was separated from her infant daughter.

7 This aspect of damage to the parent-child relationship that flows from forced separation is not new. For example, "messages of parental vulnerability and subordina-

tion were repeatedly burned into the consciousness of slave parents and children, undermining their sense of worth, diminishing the sense of family security and authority, eroding the parents' function as a model of adult agency and independence" (Davis 1997:98).

8 Processing times and bureaucratic delays can mean that "immediately" seems an overstatement, but delays here are in the application of the law, not in its substance.

9 The March 2011 Visa Bulletin shows a backlog of more than four years for a petition by a lawful permanent resident for a minor child (USDS 2011).

10 See Motomura (1995, p. 43), noting that the Immigration and Nationality Act "enumerates recognized family relationships, and the courts have consistently rejected attempts to use surrogate family relationships to meet statutory requirements."

11 *INS v. Hector* (1986, pp. 90–91), reversing a decision that nieces aged ten and eleven in the care of their aunt for three years were the "functional equivalent" of children under the Immigration and Nationality Act; see also *Moreno-Morante v. Gonzales* (2007), rejecting the argument that grandchildren were "de facto" children; *Dorado v. Gonzalez* (2006) holding that the unadopted son of the applicant's longtime girlfriend was not a "child" under the Act.

12 For an insightful discussion of the implications of this formalistic approach, *see* Zug (2009:43).

13 Describing an abusive father's failure to include his seventeen-year-old son in an immigration petition for other family members, which led to the determination to deport him alone back to Poland while leaving his mother and siblings in the United States.

14 "To the extent that the framework for family-sponsored and derivative immigration tends to achieve family integrity, it does so by ceding control over a child's status to parents and by denying opportunities for children to achieve legal status as children without their parents" (Thronson 2006, p. 1182).

15 For example, 84 percent of unauthorized migrants from Mexico and 73 percent of unauthorized migrants from Central America entered without inspection (Pew Research Center 2006, p. 4). In contrast, 91% of all other unauthorized migrants are visa overstays who escape penalties imposed for entering without inspection (Pew Research Center 2006).

16 See Personal Responsibility and Work Opportunity Reconciliation Act of 1996, Pub. L. No. 104-193, § 412, 110 Stat. 2105, 2269–70 (1996) (granting authority to states to determine eligibility of certain noncitizens for some public benefits such as Temporary Assistance for Needy Families and Food Stamps). See also Leiter, McDonald, and Jacobson (2006) noting that 1996 legal reforms "'target' social benefits to a more restricted scope of beneficiaries, and citizenship status is now one of the screens that is now used to determine eligibility."

17 See also *Plyler v. Doe* (1982), recognizing that "even aliens whose presence in this country is unlawful, have long been recognized as 'persons' guaranteed due process of law by the Fifth and Fourteenth Amendments."

18 Courts do not always understand this. See *In re* D.R. (2004), stating that a mother's "return to Honduras renders her effectively unable to serve as a responsible parent."
19 See *Gomez v. Fernandez* (2004), rejecting a father's argument that lack of employment authorization served as a defense to his child support obligation.

REFERENCES

Blair, Marianne D. and Merle H. Weiner. 2005. "Resolving Parental Custody Disputes—A Comparative Exploration." *Family Law Quarterly* 39:247–266.
Boye, Amity R. 2004. "Making Sure Children Find Their Way Home: Obliging States Under International Law to Return Dependent Children to Family Members Abroad." *Brooklyn Law Review* 69:1515.
Capps, Randy, Rosa Marie Castaneda, Ajay Chaudry, and Robert Santos. 2007. *Paying the Price: The Impact of Immigration Raids on America's Children*. Washington, DC: Urban Institute. Accessed October 19, 2014. http://www.urban.org/uploadedPDF/411566_immigration_raids.pdf.
Davis, Peggy Cooper. 1997. *Neglected Stories: The Constitution and Family Values*. New York: Hill and Wang.
Demleitner, Nora V. 2003. "How Much Do Western Democracies Value Family and Marriage?: Immigration Law's Conflicted Answers." *Hofstra Law Review* 32:273–311.
Edwards, Benjamin P. 2013. "Welcoming a Post-DOMA World: Same-Sex Spousal Petitions and Other Post-Winder Immigration Implications." *Family Law Quarterly* 47:173–189.
Fix, Michael E. and Jeffrey S. Passel. 2002. *Lessons of Welfare Reform for Immigrant Integration*. Accessed October 8, 2014. Washington, DC: Urban Institute. http://www.urban.org/url.cfm?ID=900497.
Fix, Michael E. and Wendy Zimmermann. 1999. *All Under One Roof: Mixed-Status Families in an Era of Reform*. Report. Accessed October 8, 2014. Washington, DC: Urban Institute. http://www.urban.org/UploadedPDF/409100.pdf.
Hendricks, Tyche. 2007. "The Human Face of Immigration Raids in Bay Area: Arrests of Parents Can Deeply Traumatize Children Caught in the Fray, Experts Argue." April 27, 2007. Accessed October 1, 2014. *San Francisco Chronicle*. http://www.sfgate.com/news/article/The-human-face-of-immigration-raids-in-Bay-Area-2598853.php.
Hernandez, Donald J. 2009. *Generational Patterns in the U.S.: American Community Survey and Other Sources*, paper on file with author.
Hernandez, Donald J. and Wendy D. Cervantes. 2011. *Children in Immigrant Families: Ensuring Opportunity for Every Child in America*. Report. Accessed October 8, 2014. Washington, DC: First Focus. http://fcd-us.org/sites/default/files/First%20Focus%20-%20Children%20in%20Immigrant%20Families.pdf.
Huntington, Clare. 2009. "Happy Families? Translating Positive Psychology into Family Law." *Virginia Journal of Social Policy and the Law* 16:385–424.

Johnson, Kevin R. 2007. *Opening the Floodgates: Why America Needs to Rethink Its Borders and Immigration Laws.* New York: New York University Press.

Kavanagh, Matthew M. 2004. "Rewriting the Legal Family: Beyond Exclusivity to a Care-Based Standard." *Yale Journal of Law and Feminism* 16:83–131.

Kelly, Linda. 2001. "Family Planning, American Style." *Alabama Law Review* 52:955–960.

King, Shani M. 2010. "U.S. Immigration Law and the Traditional Nuclear Conception of Family: Toward a Functional Definition of Family That Protects Children's Fundamental Human Rights." *Colombia Human Rights Law Review* 41:509–567.

Leiter, Valerie, Jennifer Lutzy McDonald, and Heather T. Jacobson. 2006. "Challenges to Children's Independent Citizenship: Immigration, Family and the State." *Childhood* 13:11–27.

Motomura, Hiroshi. 1995. "The Family and Immigration: A Roadmap for the Ruritanian Lawmaker." *American Journal of Comparative Law* 43:511–535.

Nessel, Lori A. 2005. "Forced to Choose: Torture, Family Reunification and United States Immigration Policy." *Temple Law Review* 78:897–948.

Passel, Jeffrey S. and D'Vera Cohn. 2009. *A Portrait of Unauthorized Immigrants in the United States.* Accessed October 8, 2014. Washington, DC: Pew Research Center. http://www.pewhispanic.org/2009/04/14/a-portrait-of-unauthorized-immigrants-in-the-united-states/.

Passel, Jeffrey S. and D'Vera Cohn. 2011. *Unauthorized Immigrant Population: National and State Trends.* Accessed October 8, 2014. Washington, DC: Pew Research Center. http://www.pewhispanic.org/2011/02/01/unauthorized-immigrant-population-brnational-and-state-trends-2010/.

Pew Research Center. 2006. "Modes of Entry for the Unauthorized Migrant Population." May 22, 2006. *Fact Sheet.* Accessed October 8, 2014. http://pewhispanic.org/files/factsheets/19.pdf.

Preston, Julia. 2007. "Immigration Quandary: A Mother Torn from Her Baby." November 17. Accessed October 1, 2014. *New York Times.* http://www.nytimes.com/2007/11/17/us/17citizen.html?pagewanted=all.

Romero, Victor C. 2005. "Asians, Gay Marriage, and Immigration: Family Unification at a Crossroads." *Indiana International and Comparative Law Review* 15:337–347.

Sanger, Carol. 1987. "Immigration Reform and Control of the Undocumented Family." *Georgetown Immigration Law Journal* 2:295–357.

Thronson, David B. 2006. "Choices: Deportation and the Parent-Child Relationship." *Nevada Law Journal* 6:1165–1214.

Thronson, David B. 2002. "Kids Will Be Kids? Reconsidering Conceptions of Children's Rights Underlying Immigration Law." *Ohio State Law Journal* 63:979–1016..

Urban Institute. 2006. *Children of Immigrants Facts and Figures.* Accessed October 8, 2014. Washington, DC: Urban Institute. http://www.urban.org/uploaded-pdf/900955_children_of_immigrants.pdf.

U.S. Department of Homeland Security (USDHS). 2009. *Removals Involving Illegal Alien Parents of United States Citizen Children.* Accessed October 8, 2014. Washington, DC: Department of Homeland Security, Office of Inspector General. http://www.oig.dhs.gov/assets/Mgmt/OIG_09-15_Jan09.pdf.

U.S. Department of State (USDS). 2011. *U.S. Department of State Visa Bulletin IX,* no. 30. Accessed October 8, 2014. Washington, DC: Department of State. http://travel.state.gov/content/visas/english/law-and-policy/bulletin/2011/visa-bulletin-for-march-2011.html.

WCCO-TV. 2007. "School Enrollment Down Following Swift Raids." February 12. Accessed October 8, 2014. http://www.alipac.us/f12/school-enrollment-down-following-swift-raids-50107/.

Wessler, Seth Freed. 2012. "Primary Data: Deportations of Parents of U.S. Citizen Kids." December 17. *Colorlines.* Accessed October 1, 2014. New York: Applied Research Center. http://colorlines.com/archives/2012/12/deportations_of_parents_of_us-born_citizens_122012.html.

Zug, Marcia. 2009. "Deporting Grandma: Why Grandparent Deportation May Be the Next Big Immigration Crisis and How to Solve It." *U.C. Davis Law Review* 43:193–252..

CASE CITATIONS

Dorado v. Gonzalez, 202 F. App'x 898, 899 (6th Cir. 2006).
Fiallo v. Bell, 430 U.S. 787, 798 (1977).
Flores v. Reno, 507 U.S. 292, 304 (1993).
Fornalik v. Perryman, 223 F.3d 523, 527-28 (7th Cir. 2000).
Gomez v. Fernandez, No. R-120399 (Nev. Eighth Jud. Dist. Ct. Fam. Div. hearing Mar. 22, 2004).
Hernandez-Cordero v. INS, 819 F.2d 558, 563 (5th Cir. 1987).
In re *D.R.,* 204 Conn. Super. LEXIS 325, at *34, 2004 WL 423993 (Conn. Super. Feb. 9, 2004).
In re *Monreal-Aguinaga,* 23 I. & N. Dec. 56, 65 (BIA 2001).
In re *Parentage of Florentino,* 113 Wash.App. 1002, 2002 WL 1825422 at *5, n.11 (Wash. App. Div. 2 Aug. 9, 2002).
In re *Piggot,* 15 I. & N. Dec. 129, 131 (BIA 1974).
INS v. Hector, 479 U.S. 85 (1986).
Jimenez v. INS, 116 F.3d 1485 (9th Cir. 1997).
Meyer v. Nebraska, 262 U.S. 390 (1923).
Moore v. City of East Cleveland, 431 U.S. 494, 503–506 (1977).
Moreno-Morante v. Gonzales, 490 F.3d 1172, 1173 (9th Cir. 2007).
Pierce v. Soc'y of Sisters, 268 U.S. 534–35 (1925).
Plyler v. Doe, 457 U.S. 202, 210 (1982).
Rico v. Rodriguez, 120 P.3d 812, 818 (Nev. 2005).
Sullivan v. INS, 772 F.2d 609, 611 (9th Cir. 1985).
Troxel v. Granville, 530 U.S. 57, 65 (2000).

STATUTES

8 U.S.C. § 1101(b)(1) (2006 and Supp. 2011)
8 U.S.C. § 1151(b)(2)(A)(i); (c) (Supp. 2011)
8 U.S.C. § 1151(c) (2006)
8 U.S.C. § 1153(a) (2006)
8 U.S.C. § 1153(d) (2006)
8 U.S.C. § 1182 (2006 and Supp. 2011)
8 U.S.C. § 1182(a)(3)(B) (2006)
8 U.S.C. § 1182(a)(9)(B)(v) (2006)
8 U.S.C. § 1227(a)(4)(B) (2006)
8 U.S.C. § 1229b (2006 and Supp. 2011)

2

Improving Conditions of Confinement for Immigrant Detainees

Guideposts Toward a Civil System of Civil Detention

DORA B. SCHRIRO

As a matter of law, immigration detention is unlike criminal incarceration. Criminal incarceration speaks to the authority of the government to incapacitate an individual charged with, or convicted of, a criminal offense. Immigration detention is different. It refers to the authority that Immigration and Customs Enforcement (ICE) has to civilly detain aliens who may be subject to removal for violations of administrative immigration law. ICE may detain immigrants pending removal or relief—and in a number of instances, it *must* detain aliens—however, under no circumstance is ICE authorized to detain aliens for the purpose of punishment (*Zadvydas v. Davis* 2001:690). Only persons who pled or were proven guilty of criminal offenses may be incarcerated as punishment. And despite this bright line legal limitation, immigration detainees and criminal inmates tend to be seen by the public as comparable, and both criminally and civilly confined populations are typically managed in strikingly similar ways. All too often we incapacitate individuals who could be successfully managed in the community and when we do place individuals in the community, we impose conditions when mere reporting would suffice. Likewise, the standards that ICE adopted to guide the operation of its detention facilities and community-based programs were developed to manage the movements of primarily native-born, criminally charged inmates, many of them previously incarcerated, not exclusively foreign-born, civilly charged detainees, far fewer of them previously involved with the justice system (Schriro 2009a).

Designing and delivering a national system of civil detention consistent with the law and congruent with our country's core values are our challenge and our opportunity. This chapter contemplates the principles to shape a civil system of civil detention—the case law and statutes both national and international, the professional standards, and the proven policies and practices in the disciplines of detention, as well as alternatives to detention and allied fields—principles upon which ICE could, and should, draw to inform, improve, and advance the operation of immigration detention facilities and to expand the utilization of alternatives to detention. It also considers the steps taken by ICE and those that remain to be realized since the release of the Schriro Report and the adoption of its recommendations by the Department of Homeland Security (DHS) in 2009 as the template for its detention reforms (Schriro 2009a).

High-performance organizations have three characteristics in common, characteristics that are critical to system reform: capacity, competency, and commitment (Schriro 2010:13–14). The chapter briefly considers these characteristics as well. Our conversation closes with a template to transform ICE, the country's largest system of incarceration, into a model system, one that meets and exceeds the legal and professional minimum requirements, a system worthy of emulation by other nation-states. These are guideposts toward a truly civil system of civil detention.

The History of Corrections and the U.S. Courts

The history of corrections case law is fairly short and is sometimes characterized as the "hands-off," the "hands-on," and the "one-hand-off and one-hand-on" eras (See Braham and Hamden 2005: 481–489; Collins 2005; Filter 2001; Mushlin 2002: 10–18; Wells, Eaton, and Nahmod 2004; Ross 2005: 42–47, for details). For years, the Court was reluctant to recognize inmate claims, and during the "hands-off era" routinely deferred to correctional administrators. (See, e.g., *Ruffin v. The Commonwealth* (1871) declaring incarcerated felons to be "slaves of the State" and wholly subject to the authority of the correctional authorities). Then, during the mid-1960s to the later 1980s, the "hands-on era," the Court was increasingly, even intrusively, involved with the operation of correctional institutions (e.g., *Washington v. Lee* 1966). Since then, the Court has largely moved back toward the middle, the "one-hand-on and one-hand-off era," granting relief where warranted but leaving its implementation largely to the legislative and executive branches (e.g., *Lewis v.*

Casey 1996). Civil detainees have not attracted the Court's attention until quite recently and then, quite slowly.

Before and during much of the 1960s, the Court afforded correctional systems considerable discretion, deferring to the judgment of jail and prison administrators. (See, e.g., *United States ex rel. Atterbury v. Ragen* (1956) stating that federal courts "have extremely limited area in which they may act pertaining to the treatment of prisoners confined to state penal institutions"). Starting with school desegregation cases in the 1950s, the Court became increasingly involved with conditions concerning civil rights (e.g., *Brown et al. v. Board of Education* 1954). During the 1960s, as the confined offender population increased in number and the conditions of their confinement worsened, incidents such as the riots at Attica prison in upstate New York and at the "Tombs" a jail in New York City, spilled over into the national news, raising the public's awareness.[1] The underlying facts—overcrowding, race-based treatment, inmates overseeing inmates, wholly unsanitary conditions, the absence of due process, corporal punishment, and significantly delayed and deficient healthcare, among others—shocked the conscience of an increasingly concerned community (see, e.g., *Holt v. Sarver* (1971) describing prison conditions in Arkansas as "shocking," "immoral," and "criminal"). The Court responded, reevaluating the constitutionality of a number of conditions and correctional practices (e.g., *Rhem v. Malcom* 1977, *Rhem v. Malcom* 1974). Throughout the 1970s, the Court considered the adequacy of many operational issues and enumerated remedies, sometimes quite detailed, for situations it deemed to be serious. (See, e.g., *Rhodes v. Chapman* (1981), which examines the legitimacy of "double-celling" of inmates in an Ohio prison; *United States ex rel. Wolfish v. Levy* 1977; *Bell v. Wolfish* 1979). The correction case law that followed often overtook state and local correction statutes (*Benjamin v. Fraser* 2001; *Benjamin v. Kerik* 2000).

By the 1980s, however, the Court slowed and reshaped its course, increasingly balancing the inmates' constitutionally protected interests with the legitimate interests of the correctional institution (*Bell v. Wolfish* 1979:520). Still, many of the improvements that had been put into place in the preceding years stayed in place, now ingrained in the practice of corrections systems. During the 1990s a number of "truth-in-sentencing" reforms were enacted at the state and federal levels of government, including "three strikes" laws, the civil commitment of sexual predators, and adult treatment for violent juvenile offenders.[2] As get-tough measures were adopted across the country, the inmate population increased again.[3] During this "tough on crime" era, Congress also passed into law the Prisoner Litigation Reform Act, making sterner the conditions under which inmates are incarcerated, curtailing both inmates' access to the Court and the Court's occasions to reply (Prisoner Litigation Reform Act of 1995). In just a few but significant instances, Congress and the Court have retained this tenor. Congress afforded all institutionalized persons, including inmates, more religious freedoms in general than those of us residing in the community enjoy, enabling these groups to pursue sincerely held religious beliefs in a number of particularized ways (Religious Land Use and Institutionalized Persons Act of 2000; see, e.g., *Cutter v. Wilkinson* 2005). Congress also enacted into law a zero-tolerance policy about impermissible sexual contact and conduct (Prisoner Rape Elimination Act of 2003). And, in a few notable instances, the Court shifted the burden of proof from the inmate population to the administration; for example, affirming inmates' right to be incarcerated in smoke-free facilities (*Helling v. McKinney* 1993). For the most part, however, the Court and Congress continue to be deferential to correctional administrators today.[4]

The History of Immigration Detention and the U.S. Courts

As a matter of law, immigration detention is unlike criminal incarceration. ICE does not have the authority to incarcerate aliens for criminal violations. That power resides exclusively with the Department of Justice (DOJ), subject to review of the federal courts.[5] Instead, ICE is empowered pursuant to the Immigration and Nationality Act, to detain aliens solely during the removal process, a civil proceeding.[6] Immigration detention is expressly not permitted for the purpose of punishment (Schriro 2009a:2; see also *Zadvydas v. Davis* 2001:682).

Despite these unambiguous legal distinctions, civilly held immigrant detainees are most often held in secure facilities with hardened perimeters, typically in remote locations and at considerable distances from counsel, their community, and ICE-assigned caseworker (Schriro 2009a:14).[7] With just a handful of exceptions, the facilities still used by ICE were originally built, and currently operate, as jails and prisons, secure places that primarily confine pre-trial and sentenced felons (Schriro 2009a: 21).[8] Their design, construction, staffing plans, custody management strategies and operating standards are based largely upon the correctional principles of command and control. In these places, most immigrant detainees have only limited access to essential services and basic amenities and usually, far less access to far fewer amenities than have criminal inmates. Among the material differences between the majority and minority of ICE beds are the absence of, or access to, freedom of movement within the facility and adjacent outdoors recreation yards, windows that look out into the world, a physical plant that affords privacy in sleeping quarters and bathrooms, easy access to family and counsel,[9] necessary healthcare provided in a timely manner,[10] nutritional meals and adequate clothing and footwear,[11] and opportunity to meaningfully engage in activities of daily living.[12]

Not only does the law require equitable treatment for immigrant detainees but most of the population's low custody classification scores, borne out by their institutional conduct while in ICE's custody, warrant far less restrictive treatment than they are ordinarily afforded (*Zadvydas v. Davis* 2001:702). During the intake security assessment process the majority of immigrant detainees are determined by ICE to present only minimal to moderate risk of engaging in violence in the facility, a forecast that is borne out by their institutional conduct. There have been few fights among detainees or with detention guards and no disturbances for a number of years now (Schriro 2009a:21).

The disparate treatment that many immigrant detainees experience while in the custody of ICE can be attributed at least in part to the lack of case law. Although conditions of criminal confinement have been litigated extensively, just a few cases have come before the Court that have made clearer the parameters of equal protection to be afforded aliens who are civilly detained (Schriro 2009b:26–27). Today, it is established that foreign-born persons who have been admitted to the United States as well as those who are inadmissible enjoy some due process protection. In 2001, the United States Supreme Court held that the Due Process Clause extends to aliens who have been admitted and so are "within" the United States (*Zadvydas v. Davis* 2001:693). In 2005, the Court also found that certain substantive due process protections apply to inadmissible aliens who have not entered or been admitted to our country (*Clark v. Martinez* 2005). Little else is settled.[13]

Also recently, and relevant to the reach of mandatory detention, the Court, recognizing the adverse impact of a criminal history on civil deportation determinations, held in 2005 that the Bar shall advise alien clients of deportation consequences before entering a guilty plea (*Padilla v. Kentucky* 2010). This order is far from fully implemented.

Relevant International Standards on the Human Rights of Immigrants

Many countries in the international community distinguish between immigrants who are in the territory lawfully and immigrants who are not, distinctions that often dictate the manner and means of their immigration detention (Edwards 2011:15). Despite these nation-specific differences, international associations and conventions of nation-states also assume that basic human rights always prevail. Whether or not these organizations and their treaties may impose restrictions on the treatment of aliens in either category, however, including the conditions of their detention, in conformance to international law is less clear (ibid.:32).

The Universal Declaration of Human Rights (UDCHR), specifying the rights of individuals, was adopted by the United Nations General Assembly of which the United States is a member, in 1948 (Department of Public Information 1950:535). The International Bill of Human Rights (IBHR) includes the Universal Declaration of Human Rights as well as the International Covenant on Civil and Political Rights and the International Covenant on Economic, Social and Cultural Rights, and in 1976, the IBHR took on the force of international law (Williams 1981). Article 9 of the International Covenant on Civil and Political Rights, a multilateral treaty, adopted by the UN General Assembly in 1966, and in force since 1976, committing the parties to respect basic civil and political rights of individuals, and other relevant international provisions, elaborated upon that treatment, making clear that the conditions of detention must be appropriate for each kind of immigrant such as children, the elderly, and the infirm; otherwise lawful detention may, in fact, be arbitrary and therefore unlawful (International Covenant on Civil and Political Rights, General Assembly resolution 2200A (XXI), Article 9; see also Article 3; *Muskhadzhiyeva and Others v. Belgium*, ECtHR, Application No. 41442/07, 2010; ExCom, Conclusion No. 110 (LXI), 2010, on Refugees with Disabilities and Other Persons with Disabilities Protected and Assisted by UNHCR, *paras.* 6 and 7; Article 12, ICESCR; Article 12, CEDAW; Article 24, CRC; Edwards (2011:41)). The Office of the United Nations High Commissioner for Human Rights promulgated Standard Minimum Rules for the Treatment of Prisoners, rules that are applicable to all categories of prisoners including both criminal and civil inmates, first in 1957 and again in 1977.[14] With regard to the incarceration of civil prisoners in particular, these Rules provide, "Their treatment shall not be less favorable than that of untried prisoners."[15] In 2003, the Inter-American Court of Human Rights (IACHR) held that States may establish mechanisms to control unlawful migrants' entry into and departure from its jurisdictions, but that these mechanisms must always be applied with strict regard for certain guarantees for human dignities and requirements of due process (Inter-American Court of Human Rights 2003: para. 119; see also Inter-American Commission on Human Rights 2010). The IACHR specifically noted that immigration detention is an "exceptional" measure that must be exercised in conformity with these requirements.[16] Also in 2003, and far more pointedly, the United Nations Special Rapporteur on the Human Rights of Migrant Workers expressed his view that "Irregular migrants are not criminals per se and should not be treated as such" (Pizarro 2002; see also Inter-American Commission on Human Rights 2010). Several years later, in 2008, the Inter-American Commission on Human Rights drew the brightest line to date, holding that immigrants must not be detained in prisons.[17]

More recently, the Organization of American States (OAS) issued a report by the Inter-American Commission on Human Rights on immigration detention and due process in the United States,[18] concluding that the United States, an OAS member state, is obligated to ensure the human rights of all persons including undocumented as well as documented immigrants, rights that include personal liberty, humane treatment, and minimum guarantees of due process, equality and nondiscrimination, and protection of private and family life (Inter-American Commission on Human Rights 1948, 2010).

The United States has disagreed in large part with international expectations for compliance. Responding to the draft report by the OAS on immigrant detention and due process, the government acknowledged the importance of enforcing immigration efforts "in a lawful, professional, safe and humane manner." It continued, however, ". . . contrary to the Commission's assertions, neither the American Declaration of the Rights and Duties of Man nor international law generally establish a presumption of liberty for undocumented migrants who are present in a country in violation of that country's immigration laws," and concluded with considerable finality, ". . . the advisory opinions of the Inter-American Court interpreting other international agreements, such as the International Covenant on Civil and Political Rights (ICCPR) are not relevant" (Inter-American Commission on Human Rights 2010: para. 24, 25).[19]

Standards for the Treatment of the Incarcerated Promulgated by Professional Disciplines and Government

More than 2.3 million pretrial and sentenced inmates are incarcerated today in the United States (Minton 2010; West 2010). Generally, pretrial inmates enjoy more privileges in detention than do sentenced inmates because they have not pled or been proven guilty and sentenced; thus, their incarceration is expressly not for the purpose of punishment. Sentenced inmates are incarcerated as punishment; only the few whose sentence is capital punishment are incarcerated pending imposition of their punishment. An additional 400,000 are civilly confined annually by DHS as immigrant detainees (Schriro 2009a:6). Neither immigrant detainees nor criminal pretrial detainees may be confined as punishment (*Zadvydas v. Davis* 2001:690; *Bell v. Wolfish* 1979:535).

Both case law and statute have positively impacted the operation of jails and prisons and, by and large, the conditions of criminal incarceration have improved over time. Still, these conditions vary appreciably place to place and in general, criminal inmates fare better today than do civil detainees. Striving to improve the conditions under which civil detainees—as well as criminal inmates—are held is just as important. It is consistent with our laws and those of the international community. It is congruent with our core values, our commitment to take in "the tired, the poor, the huddled masses yearning to breathe free" (Lazarus 1883). It is also beneficial to our country and to other nations because, as a matter of law, all civil inmates are to be detained only temporarily pending the determination of removal or relief, at which time they are to be returned to their native countries or released to remain in ours. The conditions of their confinement impact the extent to which they are more or less able than before to be civil and productive when they are released, and that affects us all.

Different Is Not Always Better

The Prison Rape Elimination Act, affording protections to both the criminally charged and the civilly held, was passed by Congress in 2003. National standards were to be adopted by all state and local correctional systems, DOJ's Bureau of Prison, and DHS's civil detention facilities to enact the federal legislation in 2013. DHS resisted, first requesting and receiving from DOJ a 360-day extension on compliance with PREA standards. Then, when its regulations were released, they fell short of DOJ's standards, diminished by limiting applicability to facilities with existing contracts, excluding holding facilities and transportation, and leaving unaddressed the need for strengthened oversight and accountability mechanisms.

Professional standards are based upon and sometimes build upon case law and state and federal statute and when they are adopted as regulation, standards have the effect of law. The American Bar Association (ABA) first promulgated standards on the treatment of prisoners early in 1981[20] and then supplemented them twice in 1985.[21] In 2004, the ABA Criminal Justice Standards Committee appointed a task force to propose revisions to those standards incorporating case law and improved correctional practices that had come about since 1981 to better guide the Court in its assessment of correctional systems across judicial circuits. Revised standards were approved by the ABA House of Delegates in February 2010 and, notably, included the immigrant detainee population.[22] Recognizing the need to establish standards specific to foreign-born populations detained by ICE, the ABA Commission on Immigration soon thereafter formed an expert Advisory Task Force to develop civil standards. The ABA Civil Immigration Detention Standards were adopted by the ABA House of Delegates in August 2012 (ABA 2012).

Correctional organizations and government alike have also promulgated performance standards and credentialing mechanisms to improve the delivery of pretrial detention, the incarceration of sentenced misdemeanants and felons, and the civil incapacitation of immigrants. The American Correctional Association (ACA) publishes jail standards (ACA 2010a and 1989). The ACA also publishes standards for the operation of correctional facilities for other populations including prisons and work release centers (see, e.g., ACA 2010b, 2010c). In addition, both the ACA and the American Jail Association (AJA) offer certifications of individuals in the field. The American Medical Association (AMA) National Commission on Correctional Health Care (NCCHC) also issues standards for the delivery of healthcare in correctional settings.[23] They are all elective. Correctional systems are encouraged to adopt these measures and to secure accreditations and certifications, but relatively few systems do. At the federal level, both the U.S. Department of Justice (DOJ), Bureau of Prisons (BOP),[24] and the U.S. Department of Homeland Security (DHS), Immigration and Customs Enforcement (ICE), Detention and Removal unit,[25] also promulgated standards (ICE 2008).[26] The BOP standards, called "program statements," have been incorporated into federal regulation.[27] The ICE standards have not.[28] Failure to comply with regulation is a basis for relief whereas failure to comply with elective standards is not actionable.

ICE operates the largest system of incapacitation in the nation, with more admissions and releases than the BOP or any state or local department of correction.[29] Immigration and Naturalization Services (INS), the precursor agency to ICE, introduced national detention standards in 2000.[30] ICE updated its guidelines, issuing performance-based national detention standards in 2008 (ACA 2010b). Both the original standards for civil detention and subsequent revisions largely replicate the ACA jail detention standards for pretrial criminal defendants (ACA 2010a). ICE made no modifications to tailor correctional standards to fit the unique legal, medical, and cultural requirements of foreign-born, administratively held detainees. And where its standards were modified, the standard of care was diminished; see, for example, ICE's implementation of Prison Rape Elimination Act regulations. ICE's written instruction fell short of the standards adopted by the U.S. Attorney General, limiting applicability to facilities with existing contracts, excluding holding facilities and transportation, and leaving largely untouched the need to strengthen oversight and accountability mechanisms.[31] And, although many detained aliens did not have criminal histories, and the majority of those with a record had committed drug and property offenses and not violent crimes, ICE did not modify the standards it adopted to differentiate between the detention of criminal and noncriminal aliens. Instead, ICE continues to manage all immigrant detainees as criminal defendants; by and large, it applies correctional standards across the board (Schriro 2009a:16).[32]

ICE uses approximately 250 correctional facilities today to house its average daily census of 34,000 immigrant detainees. Criminal and noncriminal aliens are assigned to the same facilities. They co-mingle with one another and frequently, with the jurisdictions' criminal defendants and sentenced inmates. None of these facilities is dedicated solely for noncriminal alien adults or for special categories of aliens such as asylum seekers, the elderly, or the ill and the infirm.

Today, ICE standards are in effect at seven of its 250-plus facilities. Several of the seven facilities failed to achieve their minimum requirements.[33] ICE intended its standards to be imposed at every facility that it uses; however, this is not yet the case (Schriro 2009:16). To its credit, ICE audits for compliance at all locations and expects both sheriffs' departments and private prison providers operating facilities that house immigrant detainees to submit action plans to cure deficiencies whenever they are identified. Enforcement is inconsistent, however. ICE continues to use facilities that have been noncompliant for two or more years (Schriro 2009:16).

The Considerable Strengths Associated with Criminal and Civil Systems of Incarceration and Opportunities to Improve Our Nation's System of Civil Incarceration

Criminal incarceration and civil detention systems perform a number of functions with exceptional efficiency. Both manage the equivalent of county-sized populations around the country with far fewer negative occurrences than do most cities. They direct the daily activities of thousands of inmates, secure the compliance of the persons involuntarily in their custody and only infrequently with force, and provide for their safety and well-being. They transport hundreds daily to court, off-site healthcare facilities and other court-mandated destinations, effectuate removals, serve millions of meals, launder tons of linens and uniforms, and deliver the mail. They operate in-house hospitals, ambulance services, and firehouses. They exercise police powers without the equipment upon which police routinely rely, render quasi-legal findings with far fewer resources than do the courts, and serve as round-the-clock emergency responders. By and large, correctional systems and ICE alike provide at least minimum levels of care and effectively control an appreciable percentage of the country's hard to control population. Many jurisdictions do much more. Some do far less. And still, every system—those that perform at a consistently high level of proficiency as well as those that perform poorly—can contribute to the commonweal by striving to do more, better.

Exceptionally high performing correctional systems, that meet and exceed both statute and standards, distinguish themselves in three appreciable ways: capacity, competency, and commitment (Schriro 2010:13–14). Similarly, our country's system of civil detention can appreciably improve its performance by distinguishing its policies and practices from those that inform criminal incarceration first by acquiring the qualities and qualifications attributed to a civil system of civil detention and then by expertly applying them to a system recognized for its capacity, competency, and commitment.

Capacity

Capacity speaks to an organization's infrastructure. It is the toolkit that an agency uses to accomplish the work it is mandated to do, the goals and objectives to be realized. Capacity is founded upon well-reasoned and well researched, published policies, procedures, and post orders to guide the workforce. It is supported by a physical plant that is congruent with the underlying assumptions about its core mission, about the operating principles upon which the persons in its custody are provided care and the manner and means by which control of the population that it oversees is exercised. Capacity also encompasses the personnel that use the toolkit, a workforce whose knowledge, skills, and abilities, as well as its reporting structure, support and sustain excellence in every rank and on every shift. Capacity is limited, or expanded, by the vision of the men and women who lead. Where expectations are clear, guidance is based upon best practices, the physical plant is consistent with core operating assumptions, and the workforce provides leadership within every level of the organization, there is an organization with capacity to perform its work well. Where there is a system that is unwilling, or unable, to expand or update its capacity, evaluate its shortcomings or other systems' successes, and meet or exceed minimum expectations, there is insufficient capacity to excel.

Here is an example. ICE had no means by which to centrally track the population it detained or to enable others, notably family members and attorneys of record, to do so. It also lacked a means by which to reconcile its count of persons in its care. Its toolkit did not include a detainee locator system, a list of all of the persons it detained with identifiers to sort through persons with the same names, the dates of their admissions, and their current locations. It added an electronic roster, updated daily, to look-up individuals in the custody of ICE and to determine their locations. When a subsequent surge occurred however, and additional facilities were quickly added, ICE neglected to update the roster to include them. Its failure to continue to maintain a complete and accurate accounting of the detained population for others suggests that ICE adopted it to placate others, not to use it as management tool to provide for those in its care.

Competency

Competency is both the means and the measurement of a system's performance. Competent systems focus on outcomes and not outputs. They have long-term goals that are reached by quickly achieving one incremental measure after the other. Competent systems strive to be consistently effective and efficient. They are safe places for innovation, professional environments that nurture a confident workforce, staffed by individuals ready to take calculated risks and able to recognize mistakes as opportunities to improve over time, to perform better next time. Competent systems are proactive—willing to find and fix root causes of real concerns regardless of whether those concerns are of their making, and to achieve measurable, meaningful results that transform the system and contribute to the body of knowledge that informs its field. The competent organization recognizes that excellence is a moving target and that it must continuously strive to succeed. Where a system is unwilling or unable to evaluate its current performance, or is closed to considering other systems' successes, or rejects feedback from others, it will fall back and fail.

The marked shift in policy from "Catch and Release" to "Catch and Remove" set a course that continues today, a course that a competent system would reconsider. Consider this. Aliens routinely released by INS, individuals who committed minor traffic offenses and misdemeanor drug and property crimes, are characterized today by ICE as "the worst of the worst," persons too dangerous to be placed anywhere but in secure detention facilities. Likewise adult family members traveling with minor children are being detained in secure facilities in unprecedented numbers. Whereas one of two family detention facilities were repurposed just several years ago, following a recent increase in unlawful admissions now several more have opened recently and more beds are being added. ICE has defaulted to policy and practice that are neither effective nor efficient. ICE continues to have difficulty making evidence-based decisions. It appears to continue to be unable or willing to take transformative steps towards excellence. Instead the census rises artificially higher, costs of every kind needlessly increase.

Commitment

Commitment keeps a system centered, steadies and sustains the agency. It is fidelity to public service and to public safety. It is fealty to constituency, both those who are lawfully present and those who are not. It is the neutrality with which government duties are performed, the fairness afforded all. The incapacitation of immigrant detainees as well as criminal inmates is a core government function, funded by government to protect and to serve all of us who live, work, and travel through this country. We are all members of this community, whether or not we are lawfully present, and each of us enjoys some rights and bears some responsibility for its size, its safety and security, its success and failures. Where the interests of any group of stakeholders—whether of one political party or another, a laborer or a labor organization, a detainee or an advocate on an alien's behalf—overtakes the interests of the others, the resulting imbalance is ultimately to everyone's detriment.

Immigration detention policy and practice has suffered from pronounced partisanship, a dearth of commitment to follow the facts. Here is an example. In each of the past several years Congress has appropriated funds to ICE to operate 34,000 beds, and each year, ICE has kept 34,000 beds full. Whereas correctional systems routinely look for ways to take beds offline and close facilities to reduce spending without impacting public safety, and reallocate those monies across categories to meet agency needs, ICE has repeatedly acquiesced to appropriations bills with language dictating its capacity. Although its own classification system has determined that the vast majority of the detained population presents little risk of harm to others in custody and evidences little risk of flight if released, ICE has increased its bed census. It has not moved any of its monies to increase community supervision, a less expensive and equally effective alternative for these individuals.

Over the years, the Court's involvement in correctional systems has occurred for many reasons, each of them fact-specific. Underlying these facts, however, and particularly today, the intensity of the Court's involvement appears to be commensurate with the degree to which individual systems evidence capacity, competency, and commitment. As the correctional field has grown in stature and individual correctional systems have evidenced higher standards of professionalism and greater proficiency, the Court's intervention in their affairs has waned. Where individual systems have performed inconsistently or poorly, the Court has interceded or continued its interventions.[34]

The discipline of immigrant detention is much newer and is not nearly as far along in its growth and development. It has not yet achieved the same levels of proficiency and professionalism as have the majority of correctional systems. To inform and improve its performance—to create capacity, build competency, and solidify commitment to constituency, the U.S. Department of Homeland Security issued a Report in 2009, the first year that the current administration took office, with key recommendations in four areas (Schriro 2009a:2).

First, ICE should establish a system of immigration detention with the requisite management tools and informational systems to detain and supervise aliens in settings consistent with assessed risk and nearby community resources. ICE should provide services to the detained population commensurate with individuals' assessed needs and create capacity within the organization to assess and improve detention operations (Schriro 2009a).

Second, in consultation with stakeholders, ICE should adopt standards, objective risk and needs assessments, and classification tools to inform care, custody management, privileges, programs, and the delivery of services consistent with assessed risks and needs of the immigrant population. It should expand aliens' access to legal materials and counsel, visitation, and religious practice and tailor its policies and practices, making special provisions for serving special populations, notably, families with minor children, women, the mentally ill and physically infirm, and asylum seekers (Schriro 2009a:2).

Third, ICE should establish an integrated and well-managed healthcare system, with comprehensive initial assessments to inform facility assignments and ongoing care management with necessary services that are readily available and timely provided regardless of the location of the detention facility and the alien's anticipated time left in detention. ICE should maintain current and complete medical records, and these records should travel with the alien if transferred or should be available electronically. ICE should establish clear standards of medical, dental, and mental healthcare for detainees and continuously monitor conditions for compliance (Schriro 2009a).

And fourth, ICE should provide federal oversight of key detention operations and adopt, audit, and enforce performance standards appropriate for immigrant detention and alternatives to detention. The outcomes should be published. ICE should place highly trained and experienced federal officials onsite to oversee detention operations, to intercede as often as necessary, and to ensure that viable grievance and disciplinary processes remain in place (Schriro 2009a).

In the several years since the release of the Report and DHS's adoption of recommendations, ICE has advanced several of its policies and practices toward less penal detention standards.[35] It has reduced the number of detention facilities by approximately 20 percent, from 341 to 270, and plans to modify conditions of detention at several of the remaining facilities, representing approximately 10 percent of its total bed capacity. When combined with several existing facilities whose conditions are similarly improved, about 14 percent of the system's total bed capacity will be less harsh and more normalized. ICE also developed and has put into use an objective risk assessment instrument to guide its assignments of aliens to community supervision, and revised its parole policy so that all detained arriving asylum seekers in an expedited removal process who pass credible fear screening interviews must be assessed for potential parole eligibility. ICE also issued guidance on the use of prosecutorial discretion by its personnel and it has trained and placed 42 monitors in the field to oversee compliance with its standards. Additionally, ICE established an online detainee locator link, updated daily, to enable family members to find loved ones and counsel to locate their clients. There is more to do (see Human Rights First 2011, 2012). The majority of immigrant detainees are still held in correctional facilities. The cost to detain immigrants pending removal or relief continues to increase and now, it exceeds two billion dollars annually (see, e.g., Department of Homeland Security Appropriations Act, 2014 (H.R. 2217)). ICE has not expanded safe and cost-effective alternatives to detention. It continues to rely on detention standards modeled on correction standards and largely disregards facilities' noncompliance with its standards. Aliens' access to legal assistance is inadequate and results in delayed and unnecessary detention.

Summary and Suggestions

High-performance systems are cognizant of the law—its letter and its spirit. They are also knowledgeable about industry standards and the field's best practices. High-performance systems draw upon their capacity, competency, and commitment to meet and to exceed legal and professional minimum requirements. ICE, the country's largest system of incarceration, can and should realize its public safety potential, improve its administration of detention facilities and alternatives to detention programs, and faithfully serve its constituencies, faithfully traveling its best path. These are guideposts toward a civil system of civil detention.[36]

Population Management

A mother and her teenage son were apprehended reentering the United States at the Canadian border nearby Buffalo, New York, and were transferred to the Berks Family Residential Facility in rural Pennsylvania. They had been removed the year before and were attempting to rejoin family members who remained in the country lawfully. Their suitcases lay open, photographs and personal items of clothes scattered on the floor in the intake area where they were being questioned. They had no recognizable claim to secure relief. They would remain together at Berks for the remainder of their time in ICE custody and then be deported again.

Population management encompasses the continuum of control exercised by ICE over aliens in its custody from least to most restrictive, and the strategies employed to supervise aliens pending their removal or relief. Population management lays out the parameters of a system specifically designed for administratively supervised and civilly detained aliens.

The following are among its most basic operating principles. One, both detention and alternatives to detention are integral to the realization of the mission of ICE. The integrity of their design and delivery is best achieved in collaboration with stakeholders so as to meet or exceed the agency's performance-based standards, optimize ICE activities and outcomes, and improve its efficiency and effectiveness, affirming government's commitment to transparency. Two, ICE's system of civil detention and alternatives to detention should be specifically designed for administratively held aliens, informed by correction law and correctional practices but not governed by them. Three, an integrated network of detention facilities and alternatives provided when possible by not-for-profit providers and nongovernmental organizations affords a continuum of control and ensures adequate capacity from least to more restrictive. When supervision of an alien is determined to be necessary—because it is mandated by law or warranted by objective assessment of risk of flight—ICE should opt for the least restrictive means of management. Four, management practices must be firm, implemented in full and periodically updated. These include (a) publishing a real-time, online roster of detainees with the locations at which they are being held by ICE; (b) maintaining a current list of all facilities in use with basic information about each of them, such as their capacity by custody level, availability of healthcare, and handicap accessibility; (c) training and technical manuals; (d) centralized acquisition of beds and community supervision slots, and a schedule of contract reviews with contract renewals predicated upon compliance with ICE performance-based standards; and (e) objective and periodically recalibrated risk and needs assessment instruments. Five, ICE may delegate certain duties by means of contracts, intergovernmental service agreements or memoranda of agreement; however, as a matter of law, ICE must never delegate to others the government's fundamental responsibility to operate a safe, secure, and humane system of civil detention and supervision.

When improved population management practices are in place, a civil system of civil detention and alternatives will emerge. These are its characteristics. ICE will operate the fewest number of detention facilities necessary, their locations will be near population centers, transportation networks, 24-hour emergency healthcare, and a qualified workforce; their design and construction will be suitable for administratively held individuals, the majority of whom present little to no assessed risk of violence or escape, their capacity consistent with each region's rates of apprehensions to minimize the need for transfers elsewhere. Hardened physical plants, augmented perimeters, and surveillance equipment are used only to the limited extent necessary. Likewise, its continuum of control distinguishes alternative *forms* of detention such as electronic monitoring, from alternatives *to* detention, assigning aliens eligible for community supervision to the least restrictive supervision strategies warranted to achieve their timely reporting. Accordingly, ICE assigns aliens to detention facilities and alternatives to detention programs based upon assessed risk and need and not availability. To accomplish these tasks, ICE will develop objective risk assessment instruments to ascertain each alien's propensity for fight and for flight. ICE will also conduct periodic population forecasts to ensure it secures adequate funding to maintain sufficient secure and community-based capacity. Staffing, supervision strategies, and program offerings will also align with individual aliens' anticipated length of stay. Special needs populations including women and children, the elderly and mentally or physically infirm, and asylum seekers, as well as low custody detainees will not be placed in high custody correctional settings or assigned to segregation cells. Every facility and alternative to detention provider used by ICE will meet or exceed the standards that it adopts and the terms and conditions for which it contracts. ICE will no longer use facilities and providers whose performance is subpar. Similarly, ICE agents will maintain contact with their assigned caseloads, providing in person up-to-date, individualized information.

Detention management describes how a national system of detention can be organized and operated to inform and improve the conditions of detention and detention alternatives so that they are level with, if not better than, conditions under which pretrial, criminal inmates are kept. Adoption also enhances ICE's efficiency and effectiveness in all types of facilities it operates, holding facilities where detainees are assigned temporarily prior to booking, and detention facilities where they are transferred afterward, as well as during transport between facilities and from the United States when removed.

Detention Management

About 100 detainees, all of them assessed by ICE agents to be maximum custody, and dressed in red jumpsuits signifying their high custody classification, were escorted to the recreation yard by two guards who stayed to supervise them. There were wooden bats and hard balls and metal horseshoes and stakes on the field. The detainees took turns playing baseball and tossing horseshoes for the next hour without incident. They did not behave like the "worst of the worst" and were not managed by ICE as if they were. In a correctional facility, only small numbers of high custody inmates, supervised by more officers, would be permitted to recreate together. Any sports equipment that could be used as weapons would be expressly prohibited. These detainees' risk to themselves and others was clearly misclassified. Had they been maximum custody, the conditions under which they had been supervised would have placed both the population and the staff at significant risk.

Detention management's key components are fairly few in number and feature due process proportionate to the rights at risk, adopting Miranda-like warnings and providing publically funded counsel; the means to timely redress rights denied; the right to remain in the region where one resided; the right to personal expression, specifically to wear one's own clothes and maintain one's own appearance; and the ability to communicate in one's primary language, prepare one's own meals and eat familiar foods; and move with some freedom within the detention facility and on its grounds. Core governmental duties, particularly detention oversight, detainee classification, and determinations of disciplinary infractions and sanctions and detainee grievances, are never delegated by government agents to others secured to act on their behalf. To perform its duties with excellence, ICE agents acquire the education, experience, and expertise to effectively maintain continuous oversight of detention and alternatives to detention management activities and outcomes, conduct interim assessments and annual evaluations, and direct improvement efforts. Finally, whereas the standards that guide ICE activities today represent minimum expectations for conditions in detention and the community and not maximum expectations, and need to be reviewed regularly and updated periodically, prospectively, ICE tailors detention and alternatives to detention standards to administratively held aliens.

Healthcare

The medical file that is started at intake remains at the sending facility when a detainee is transferred to another location. The receiving facility creates a new file. A summary of the detainee's healthcare is supposed to follow shortly after arrival, but that does not always occur. If the detainee is transferred again or re-admitted at a later date, the process begins anew.

Improved detention management manifests in many ways. The objective methods by which ICE assesses individual aliens' risks and needs will measurably reduce its reliance on detention and on correctional facilities when detention is warranted. Similarly, it will lower utilization of electronic monitoring when community supervision is warranted. Additionally, placements will be better informed. Aliens will be assigned to facilities where the level of medical care meets their needs and the level of supervision is consistent with the risk they present. Avoidable medical deaths are averted. Activities occur in congregate settings. Recreation is outdoors, religious services are held in a chapel, visitation is family friendly. Facilities comply with federal law, notably, the Prisoner Rape Elimination Act and the Religious Land Use and Institutionalized Persons Act. Communication is improved. Translation services are readily available, correspondence and phone calls with family members and counsel increases. Detainees are also conversant about the status of their cases; they do not seek relief where none is provided in the statute. Their time in detention decreases. Onsite oversight by qualified government agents helps identify problems early and see them through to satisfactory conclusions. ICE also elicits feedback from detainees, counsel, nongovernmental organizations and other stakeholders. Extreme correctional measures such as nonlethal force including stun guns, punitive segregation, and strip searches are only used under exigent circumstances and are always subject to review by ICE. Lethal force is expressly prohibited.

Healthcare is a fundamental right to which every detainee should have access and includes medical, mental health, and dental assessments and services. Responsible delivery requires an integrated system that takes into consideration the public health needs of the workplace, the communities in which the facilities are located, and the countries to which many of the aliens will return. Healthcare includes wellness and prevention as well as routine and emergency intervention. Healthcare is never conditioned upon the facility's location or the alien's anticipated date of removal or relief. It always meets or exceeds community standards.

Programs Management

The law library at a men's detention facility operated for ICE in southern Louisiana was "staffed" solely by state inmates who were incarcerated at a nearby prison. Women detained in a county jail in a southeastern city for ICE could only access the law library when none of the female offenders wanted to use it.

Execution is as important as conceptualization. Comprehensive care requires that emergency care is available on an ongoing and as-needed basis and routine care is available at least weekdays, for eight or more hours daily. Good nutrition, adequate exercise, access to accurate healthcare information, and contact with community providers furthers prevention and wellness. Neither transfers between facilities nor deportation from the United States may interrupt or delay essential medication or care. Healthcare records are current, complete, confidential, travel with aliens during transport, and are kept secured either electronically or at an easy-to-retrieve location in the event that they return to ICE custody. Healthcare staff members are fully credentialed; impaired providers and healthcare professionals with restricted licenses are disqualified. Chronic conditions are effectively managed;

acute conditions are diagnosed quickly and treated appropriately. ICE communicates with receiving countries prior to repatriation, ensuring a continuum of care is in place for returning immigrants and the receiving nations' public health issues are fully addressed.

Programs management encompasses the several services that are currently required by ICE and other activities that ought to be provided by ICE consistent with aliens' anticipated time in detention, special population characteristics, and individually assessed need. There are four mandated services, all of them based upon corrections case law. They are legal research in the area of immigration law,[37] outdoor recreation, religious services, and family contact including visitation and communication by mail and phone. Several other activities ought to be added to meet the unique requirements of the foreign-born. They include (a) expanding legal research materials to include criminal and family law; (b) increasing DOJ funding to be able to offer the Legal Orientation program to immigrant detainees at every facility to which they are assigned by ICE; (c) developing age- and gender-appropriate and culturally sensitive recreation programs, both indoors and outdoors; (d) expanding ministerial services to meet the spiritual needs of all faiths, eliciting the input and involvement of nearby religious communities and by adding religious study and related activities; (e) normalizing visitation with furnishings appropriate for family gatherings and dedicating partitioned areas to assure the confidentiality of attorney-client consultations; and (f) offering English-as-a-Second-Language classes to augment mandated translation services. The addition of these and other programs services will reduce idleness and enhance wellness. Finally, ICE should offer discharge planning and pre-release preparation to ready aliens who have been identified for release to the community and to expand the pool of aliens who are otherwise eligible for alternatives to detention.[38]

Special Populations

In a number of locations, a seriously medically ill alien or an alien on suicide watch is assigned to a single cell in a punitive segregation unit or to a holding pen in the new admissions area alongside inmates serving infractions or being processed in or out of the facility. Medical and mental health staff come by infrequently.

Special populations include families with minor children, females, unaccompanied minors, aliens with handicapping conditions, the ill, the elderly and the infirm, asylum seekers, and other vulnerable populations, including for example transgender detainees. The effective implementation of reform efforts anticipates adjusting the design and delivery of Population Management, Detention Management, Programs Management, and Healthcare as warranted, to meet the unique requirements of special populations. Modifying population management as needed ensures that the conditions of detention and opportunities for participation in alternatives are comparable and that the management of special populations is not disadvantaged by virtue of their unique requirements. Adjusting as necessary detention management ensures that it is always age- and gender-appropriate and culturally sensitive and that programs management is inclusive. Meaningful access to critical programs services is essential both to equitable treatment and effective detention management. To this end, special populations are also mainstreamed with the general population whenever possible and appropriate. Similarly situated detainees are assigned to detention facilities that are designed or retrofitted and staffed to meet their unique requirements for both custody and care; they are not placed in facilities where their mobility will be curtailed and access to services disparate.

Accountability

ICE maintains a presence at every facility it uses, primarily through the detention officer (DO). Every detainee is assigned a DO, an official point of contact to provide weekly face-to-face updates about the status of their removal or petition for relief. Aliens, whose cases move slowly, are frequently reassigned to facilities aurther away, often to more remote locations in other regions. There, they lose contact with their assigned DO and are not transferred to another at the new location.

Accountability brings this conversation full circle. Accountability speaks to the operating framework, the processes and the tenets for decision-making. It is the means, the manner, and the methods by which ICE provides oversight, pursues continuous improvement, and achieves transparency in the execution of its reforms.

Accountability embodies several operating principles. One, government's improved system civil detention and alternatives to detention is specifically designed for administratively referred aliens pending civil resolution of immigration matters; it is informed by correction law and criminal justice practices but it is not governed by them. Two, its detention standards represent minimum expectations, and not maximum expectations, for conditions of civil detention. ICE commits to exceed minimum standards and strives toward the realization of maximum standards and continuous improvement. Its benchmarks are specific to civil detention and are consistently enforced. Failure to reach minimum standards results in real consequences. Three, ICE also incorporates its minimum operating expectations and requirements in its intergovernmental service agreements, contractual terms and conditions, and policy and procedure manual. In its entirety, all of these documents form the foundation for assessing the performance of individual facilities and contractor providers, each field and every regional office, and the system overall. Four, ICE is charged with the execution of a number of core governmental functions including detention oversight, onsite administrative coordination, and the adjudication of detainee classification, discipline, and grievances. ICE may delegate certain duties by means of contracts, intergovernmental service agreements, and memoranda of agreement; however, ICE may never delegate the fundamental responsibility to operate a safe and secure system of civil detention and alternatives to detention. To that end, ICE must take back from the private sector the oversight of detention management activities and assume responsibility for outcomes by conducting regular and random assessments and annual evaluations. ICE must advance its influence and impact on outcomes through the workforce, ensuring its agents maintain meaningful contact with all of the detainees on their caseload, to be alert to and immediately report issues impacting the alien population, the facility, or the system's overall operation.

Earnest execution of these reforms will yield optimal results. The United States's system of civil detention will reflect our vision of ourselves and our core values as a welcoming and caring nation. Aliens within our borders as well as those under the authority of ICE will enjoy protections provided by law. ICE will exercise discretion provided in statute and in accordance with the field's evidence-based practices. Aliens under ICE authority will be supervised only when necessary and by the least restrictive means. Time spent in detention will be as short as necessary. Conditions of civil detention will be comparable to or better than those of the criminally detained. Those warranting detention will be assigned to facilities that meet their needs and manage their risk. All detention facilities will meet or exceed ICE detention standards. They will all be places where immigrant detainees receive good care. ICE will be adequately funded and will wisely expend government resources, utilizing the whole of the continuum of control to realize its mission. The system of oversight that ICE institutes will identify root causes of real concerns. Its assessments will be accurate and its interventions, timely and effective. Issues, once resolved, are abated and do not reoccur. Its findings are published; its reports invite and incorporate public comment. ICE continues to strive toward excellence.

NOTES

1 See, e.g., New York Special Commission on Attica Hearings (1972); available at http://talkinghistory.org/attica/mckay.html; Autopsies Show Shots Killed 9, *New York Times*, September 15, 1971:1; State Official Admits Mistake, *New York Times*, September 17, 1971:1; A Year Ago at Attica, *TIME*, September. 25, 1972: 42–43; Use of Shotguns in Attica Revolt Deplored in House Unit's Report, *New York Times*, June 27, 1973:37.

2 Violent Offender Incarceration and Truth-In-Sentencing Incentive Grants Program, 42 USC §§ 13701-04 (2006). As to the civil commitment of sexual predators, see, e.g., NY Correct. Law § 500-a (1) (f) (Consol. 2009); N.Y. Crim. Proc. Law, Section 720.10 (Consol. 2009).

3 The federal VOI/TIS statute was enacted in 1994. By 2009, the inmate population had increased 79 percent (Bureau of Justice Statistics 2014).

4 See, for example, *Lewis v. Casey* (1996): "It is for the courts to remedy . . . interference with [inmates' constitutional rights]; it is for the political branches . . . to manage prisons"; *Sandlin v. Conner* (1995); *Bounds v. Smith* (1977), stating that judicial restraint is appropriate in prisoners' rights cases, but that it does not extend to ignoring valid constitutional claims; *Wolff v. McDonnell* (1974) noting the folly of ignoring the judgment of correctional administrators by "encasing the disciplinary procedures in an inflexible constitutional straitjacket."

5 For instance, although an alien who enters illegally may have committed a misdemeanor criminal offense in violation of 8 U.S.C. § 1325, ICE does not have authority to detain an alien for that criminal violation while criminal proceedings are pending. Instead, the Department of Justice holds that authority. 8 U.S.C. §§ 1226, 1231 (2006).

6 The duration of confinement in immigration detention may be modified, however, based upon an alien's criminal and immigration record and institutional conduct (*Zadvydas v. Davis* 2001).

7 In 2009, three facilities, a total combined capacity of 1,137 beds, about 3 percent of the inventory of beds used by ICE, afforded conditions approximating those of DHS's envisioned reforms. One of them was of a noncorrectional design; a facility in rural Pennsylvania was first a residence for the indigent elderly. The other two were of correctional origins. One was used previously as a work release center for low custody sentenced inmates in suburban Florida and the other was built in rural Texas to detain sheriff's prisoners and was later modified.

8 Among the reform announcements by DHS in 2009, following its adoption of the recommendations in the Schriro Report, ICE committed to build several new generation facilities with a combined total capacity of 3,485 new beds (Human Rights First 2011).

9 Access encompasses contact visitation, mail, email, and low-cost phone calls as well as confidential communication with counsel.

10 ICE performance-based detention standards do not prohibit preventive, emergent, and urgent healthcare that is conditioned upon the anticipated length of stay prior to removal or release.

11 Adequate clothing is weather-, gender-, and age-appropriate and respectfully accommodates religious and cultural requirements.

12 Activities of daily living include, for example, preparing one's own meals, laundering one's own clothes, and bathing consistent with one's own needs.

13 In the Ninth Circuit, the U.S. Court of Appeals added its own guidance, holding that conditions of confinement for civil detainees must be superior to those provided pretrial criminal detainees as well as convicted prisoners; see *Jones v. Blanas* (2004). The Court wrote that if a civil detainee's conditions of confinement are the same, similar, or more restrictive than those of pretrial or sentenced felons, then those conditions are presumptively punitive and therefore unconstitutional (*Jones v. Blanas* 2004:934). The 9th Circuit did not prevail (*Cert. denied* 2005).

14 Standard Minimum Rules for the Treatment of Prisoners (United Nations Economic and Social Council Resolutions 663 C (XXIV) 1957 and (LXII) 1977).

15 Ibid. at Civil Prisoners, para. 94.

16 For elaboration on the principle of exceptionality of pretrial detention pursuant to international human rights law, see IAHCR Report No. 86/09, Case 12.553, para. 93 et seq. (2009); see also Inter-American Commission on Human Rights (2010).

17 Inter-American Commission on Human Rights, res. 03/08, Human Rights of Migrants, International Standards and the Return Directive of the EU, at 2.

18 Organization of American States: Inter-American Commission on Human Rights. *Report on Immigration in the United States: Detention and Due Process* 2010.

19 The United Nations Human Rights Committee oversees the ICCPR's implementation of the covenant.

20 American Bar Association (ABA). *Criminal Justice Standards on the Legal Status of Prisoners* §§ 23-1.1—23-8.8 (1981).

21 Ibid. (1985).

22 American Bar Association (ABA). *Standards for Criminal Justice: Treatment of Prisoners.* 2009. (3rd ed.). See also Criminal Justice Section, The Report of the ABA Draft Treatment of Prisoners Standards, Documents submitted to the ABA House of Delegates 5 (November 2009).
23 National Commission on Correctional Health Care. *Standards for Health Services.* (2008).
24 U.S. Department of Justice. Bureau of Prisons. (2010). *Program Statements.*
25 Detention and Removal Operations (DRO) was renamed Enforcement and Removal Operations (ERO) several years ago.
26 U.S. Department of Homeland Security. Immigrations and Customs Enforcement. (2008). *Performance-Based Standards.*
27 28 C.F.R. 500–599 (2009).
28 Pursuant to the Prisoner Rape Elimination Act (PREA). the PREA Commission submitted draft standards to the U.S. Attorney General for the implementation of the Act, including the recommendation that they apply to immigrant detainees in the custody of ICE as well as to criminal inmates incarcerated by the Bureau of Prisons and all state and local correctional systems. ICE objected. Instead, ICE developed standards to which it will adhere. See U.S. Department of Homeland Security (2006).
29 ICE detains over 400,000 aliens annually, far more than the U.S. Bureau of Prisons or any state or local correctional system (Minton 2010; West 2010; Schriro 2009a:1445).
30 Immigration and Naturalization Service (2000). *National Detention Standards.*
31 See Comments by the American Bar Association at www.americanbar.org/ . . . 2013fed26_abuseinconfinementfacilities_l.auth; Sign-on Letter to the White House Urging PREA to Cover. Accessed November 11, 2014; www.aila.org/content/default.aspx?docid=39227; and Letter on PREA Standard in Immigration Detention. Accessed November 11, 2014; http://www.hrw.org/news/2011/02/15/us-immigration-facilities-should-apply-prison-rape-elimination-act-protections.
32 Where ICE does not apply correctional standards across the board, it requires less, not more, of its providers. Two notable examples of this exception include PREA; see U.S. Department of Homeland Security (2006), and Healthcare, as discussed in this chapter.
33 These seven facilities, all of them "legacy" facilities previously used by INS, are called Service Processing Centers (SPCs). They are owned by the government and operated by private prison providers. They are the El Paso SPC, Krome SPC, Port Isabel SPC, Batavia SPC, El Centro SPC, Florence SPC, and Aguadilla SPC (Schriro 2009a:10).
34 Congress enacted the Prison Litigation Reform Act, which precluded bringing any action until available administrative remedies were exhausted, affording corrections officials an opportunity to address complaints internally, to reduce the quantity and to improve the quality of prisoner suits. Where corrections officials successfully took steps to avert litigation, both inmate filings and court findings were positively impacted. See Branham (1997:56–97); Hanson and Daley (1994).

35 ICE Detention Reform Accomplishments. Accessed November 11, 2014; http://www.ice.gov/detention-reform/detention-reform.htm.
36 The suggestions in this section build upon recommendations included in the 2009 report; see Schriro (2009a:18–19, 22–23, 24–25, 26, 27–28, 28–29).
37 Correctional standards require legal research materials in the area of criminal law. ICE substituted immigration law for criminal law. In fact, immigrant detainees need access to immigration, criminal, and family law: immigration law to address the underlying issues in the detainer, criminal law to assist criminal aliens with petitions of relief, and family law to aid parents at risk of losing their custodial rights for their minor children.
38 Pursuant to *Zadvydas v. Davis* (2001), removable aliens who will not be deported in the foreseeable future must be released. Other aliens will receive relief. Still others will be eligible for placement in an alternative to a detention program pending determination of removal or relief. Aliens in each of these categories will benefit from discharge planning and pre-release preparation.

REFERENCES

American Bar Association (ABA). 1981. *Criminal Justice Standards on the Legal Status of Prisoners.* Washington, DC: American Bar Association.

American Bar Association (ABA). 2012. *ABA Civil Immigration Detention Standards.* Washington, DC: American Bar Association.

American Correctional Association (ACA). 1989. *Standards for Small Jail Facilities.* Alexandria, VA: American Correctional Association.

American Correctional Association (ACA). 2010a. *Core Jail Standards.* Alexandria, VA: American Correctional Association.

American Correctional Association (ACA). 2010b. *Performance-Based Standards for Adult Community Residential Services.* Alexandria, VA: American Correctional Association.

American Correctional Association (ACA). 2010c. *Standards for Adult Correctional Institutions.* Alexandria, VA: American Correctional Association.

Branham, Lynn S. 1997. Limiting the Burdens of Pro Se Inmate Litigation: A Technical Assistance Manual for Courts, Correctional Officers and Attorneys General. Washington, DC: American Bar Association.

Branham, Lynn S. and Michael S. Hamden. 2005. *Cases and Materials on the Law and Policy of Sentencing and Corrections* (7th ed.). St. Paul, MN: Thomson West.

Bureau of Justice Statistics. 2014. *Key Facts at a Glance (2010).* Washington, DC: U.S. Department of Justice. Accessed November 5, 2014. http://www.bjs.gov/glance_redirect.cfm.

Collins, William C. 2005. *Correctional Law for the Correctional Officer* (4th ed.). Alexandria, VA: American Correctional Association.

Department of Public Information. 1950. *Yearbook of the United Nations, 1948–1949.* New York: United Nations Publications. Accessed November 12, 2014. http://www2.ohchr.org/english/issues/education/training/docs/UNYearbook.pdf.

Edwards, Alice. 2011. *Back to Basics: The Right to Liberty and Security of Person and 'Alternatives to Detention' of Refugees, Asylum-Seekers, Stateless Persons and Other Migrants.* Switzerland: UN High Commissioner for Refugees.

Filter, John A. 2001. *Prisoners' Rights: The Supreme Court and Evolving Standards of Decency.* Westport, CT: Greenwood Press.

Hanson, Roger A. and Henry W. K. Daley. 1994. *Challenging the Conditions of Prisons and Jails: A Report on Section 1983 Litigation.* Washington, DC: U.S. Department of Justice. Accessed November 12, 2014. http://cacs.unlv.edu/pdf/ccopaj.pdf.

Human Rights First. 2011. *Jails and Jumpsuits: Transforming the U.S. Immigration Detention System—A Two-Year Review.* New York: Human Rights First. Accessed November 12, 2014. http://www.humanrightsfirst.org/wp-content/uploads/pdf/HRF-Jails-and-Jumpsuits-report.pdf.

Human Rights First. 2012. *How to Repair the U.S. Immigration Detention System: Blueprint for the Next Administration.* New York: Human Rights First. Accessed November 12, 2014. http://www.humanrightsfirst.org/wp-content/uploads/pdf/immigration_detention_blueprint.pdf.

Inter-American Commission on Human Rights. Organization of American States. 1948. *American Declaration on the Rights and Duties of Man.* Accessed November 12, 2014. https://www.cidh.oas.org/Basicos/English/Basic2.American%20Declaration.htm.

Inter-American Commission on Human Rights. Organization of American States. 2010. *Report on Immigration in the United States: Detention and Due Process.* Accessed November 12, 2014. https://www.oas.org/en/iachr/migrants/docs/pdf/Migrants2011.pdf.

Inter-American Court of Human Rights. 2003. *Juridical Condition and Rights of the Undocumented Migrants, Advisory Opinion.* Accessed November 12, 2014. http://www.unhcr.org/4bfb8e2c9.html.

Lazarus, E. 1883. *The New Colossus.* Accessed November 3, 2014. http://xroads.virginia.edu/~cap/liberty/lazaruspoem.html.

Minton, Todd D. 2010. *Jail Inmates at Midyear 2009—Statistical Tables.* Washington, DC: U.S. Department of Justice, Bureau of Justice Statistics. Accessed November 12, 2014. http://www.bjs.gov/content/pub/pdf/jim09st.pdf.

Mushlin, Michael B. 2002. *Rights of Prisoners* (3rd ed.). St. Paul, MN: Thomson West.

New York Special Commission on Attica. 1972. *Attica: The Official Report on the New York State Special Commission on Attica.* New York: Bantam Books.

Pizarro, Gabriela Rodriquez. 2002. *Report of the United Nations Special Rapporteur on the Human Rights of Migrant Workers.* Commission on Human Rights. Accessed November 12, 2014. http://daccess-dds-ny.un.org/doc/UNDOC/GEN/G02/162/55/PDF/G0216255.pdf?OpenElement.

Ross, Darrell L. 2005. *Civil Liability Issues in Corrections.* Durham, NC: Carolina Academic Press.

Schriro, Dora. 2009a. *Report on ICE Detention Policies and Practices: A Recommended Course of Action for Systems Reform.* Washington, DC: Department of Homeland Security.

Schriro, Dora. 2009b. "Rethinking Civil Detention and Supervision." *Arizona Attorney* Fall 2010, pp. 13–14 *(Special Issue Immigration: 2009 and Beyond).*

Schriro, Dora. 2010. "Improving Conditions of Confinement for Criminal Inmates and Immigrant Detainees." Arthur Liman Public Interest Program at Yale Law School, *Public Interest Newsletter.* Accessed November 12, 2014 www.law.yale.edu/document/pdf/Liman.NL.2010.final.pdf

U.S. Department of Homeland Security. 2006. *Treatment of Immigration Detainees Housed at Immigrations and Customs Enforcement Facilities.* Accessed November 12, 2014. http://www.oig.dhs.gov/assets/Mgmt/OIG_07-01_Dec06.pdf.

U.S. Department of Homeland Security. U.S. Immigration and Customs Enforcement (ICE). 2008. *Performance-Based National Detention Standards.* Accessed November 12, 2014. http://www.ice.gov/detention-standards/2008.

U.S. Immigration and Naturalization Service. (2000). *National Detention Standards.*

Wells, Michael, Thomas A. Eaton, and Sheldon H. Nahmod. (2004). *Constitutional Torts* (2nd ed.). Lexus/Nexus. Book 58. http://digitalcommons.law.uga.edu/books/58.

West, Heather C. 2010. *Prisoners at Yearend 2009—Advance Counts.* Washington, DC: U.S. Department of Justice, Bureau of Justice Statistics. Accessed November 12, 2014. http://www.bjs.gov/content/pub/pdf/py09ac.pdf.

Williams, Paul. 1981. *The International Bill of Human Rights.* New York: Entwhistle Books.

CASE CITATIONS

Bell v. Wolfish, 441 U.S. 529 (1979).
Benjamin v. Fraser, 161 F. Supp. 151 (S.D.N.Y. 2001).
Benjamin v. Kerik, 102 F. Supp. 2d 157 (S.D.N.Y. 2000).
Bounds v. Smith, 430 U.S. 817, 832 (1977).
Brown et al. v. Board of Education, 347 U.S. 483 (1954).
Cert. denied, 126 S .Ct. 351 (2005).
Clark v. Martinez, 543 U.S. 371, 3810-3 (2005).
Cutter v. Wilkinson, 544 U.S. 709 (2005).
Helling v. McKinney, 509 U.S. 25 (1993).
Holt v. Sarver, 442 F.2d 304, 309-10 (8th Cir. 1971).
Jones v. Blanas, 393 F.3d 918 (9th Cir. 2004).
Lewis v. Casey, 518 U.S. 343, 349 (1996).
Padilla v. Kentucky, 130 S. Ct. 1473 (2010).
Rhem v. Malcolm, 432 F. Supp. 769 *passim* (S.D.N.Y. 1977).
Rhem v. Malcolm, 371 F. Supp. 594, 600 (S.D.N.Y. 1974).
Rhodes v. Chapman, 452 U.S. 337 (1981).

Ruffin v. The Commonwealth, 62 Va. (21 Gratt.) 790, 796 (1871).
Sandlin v. Conner, 515 U.S. 472, 482-83 (1995).
United States ex rel. Atterbury v. Ragen, 237 F.2d 953, 955 (7th Cir. 1956).
United States ex rel. Wolfish v. Levy, 439 F. Supp. 114 *passim* (S.D.N.Y. 1977).
Washington v. Lee, 263 F. Supp. 327, 333-34 (M.D. Ala., 1966).
Wolff v. McDonnell, 418 U.S. 539, 563 (1974).
Zadvydas v. Davis, 533 U.S. 678 (2001).

STATUTES

Prisoner Litigation Reform Act of 1995, Title VIII of Pub.L. 104–134; 28 U.S.C. § 1932.
Prisoner Rape Elimination Act of 2003, Pub.L. 108–79; 42 U.S.C. ch. 147 § 15601 et seq.
Religious Land Use and Institutionalized Persons Act of 2000; Pub.L. 106–274; 42 U.S.C. § 2000cc et seq.

3

You Be the Judge

Who Should Preside Over Immigration Cases, Where, and How?

DENISE NOONAN SLAVIN AND DANA LEIGH MARKS

As we write this chapter, some 242 Immigration Judges across the United States face approximately 408,037 pending cases (TRAC Immigration 2014).[1] These seemingly dry statistics relate to life-altering proceedings where the fates of innumerable noncitizens and their families (who may be citizens) lie in the hands of these Immigration Judges. Noncitizens come before the Immigration Court because the Department of Homeland Security has alleged that they have violated our country's immigration laws.[2] Immigration Judges determine at the trial level whether these individuals are in fact "deportable" from the United States. The array of possible charges is vast. Some noncitizens (referred to as respondents when in proceedings) face deportation (formally called removal) because they entered illegally. Others may have violated conditions of their authorized status or stayed beyond the period authorized for their lawful status. Hundreds of thousands of noncitizens in otherwise lawful status (such as legal permanent resident status) also have faced removal in recent years because of criminal conduct in the United States.

In these proceedings, Immigration Judges also frequently rule on applications from individuals who, although in the country unlawfully or subject to removal due to illegal conduct, may qualify for some discretionary "relief" which would allow them to remain here legally. One common example is a request for asylum, which requires a showing of either past persecution or a well-founded fear of future persecution in the country of intended deportation due to race, religion, nationality, political opinion, or membership in a particular social group. Another example is "cancellation of removal," a remedy available when an individual can show that removal would cause exceptional hardship to certain specified immediate family members. In addition, immigration law—famous (or infamous) for its complexity—provides several other more esoteric remedies, too numerous to discuss here. Simply put, Immigration Judges are charged with the grave, complex, and multi-layered decisions about who should be deported and who should be granted lawful status in the United States.

The U.S. Supreme Court has called the effect of deportation the equivalent of banishment, a sentence to life in exile, loss of property or life or all that makes life worth living, and, in essence: a "punishment of the most drastic kind." (*See*, e.g., *Fong Haw Tan v. Phelan* (1948); *Jordan v. DeGeorge* (1951); *Ng Fung Ho v. White* (1922); *Lehman v. United States* (1957).) An order of deportation can effectively amount to a death sentence, when an individual will be subject to persecution upon return to his or her country. Yet in the post–9/11 era, legitimate concerns regarding national security and terrorism also are crucial factors which can be implicated in these cases. Herein lies the inescapable challenge: The system has been changed in many ways since 2001 including, most significantly, having many immigration functions placed under the jurisdiction of the Department of Homeland Security, but the Immigration Courts are housed, as they have long been, within the Department of Justice. While this has enabled continuity, removing the Immigration Courts from a law enforcement agency would result in significant improvements that would allow this crucially important adjudications system to function better.

Despite their exceedingly high stakes, immigration cases are significantly complicated by mundane administrative realities. The complexity of the law and the paucity of resources available to the Immigration Courts contribute to a court system that has been widely described as overburdened and overwhelmed. Immigration law has been repeatedly recognized by the federal courts as being second only to tax law in its complexity. The statute itself is an ever-changing labyrinth of idiosyncratic terminology and seemingly conflicting provisions, which is continually generating circuit court and Supreme Court interpretations. Major decisions, such as *Padilla v. Kentucky* (2010), which affects the legal advice required for noncitizen criminal defendants, dramatically impact day-to-day proceedings in our courts. One must also add into the mix the myriad of languages and cultural contexts in which these matters arise, the staggering numbers of cases on the docket, and the fact that less than half of the people who appear before the Immigration Courts are represented by an attorney.[3] Only then can one begin to appreciate the full array of challenges faced by Immigration Judges, whose mission is to decide these cases fairly and expeditiously.

One goal of this chapter is to describe certain structural impediments that undermine the optimal functioning of these important tribunals. These systemic impediments range from such macro-level concerns as where Immigration Courts should be properly housed in our legal system, to such micro-level issues as how to alleviate workload pressures and ensure that judges have the ability to render decisions independently and expeditiously. In order to fairly assess the competing concerns, we will particularly examine the conflicting roles currently imposed on Immigration Judges.

What should an individual expect from the Immigration Judge who is to decide his or her future? An Immigration Judge is required by law to exercise independent judgment and discretion, consistent with the law and regulations, to render a decision (8 C.F.R. Section 1103.10(b)). The fundamental expectations of a judge in the United States are to be impartial and independent. Legal scholars would surely agree that without an independent and neutral decision-maker, due process cannot be achieved. The independence of the judiciary in our federal and state systems is of course mandated aspirationally by the separation of the judiciary from the legislative and executive branches. Although many are executive branch agencies, administrative tribunals provide a well-accepted and valuable method for high-volume adjudications by specialized adjudicators. These tribunals, most of which are governed by the Administrative Procedure Act, safeguard decisional independence by specific provisions to protect against any commingling of investigative and prosecutorial functions, thereby assuring impartiality and independence.[4]

The Immigration Courts, however, are unique. They lack clear statutory structure and provisions to safeguard impartiality and independence. They are not in the judicial branch of the government, nor does the Administrative Procedure Act clearly cover them. Despite this, *Judulang v. Holder* (2011) holds immigration decisions of the government to essentially the same standard of judicial review as applied to other agency action. Indeed, after the Administrative Procedure Act was enacted, Congress exempted deportation proceedings from its protections, concluding that adherence to the statute would be too costly or cumbersome (*see* Rawitz 1988 for a thorough history).

The Immigration Court system is part of the executive branch of government, located in an agency called the Executive Office of Immigration Review, which, in turn, is a component of the Department of Justice. Until March 1, 2003, the Department of Justice also housed the Immigration and Naturalization Service (INS), the same office that employed the prosecutors appearing before the Immigration Court. Since 2003, those prosecutors have been housed in the Department of Homeland Security. This has provided some important separation of functions for the Immigration Courts; however, as employees of the executive branch rather than the judicial branch of government, the Department of Justice characterizes Immigration Judges as "attorneys" employed by the U.S. government, rather than as judges.

This rather unique (and anachronistic) model causes actual and potential conflicts. The overarching issue is this: Immigration Judges are treated as attorneys working for or representing the U.S. government, while at the same time, their daily role and the duties they discharge mandate the traditional responsibilities that the title of "judge" implies. There is a deep, inherent tension between these conflicting functions. These tensions are apparent when you review the implementation and impact of case completion goals, the practical effects that placement of these courts in a law enforcement agency has had, the lack of even-handed sanctions authority that has resulted, and questions that are arising in the rapidly emerging area of post-deportation law. Finally, we will discuss the provisions relating to the Immigration Courts in Senate Bill 744 on comprehensive immigration reform, and provide an alternative blueprint for reform.

Case Completion Goals: Timeliness versus Quality

Consider the following typical scenario:

> An Immigration Judge is instructed by her superior to conduct four "merits" (i.e., full hearings) cases in a day. In addition, she is tasked with completing all cases within a specified number of months after they ap-

pear on her docket. As an attorney working for the government, her performance is subject to performance evaluation and she is subject to the rules relating to employee insubordination if she fails to follow her supervisor's instructions.

As a judge, in her first case of the day, which has been long pending, she must decide whether to grant a continuance to a party who asserts he needs more time to obtain vital evidence from a foreign country. Then, during her third case of the day, she must decide whether an additional witness should be allowed to testify, although that would necessitate another hearing session at a later date or require her to reset the fourth case on her docket that day to a later date.

This judge faces a real dilemma: Should she act as an attorney or as a judge? How do the personal consequences to the judge differ based on whether she is considered a government attorney or a judge? Clearly, her answer will influence the choices she must make.

We believe that this dilemma is an all too common reflection of the systemic problem of placing the Immigration Court in an executive branch law enforcement agency. It is axiomatic that "justice delayed is justice denied." Litigants should be able to have their cases heard fairly and in a timely fashion. In federal, state, and local courts judges struggle to keep up with burgeoning caseloads. The same is true in Immigration Court, but because it is a court within a federal agency, there are unique mechanisms in place outside the control (and frequently outside the knowledge) of the litigants that impose timeliness constraints on Immigration Judges. These are called "case completion goals." In the Immigration Court system, these "goals" have become an undue and sometimes unseen pressure on an Immigration Judge's ability to render a thorough, well-reasoned decision.

In June 2000, the Immigration Court system began formulating the case completion goals, which were formally implemented in May 2002. They were the result of requirements imposed by the Government Performance and Results Act of 1993. Bound by its mandate, the Department of Justice had to quantify its achievements and provide accountability. To comply, the Department chose to establish "adjudication priorities" for the Immigration Courts and elected to measure its success by evaluating whether the court met case completion goals (U.S. GAO 2006:20–21).

The stated purpose of these goals is to assure that the Immigration Courts "adjudicate cases fairly and in a timely matter" (U.S. GAO 2006). To that end, a target time frame was established for the completion of every case, based on the existing resources and case type. Then the agency set expectations for the percentage of such cases to be completed within that time frame. Providing some flexibility, the Executive Office for Immigration Review (EOIR) determined that, for the most part, completing 90 percent of the cases within the established time frame would be an "acceptable result." The agency monitors each local Immigration Court to identify cases that have not met the established time frames and takes action to assist courts that are not meeting the goals.

Clearly it is in the public interest to have measures that facilitate objective evaluation of the Immigration Court system as a whole. This is the core objective of case completion goals. In fact, the ability to evaluate how long cases remain pending on the docket is essential to any determination of the appropriate level of resources necessary to address the needs of a seemingly ever-increasing caseload. This is a considerable challenge, particularly in the current climate where ever-increasing resources are directed toward immigration enforcement efforts, while at the same time the impact these increased enforcement measures have on the caseload at our Immigration Courts is consistently overlooked. However, when case completion goals are implemented and increased numbers of cases are fed into the system without a concomitant increase in resources, the goals do not serve as "resource allocation tools." Instead, they are perceived as performance measures, and individual judges are placed in the untenable position of potentially being forced to choose between their personal interest to maintain their own job security and the competing due process needs of a given case.

EOIR has not stated publicly that actions can be taken against an individual Immigration Judge for failure to meet a goal in any given case and repeatedly asserts in meetings and discussions relating to discipline cases that the goals are aspirations, not inflexible mandates. However, narrative responses from Immigration Judges in a recent study revealed that they perceive these goals to be mandatory, and frequently in conflict with ideal conditions for adjudicating cases fairly and independently (Lustig et al. 2008). Immigration Judges noted: "In those cases where I would like more time to consider all the facts and weigh what I have heard I rarely have much time to do so simply because of the pressure to complete cases"; and: "What is required to meet the case completions is quantity over quality." The agency's monitoring of case completions has been described as:

> the drip-drip-drip of Chinese water torture that I hear in my mind (i.e. in my mind I hear my boss saying: "more completions, more completions, bring that calendar in, you are set out too far, you have too many reserved decisions, why has that motion been pending so long, too many cases off calendar." (Lustig et al. 2008:64–65)

Based on these reports, the way in which these goals are being imposed by Immigration Judges' supervisors may not comport with what is expected of an independent and fair judge, even though they may be in line with appropriate expectations for an attorney for the government. Judges, who are accustomed to succeeding and achieving, may well fear disapproval or even discipline from their supervisors if they fail to meet expectations. Certainly each situation is different. Yet perhaps most problematic is the fact that litigants might not be aware of these goals or the pressures they place on Immigration Judges, since these internal management directives are not "on the record" with regard to how they may apply to a particular case.

The reality of this pressure and the role it can play is illustrated in a published 2008 case. In *Hashmi v. Attorney General of the United States* (2008), an Immigration Judge referenced the case completion goals and noted that the goal for this case type had been exceeded when he denied an unopposed motion to continue the case. The Circuit Court found that: "the sole basis for the Immigration Judge's exercise of discretion was the Immigration Judge's perceived 'obligation []' to 'manage [his] calendar' []" (*Hashmi v. Attorney General of the United States* 2008:261). The court cautioned:

> Case completion goals are ordinarily implemented as guidelines to promote reasonable uniformity and to help judges schedule and effectively manage their caseloads. As guidelines, they should not be read as an end in themselves but as a means to prompt and fair dispositions, giving due regard to the unique facts and circumstances of the case. (ibid.)

Finding that the Immigration Judge had reached the decision on whether to grant or deny the motion based "solely" on case completion goals, the Circuit Court found that the decision was "impermissibly arbitrary" and an abuse of discretion (*Hashmi v. Attorney General of the United States* 2008).

One would think that such criticism from "above" would be compelling. On remand, however, the Board of Immigration Appeals apparently disagreed with the Circuit Court's characterization of the Immigration Judge's decision. The Board noted it had affirmed the initial decision to deny a continuance because it agreed with the Immigration Judge that "a further continuance was unwarranted in light of the numerous continuances already granted" (*Matter of* Hashmi 2009). It further held that there was no prejudice to the respondent and the delay was caused, in part, by the respondent's failures. Nevertheless, the Board went on to articulate factors to be considered in determining if a continuance was warranted, and noted that while "other procedural factors" may be considered, "[c]ompliance with an Immigration Judge's case completion goals, however, is not a proper factor in deciding a continuance request, and Immigration Judges should not cite such goals in decisions relating to continuances" (*Matter of* Hashmi 2009).

This illustrates well the conflicts Immigration Judges face. They are torn between their classification as government attorneys and their duties as judges. While the Circuit Court made clear that case completion goals should not be a factor in a decision, the comments of the judge in that case and the comments of the judges in response to the survey noted above reveal that case completion goals *are* often a factor in the decision-making process. Reinforcing the mixed message that judges receive, it is noteworthy that the Board referenced "the *Immigration Judge's* case completion goals," reflecting an agency view that these goals are imposed on individual judges, not on the courts as a whole. The admonition not to *cite* them merely hides the dilemma.

Such mixed messages cannot help but create further unease for Immigration Judges who only recently have become subject to performance evaluations after years of exemption from this process (U.S. Department of Justice 2006). Under these circumstances, and in light of the fact that the Department of Justice has made it clear that these goals are essential to its compliance with the Government Performance and Results Act, it is easy to understand how an Immigration Judge would have uppermost in her mind the concern for the agency's success in meeting case completion goals. How this consideration is weighed when competing against other fundamental due process concerns is a choice that plays out daily, unfolding on a case-by-case basis. The questions are: Does this tension have to exist, and could structural reform resolve this conflict once and for all?

It is certainly necessary for a court to establish a system to estimate the time needed to complete cases in order to assure proper resource allocation and timely completion of cases. However, judges should not be made to feel that these are quotas or goals for them, and they should be consulted as to how the goals are set. Indeed, the federal judiciary has done this, but in a much different manner. In determining how to measure the time needed for case processing, the Federal Judicial Center, in cooperation with the Administrative Office of U.S. Courts, used over one hundred district court judges as consultants, reviewers, and study participants. To our knowledge, not a single sitting Immigration Judge was consulted in setting the Department of Justice case completions goals, and the Department has not revealed if any "study" was done to set them.

As we explain in our suggestions for reform that follow, we propose a solution that would alleviate much of the tension and resolve these conflicts.

Potential Conflicts for Judges Working in a Law Enforcement Agency

> Picture an Immigration Judge who is presiding over a case where the individual is applying for asylum because he was jailed and tortured for engaging in a protest against the ruling party of his homeland. In his country, the judicial branch is corrupt and widely seen as a "puppet" of the government.
>
> How should the Immigration Judge convincingly assure the asylum applicant that the U.S. Immigration Court is not a "puppet" of or "rubber stamp" for the Department of Homeland Security, which had previously denied his asylum application?

One predominant theme that permeates the conflicts facing Immigration Judges on a day-to-day basis is the placement of the court within the

Department of Justice, a law enforcement agency.[5] Many of the conflicts this creates involve perceptions and appearances; but some are much more tangible and specific. Unfortunately, the history of the Immigration Court system is rife with instances where undue law enforcement pressures were placed on Immigration Judges. Judges in the Immigration Courts are aware of that history and mindful of it. In its early years, when the Immigration Court and the prosecutor's office (then the Immigration and Naturalization Service) were both housed within the Department of Justice, Immigration Judges were dependent on the INS District Directors (in essence the client of the prosecutors) for hearing facilities, office space, and supplies. Even today, many Immigration Courts remain located inside detention centers operated and/or controlled by the Department of Homeland Security (DHS) and many other courts are located in the same building as DHS offices and prosecutors. All Immigration Judges are familiar with the old rumor that a Texas Immigration Judge lost his parking space when the INS District Director was upset with his decision. While this rumor may seem laughable, the discomfort among the Immigration Judges who were at the mercy of the INS for worksite conditions was all too real and contributed to a desire to not "rock the boat." A similar uneasiness still exists today while the Immigration Courts remain housed in the Department of Justice, which is closely aligned with DHS and shares with it the primary mission of law enforcement rather than neutral adjudications.

In addition, there is the day-to-day problem of the perception of being housed inside the same building as the prosecutor, and using some of the same resources. The public and even members of the press all too frequently refer to the Immigration Courts as the "INS Courts" and fail to note that they are part of the Department of Justice, a completely separate department. Many of the respondents appearing before the Immigration Courts come from countries "where a courtroom is not an institution of justice, but rather an extension of a corrupt state" (Appleseed 2009:7). It is not infrequent in Immigration Court for an unrepresented individual to assume that the Immigration Judge works for the same entity as the DHS prosecutor. Frequently in Court, a respondent will indicate that he gave a document to an Immigration Judge "before." Further inquiry will reveal that the document was actually given to a DHS representative. Many respondents come to court with the perception that their deportation is a foregone conclusion, claiming that's what the DHS representatives told them. It is difficult to elicit cooperation and forthrightness from a respondent who believes the deck is already stacked against him or her. These perceptions are even more difficult to dispel when the Immigration Judge's courtroom door is located directly across from the prosecutors' door. This is most difficult in the detained setting, when the guard providing security for the courtroom may be the same guard who is watching over the respondent in his or her "barracks."

It is not just the co-location of Immigration Courts with a prosecutorial party that has caused charges that the Immigration Court is subject to undue pressure from the government. Allegations also have persisted that government prosecutors have had inappropriate *ex parte* contact with the Immigration Court system. The allegations that the Immigration Court has undue bias toward the government persist to this day. A report from the Chicago Appleseed Fund for Justice (2009) noted, "[t]he Immigration Courts and the BIA [Board of Immigration Appeals] [have] never enjoyed a stellar reputation for impartiality. But that reputation fell to a new low after a deliberate effort to stack the Immigration Courts . . . in favor to the government between 2004 and 2006."[6] The report also claimed that the composition of the Immigration Courts favors the government, stating that "almost 80 percent of Immigration Judges have professional backgrounds that tend to cause them to find in favor of the government significantly more often than judges without those backgrounds" (Appleseed 2009).

This public perception of the Immigration Court affects the ability of Immigration Judges to do their jobs. As noted above, an Immigration Judge is expected to use his or her independent judgment and to be impartial. As the Appleseed Report (2009) noted, "John Adams urged that judges should be 'impartial and independent as the lot of humanity will admit.'" Immigration Judges are aware of the public perception that they are partial toward the government, and have been subjected to incredibly increased scrutiny as a result. Specifically, in 2006, the Attorney General created a "performance evaluation" process for judges, and in 2010, created a process for filing complaints against Immigration Judges online (U.S. Department of Justice 2010). Unfortunately, this process has not been patterned after judicial performance evaluations, which provide safeguards against political influence and retribution for good faith legal decisions, but instead includes factors such as success or failure to achieve agency goals, a factor that may at times be at odds with the due process concerns raised in a particular case. In addition, this process is internal and not disclosed to the public. At this time, there is a real concern that these allegations of government bias could cause Immigration Judges to over-compensate, to "bend over backwards," or worse, exhibit a bias against the government, to avoid being the object of complaint or discipline. As noted in a letter to the Attorney General from Ranking House Minority Member Lamar Smith:

> Under its practice, OPR [Office of Professional Responsibility] will usually investigate immigration judges only in cases in which they deny relief that is later granted by the federal courts. The course of least resistance is therefore for immigration judges to grant relief in many cases despite their beliefs about the merits of the cases. . . . This perceived pressure ultimately frustrates the integrity of our immigration laws and the American people's interest in the laws being enforced in a fair and orderly manner.[7]

This perception and the complaint process certainly create pressure for Immigration Judges. Responses by Immigration Judges to the survey noted above indicate that the negative perception of the public and fear of investigation is a driving and stressful force in the decision-making process (Lustig et al. 2008). One description of these pressures aptly captures the essence of this concern:

> Fear that every decision or proceeding may trigger a "personalized" and scathing published criticism from the reviewing circuit court and/or an Office of Professional Responsibility investigation into the judge, which may destroy the judge's professional reputation and career without the ability to rebut or defend. (ibid.)

Another judge noted that he or she was "demoralized by being made the 'whipping boy' by the press and public, when it is the system we are forced to follow that contributes so greatly to the errors I make" (Lustig et al. 2008). These comments reveal that the negative perception of the Immigration Court system, coupled with the mechanisms the Department of Justice has put in place to deal with these perceptions, create a potentially coercive influence on Immigration Judges. At a minimum, they indisputably have been found to be corrosive to morale and have increased stress and burnout in the Immigration Judge corps. While we fully endorse a transparent evaluation process modeled on accepted standards for the judicial branch of government, the system currently in place unfairly places Immigration Judges at personal peril for good faith legal decisions, an unnecessary and counterproductive situation.

Thus, being housed within the Department of Justice creates several conflicts for Immigration Judges on a daily basis. Because many of the workplace resources for the Court are inextricably tied to those of the Department of Homeland Security, a sister agency, the public perception of the independence of the Immigration Court system is harmed, the Immigration Judges' ability to do their jobs is impaired, and a chilling effect on them is created. In addition, the inescapable impression of government bias created by being housed in a law enforcement agency may actually cause a backlash and encourage appeals by respondents who may have accepted a decision by a court perceived to be truly independent. Taking the Immigration Court out of the Department of Justice and making it an Article I court, as discussed below, would resolve these problems.

Concerns about the Lack of Even-Handed Sanctions Authority

> With the mountain of cases facing Immigration Judges every day, judges need to run their courtrooms as efficiently as possible; this necessarily requires the power to discipline all attorneys who come to court unprepared (Appleseed 2009:11).
>
> Imagine an Immigration Judge who has had numerous problems with two attorneys who appear before her regularly. They are both routinely late, unprepared, rude, and belligerent, and have even made misrepresentations in court. One is a government attorney, and one is a private attorney. This Immigration Judge can refer the private attorney for possible sanctions, but cannot take such action against the government attorney. What can or should the judge do in order to maintain control of her court in a fair manner? (Appleseed 2009:11)

While Immigration Judges have had statutory authority to sanction attorneys by civil monetary penalties since 1996, the Department of Justice has failed to promulgate the regulations needed to implement this authority (*See* Illegal Immigration Reform and Immigrant Responsibility Act of 1996 (IIRIRA), Pub. L. No. 104-208, Section 304, 110 Stat. 3009, 3009-589 (IIRIRA) codified as amended at Section 240(b)(1) of the Immigration and Nationality Act, 8 U.S.C. Section 1229a(b)(1)). This lack of an appropriate sanctions mechanism for attorneys appearing before the Court has led to pressures that may contribute to stress and intemperate behavior by Immigration Judges.

The current procedures available to Immigration Judges for sanctioning lawyers appearing before the Immigration Court are one-sided. The procedures for sanctioning "practitioners" before the Immigration Court for "criminal, unethical, or unprofessional conduct" apply only to an attorney "who does not represent the federal government" (8 C.F.R. Sections 1292.3(a)(1) and (2)). Since this process can only be used against a private attorney, some Immigration Judges are reticent to use it, believing it may create the appearance of a lack of impartiality. Yet, without the ability to impose sanctions, an Immigration Judge lacks a vital tool to address attorney misconduct. This situation leaves Immigration Judges without a mechanism to punish recalcitrant private attorneys, short of resorting to punitive rulings which may harm the respondent far more gravely than his attorney. Judges are also unable to punish recalcitrant government attorneys, short of bestowing an immigration benefit on a respondent who may not deserve it. The danger of employing one-sided procedures against the private bar is that such actions could be viewed as another example where Immigration Judges are providing preferential treatment to government attorneys.

In the survey noted above, one Immigration Judge commented, "We have been intentionally deprived by the Department [of Justice] and DHS of the tools and rules necessary to make DHS function in court in a reasonably professional and competent manner" (Lustig et al. 2008). This belief that the DHS has obstructed the implementation of contempt authority rules is not unfounded. It appears that the situation remains unresolved, at least in part because of historical opposition of the Department of Homeland Security. As one commentator noted, "The INS has generally opposed the application of the [contempt] authority to its attorneys. In more than three years since the enactment of IIRIRA, the [EOIR] and the DOJ have failed to resolve this issue, apparently still paralyzed by the legacy of their relationship with INS" (Creppy et al. 1999). Lamentably, the continued lack of implementing regulations demonstrates that no progress has been made in this regard despite the establishment of DHS more than a decade ago.

While Immigration Judges repeatedly have protested the lengthy delay (eighteen years) in enacting regulations to enforce the contempt power, the regulations remain stalled, as the DOJ continues to view Immigration Judges and DHS prosecutors as equivalent, i.e., attorneys whose client is the U.S. government. Because of this inaction, the Immigration Judges lack a vital tool to do their jobs. Federal and state court judges are not so constrained. NAIJ is unaware of any administrative law judges who have contempt power, but such authority is not as necessary in their setting since the government is rarely represented by an attorney in most other tribunals. This fact exemplifies how the classification of Immigration Judges as both attorneys and judges has contributed to dysfunction in an already overburdened system.

Post-Removal Bars to Immigration Judge Authority

Among the most difficult cases encountered by Immigration Judges are post-deportation matters. These involve exceptionally complex statutory and regulatory interpretations, and various types of discretion. Here is a scenario that exemplifies the complexities with which Immigration Judges must grapple.

> Respondent Y became a lawful permanent resident at age two years when he immigrated with his entire nuclear family. At age 19, while attending a fraternity party at the university where he was a freshman, he was arrested for possession with intent to sell marijuana. Afraid that his parents would find out and that he would miss his final exams, he pled no contest to the charges, thinking this is a good deal because his harried public defender told him the judge would "withhold adjudication" and he would be sentenced to time served and immediately released.
>
> On the day of his release from state custody, Y was picked up by Immigration and Customs Enforcement officials. He was told he would

be subject to mandatory detention and removal as an aggravated felon. Overwhelmed by the jail experience and embarrassed for having jeopardized his chance to be the first college graduate in his family, he told Immigration Judge X that he wanted to be deported to Mexico immediately. He was ordered removed and put on the bus to Mexico that afternoon.

Months later, when Y's predicament is discovered by his family, they retain an attorney who relies on the U.S. Supreme Court case of *Padilla v. Kentucky* to file a motion to vacate the conviction. The motion is granted and the charges are dropped. Y's attorney immediately files a motion to reopen the removal proceedings in Immigration Court before Judge X.

Should Judge X grant such a motion? What process should be followed? Can Judge X order DHS to return Y to the United States to appear again in Immigration Court?

The effects of deportation on possible subsequent claims of right to reenter the United States is itself deserving of in-depth analysis. In fact, it is the subject of entire books. For our purposes, however, it will be explained only briefly in this chapter. Nonetheless, it is an important topic to consider as it provides an excellent example of the relative lack of authority and power of Immigration Judges versus that of government prosecutors as compared to how that balance is struck by other courts.

The congressional trend in immigration law over the past few decades has been to deformalize deportation proceedings and to move increasingly toward more administrative, fast-track models. Such mechanisms as administrative removal, expedited removal, and reinstatement of prior deportation orders take thousands of cases out of the Immigration Courts entirely. Some argue that such expeditiousness comes at an unacceptably high cost. At least one study of the expedited removal process found serious flaws with the implementation of the idea of streamlining cases out of the hands of Immigration Judges. That report found that asylum seekers in expedited removal proceedings were at risk of being returned to countries where they may face persecution. Some asylum seekers who succeeded in obtaining referrals to Immigration Court were plagued by problems created by unreliable documents generated in the expedited removal process.

Such problems—and many other difficulties in the immigration adjudication system—have led to a rise in post-deportation claims for relief for a wide variety of reasons. For example, some allege evidentiary error (e.g., incorrect criminal records, incorrect assessment of immigration status). Others base their claims on judicial holdings that the government's theory of prosecution in a class of cases was incorrect, such as the long-standing debate over whether drunk driving could be considered a "crime of violence."

For many years, however, such claims were completely barred in Immigration Courts. A regulatory rule known as the "departure bar" has long provided a definitive ending point for possible review of deportation or removal orders. Dating its reasoning back to a 1952 regulation, the BIA consistently has held that "reopening is unavailable to any alien who departs the United States after having been ordered removed." While at first blush this may seem like a sensible and straightforward bright line for jurisdiction, changes in the statute wrought by the Illegal Immigration Reform and Immigrant Responsibility Act (IIRIRA) have led to successful legal challenges of this regulation and the Board's interpretation in many circuit courts.

Before 1996, motions to reopen removal proceedings, which were based on regulations, were generally disfavored for the same reasons that a petition for rehearing or motion for new trial is disfavored. Motions to reopen were especially disfavored in immigration proceedings, "where, as a general matter, every delay was to the advantage of the deportable alien who wishes merely to remain in the United States." The motion to reopen was statutorily codified for the first time in 1996, with certain evidentiary requirements. Such motions are circumscribed by strict statutory numerical and time limits. However, the old 1952 departure bar rule was *not* part of the new statute. The Attorney General nevertheless determined that the bar survived, and reissued it in regulatory form. Because Immigration Judges are part of the Department of Justice they were bound to apply this interpretation, whether they agreed it was legally correct or not.

For a variety of reasons, the circuit courts have now split on the issue of post-departure jurisdiction, leaving crucial rights hanging in the balance. There is an understandable need for finality in the removal process. However, consider the fact that the statute, which had previously provided automatic stays during the appeal process, has now been repealed. Thus, after an Immigration Judge issues an order of removal and the Board of Immigration Appeals affirms the order (if the respondent has sought such administrative review), the noncitizen will in all likelihood now be physically removed. Some challenges to deportation in the courts may proceed from abroad as "direct" appeals. But motions to reopen based on later-discovered factual errors or changes to the law have been barred once removal takes place. Thus, a potentially meritorious challenge to deportation can be forestalled by the actions of one party, i.e., the government's execution of a removal order.

Further complicating the analysis in these cases, the split structure of authority for these motions has led some circuit courts to differentiate between "statutory" motions and those potentially authorized by regulation. Nowhere is this more stark than in the regulation that allows Immigration Judges to grant motions to reopen or reconsider on their own, i.e., *sua sponte*, and not based on a motion from either party (8 C.F.R. §1003.23(b)(1)). Although authorized by regulation, this remedy places Immigration Judges in an extremely challenging position, particularly since the extent of their authority has not been clearly defined.

It is not uncommon for motions to reopen to implicate weighty due process concerns. For example, cases present issues of "equitable tolling" due to allegedly ineffective assistance of counsel when respondents were not properly advised of available relief or when their lawyer's alleged negligence has caused applications to go unfiled. In other cases, changes in accepted interpretations of the governing law can mean that a respondent is removed only to discover later that he or she was not removable had the law been properly understood. For example, *Vartelas v. Holder* (2012) held that IIRIRA's changes to the INA's treatment of returning lawful permanent residents did not apply retroactively to people who were convicted prior to IIRIRA's effective date. Strict time limitations on such motions can limit the ability of a respondent to obtain review of a previously denied application for relief, notwithstanding significant changes in personal circumstances, such as the vacature of his or her criminal conviction or an illness threatening the health or life of someone in respondent's immediate family. Simply put, neither the law nor the lives it affects are static, and it is not uncommon for circumstances to arise that cry out for a second look by the decision-maker. Who better than the Immigration Judge to be in a position to review such circumstances and issue a decision based on all the facts?

Cases such as these thus present thorny issues deserving of solutions which can more effectively be crafted by a decision-maker acting with traditional judicial tools rather than a government attorney with limited authority or a deportation officer with no legal background. For now, more issues exist than solutions in this evolving legal context. With scarce resources creating lengthy dockets at the Board of Immigration Appeals and circuit courts, how should changes in personal circumstances, such as marriage or illness or changes in country conditions, be properly addressed to assure that fairness is achieved? Although equitable tolling to address time bar issues has been widely accepted in our legal system, should it apply to the numerical limitation on motions (allowing only one motion) now imposed by statute?

These cases also implicate enormous practical complications. What tools does an Immigration Judge have to compel the government to return a respondent to the United States after a conviction has been vacated? This issue has received considerable scrutiny in light of an ongoing controversy regarding exactly what steps the government is willing to undertake in these situations. Indeed, there has been some controversy about the government's representations about its ability to locate and return deported noncitizens. For example, following the Supreme Court decision in *Nken v. Holder* (2009), District Court Judge Jed Rakoff found that materials obtained under the Freedom of Information Act showed that the government had provided the Supreme Court a "distorted or inaccurate factual representation" on this issue.

These are but a handful of examples of the difficult issues Immigration Judges routinely confront that directly implicate the dimensions of their proper authority and the tools at their disposal—including discretion—necessary to assure that the impact of their decision provides respondents with the fundamental fairness that the Constitution guarantees them. We posit that whatever procedural or substantive parameters are applied, the integrity of these decisions will be greatly enhanced by having them made by a judge rather than a government attorney.

How Can Congressional Action Address These Problems?

Comprehensive immigration reform is all the talk these days. No one can predict what shape or form comprehensive immigration reform will take, or even if any immigration reform measure will become law. As of this writing, the Senate has passed an immigration reform package which in part attempts to address crushing caseloads of the court by providing more judges and law clerks. While the provision of resources to the Immigration Courts is a laudable first step, the Immigration Courts need both adequate resources and iron-clad independence to function fairly and efficiently.

History has shown that incremental modifications to the Immigration Courts have not resolved the pernicious problems created by placement of the Court within a law enforcement structure. There has been a gradual shift toward a structure that has increasingly insulated the Court from encroachments on decisional independence and political manipulation. Over the past 60 years, the Immigration Courts have evolved from a system internal to, and at the mercy of, the prosecutors of the INS, to the status of a sibling component of the primary immigration law enforcement agency to a component of an executive branch agency whose primary mission is law enforcement, ostensibly removed from direct immigration law prosecutions (American Bar Association 2010, ES-9; U.S. Department of Justice 2014; Rawitz 1988:453–459). However, these gradual steps have proven inadequate to safeguard true independence and quality decision-making. Indeed, illegal, politicized hiring of Immigration Judges occurred subsequent to the last major step to reform the Immigration Courts in 2002.

The idea of an independent agency or Article I Court has been seriously considered for more than 25 years. Many have concluded that the creation of an Article I Immigration Court, or the establishment of an Immigration Court in an independent agency outside the Department of Justice, is needed. After years of thorough study, the bipartisan Select Commission came to this conclusion in 1981. The same conclusion was reached recently by the comprehensive study commissioned by the American Bar Association and the Chicago Appleseed Fund for Justice. The National Association of Women Judges (NAWJ) has endorsed the concept as well. The American Immigration Lawyers Association also reportedly backs the creation of an independent court. Most recently, the Federal Bar Association has endorsed the creation of an Article I Immigration Court and has taken steps to lobby for its creation.

Comprehensive immigration reform presents the ideal opportunity for reforming the Court. In our experience, immigration reform that creates new applications for relief or paths to citizenship usually results in a short-term decrease in cases pending at the Immigration Court while these applications are being processed but a subsequent spike in cases when unsuccessful applicants return to the court system. This brief calm before the storm is the perfect time to restructure the court without unduly burdening those appearing before it, also providing the optimal opportunity for the court to respond in real time to any changing needs which unexpectedly may result as reform is implemented.[8]

Senate Bill 744 would create at least one new discretionary application for relief. For decades Immigration Judges had the authority to grant discretionary relief from deportation to immigrants with lawful status in the United States (e.g., people with "green cards") who had committed crimes making them deportable, based on a consideration of countervailing positive factors such as U.S. military service, family ties, medical issues, and rehabilitation. In the 1990s, Congress severely curtailed this discretion. Senate Bill 744 would restore some of this discretion, and many are saying that even more discretion should be returned to Immigration Judges. Restoring discretion to Immigration Judges would result in an improved system with more efficient checks and balances.

Conclusion

This chapter has explored some of the real and potential conflicts created for Immigration Judges, in their dual roles as U.S. government "attorneys" and as "judges." Immigration Judges face several pressures due to the unusual placement of the Immigration Court within a federal law enforcement agency: (1) case completion "goals" that are perceived to be mandatory deadlines and frequently are perceived to be in conflict with adjudicating cases fairly; (2) the pressures of exposure to personal discipline for good faith legal decisions; (3) the public perception of a "government bias" of the Immigration Court and the effect that this perception has on the Immigration Judges; and (4) the lack of even-handed tools to deal with misconduct by government attorneys appearing before them.

We believe that the best solution to these and other problems caused by this structural flaw would be the creation of an Article I Immigration Court, or, as an alternative, the establishment of an Immigration Court in an independent agency outside the Department of Justice. We applaud many of the efforts that the Department of Justice has made and continues to make over the years to provide for fair and full adjudications in the Immigration Court system. Nevertheless, it is only through an Article I court or separate agency that complete independence and impartiality can be achieved, both in reality and in public perception.

NOTES

Earlier versions of portions of this chapter were previously published as Conflicting Roles of Immigration Judges: Do You Want Your Case Heard By a "Government Attorney" or By a "Judge"? in 16 *Bender's Immigration Bulletin* 1785 (November 15, 2011). Reprinted with permission. Copyright 2011 Matthew Bender & Company, Inc., a LexisNexis Company. All rights reserved.

1 The views expressed here are those of the authors in their individual personal capacities and as executive vice president and president of the National Association of Immigration Judges (NAIJ), not as official spokespersons for the U.S. Department of Justice (DOJ). The NAIJ is a professional association of Immigration Judges, and also the certified representative and recognized collective bargaining unit that represents the Immigration Judges of the United States. The views expressed herein do not purport to represent the views of the U.S. DOJ, the Executive Office for Immigration Review, or the Office of the Chief Immigration Judge. Rather, they represent the personal opinions of the authors, which were formed after extensive consultation with the membership of the NAIJ.

2 Before April 1, 1997, proceedings before the Immigration Court were either "deportation" or "exclusion" proceedings, depending on the manner in which an individual had come to the United States. The Illegal Immigration Reform and Immigrant Responsibility Act of 1996 (IIRIRA), Pub. L. No. 104-208, 110 Stat. 3009, changed the terminology from "deportation" and "exclusion" proceedings to "removal" proceedings, but for purposes of clarity since the general public is more familiar with the term of "deportation," this term will be used throughout.

3 For an inside perspective from an Immigration Judge on the topic of attorney representation, including the laudable efforts by New York *pro bono* programs, see Brennan (2009), U.S. Department of Justice (2012).

4 The Administrative Procedure Act, 5 U.S.C. Section 553(a)(1), requires that administrative policies affecting individual rights and obligations be promulgated pursuant to certain stated procedures so as to avoid the inherently arbitrary nature of unpublished *ad hoc* determinations (*Morton v. Ruiz* 1974).

5 The mission statement of the Department of Justice is "to enforce the law and defend the interests of the United States according to the law; to ensure public safety against threats foreign and domestic; to provide federal leadership in preventing and controlling crime; to seek just punishment for those guilty of unlawful behavior; and to ensure fair and impartial administration of justice for all Americans" (U.S. Department of Justice 2014).

6 This was based on a 2008 report by the DOJ Inspector General and the Office of Professional Responsibility that found a systematic campaign by members of the previous administration to pack the court with "good Republicans" who were "on the team."
7 Letter of May 26, 2010 to the Honorable Eric Holder, Attorney General from Lamar Smith, Ranking Member, House of Representatives, on file with the authors.
8 The rise of prosecutorial discretion initiatives in recent years could in fact be a reaction to the stripping of discretionary authority from the Immigration Courts, which has left us with a system where, ironically, the prosecutors have more discretion than the judges.

REFERENCES

American Bar Association. 2010. *Reforming the Immigration System: Proposals to Promote Independence, Fairness, Efficiency and Professionalism in the Adjudication of Removal Cases.* Executive Summary. Washington, DC: ABA, Commission on Immigration.

Appleseed and Chicago Appleseed for Justice. 2009. *Assembly Line Injustice: Blueprint to Reform America's Immigration Courts.* Report. Accessed November 5, 2014. http://appleseednetwork.org/wp-content/uploads/2012/05/Assembly-Line-Injustice-Blueprint-to-Reform-Americas-Immigration-Courts1.pdf.

Brennan, Noel. 2009. "A View from the Immigration Bench." *Fordham Law Review* 78:623.

Creppy, Michael J. et al. 1999. "Court Executive Dev. Project, Inst. for Court Mgmt." In *The United States Immigration Court in the 21st Century*, 109 n. 313. Copy on file with the authors.

Lustig, Stuart L., Karnik Niranjan, Kevin Dellucchi, Lakshika Tennakoon, Brent Kaul, Dana Leigh Marks, Denise Slavin. 2008. "Inside the Judges' Chambers: Narrative Responses from the National Association of Immigration Judges Stress and Burn-out Survey." *Georgetown Immigration Law Journal* 23:57.

Rawitz, Sidney B. 1988. "From Wong Yang Sung to Black Robes." *Interpreter Releases* 65:453.

Slavin, Denise N. and Dana L. Marks. 2011. Conflicting Roles of Immigration Judges: Do You Want Your Case Heard By a "Government Attorney" Or By a "Judge"? *Bender's Immigration Bulletin* 16:1785 (November 15).

TRAC Immigration. 2014. *Immigration Court Backlog Tool.* Accessed November 4, 2014. TRAC Reports. http://trac.syr.edu/phptools/immigration/court_backlog/.

U.S. Department of Justice. 2014. *United States Department of Justice.* Accessed November 5, 2014. http://www.justice.gov/about/about-doj.

U.S. Department of Justice. 2012. *FY 2012 Statistical Yearbook.* Accessed November 5, 2014. http://www.justice.gov/eoir/statspub/fy12syb.pdf.

U.S. Department of Justice. 2010. "The Executive Office for Immigration Review Announces New Process for Filing Immigration Judge Complaints." Press release. Accessed November 5, 2014. http://www.justice.gov/eoir/press/2010/IJConduct-ProfComplaints05192010.pdf.

U.S. Department of Justice. 2006. "Attorney General Alberto R. Gonzales Outlines Reforms for Immigration Courts and Board of Immigration Appeals." Press release. Accessed November 5, 2014. http://www.justice.gov/archive/opa/pr/2006/August/06_ag_520.html.

U. S. Government Accountability Office (GAO). 2006. *Executive Office for Immigration Review Caseload Performance Reporting Needs Improvement.* Report. Accessed November 5, 2014. http://www.gao.gov/assets/260/251155.pdf.

CASE CITATIONS

Fong Haw Tan v. Phelan, 333 U.S. 6 (1948).
Hashmi v. Attorney General of the United States, 53 F. 3d 256 (3rd Cir. 2008).
Jordan v. DeGeorge, 341 U.S. 223 (1951).
Judulang v. Holder, 132 S. Ct. 746 (2011).
Lehman v. United States, 353 U.S. 685, 691 (1957).
Matter of Hashmi, 24 I&N Dec. 785, 787 (BIA 2009).
Morton v. Ruiz, 415 U.S. 199 (1974).
Ng Fung Ho v. White, 259 U.S. 276 (1922).
Nken v. Holder, 556 U.S. 418 (2009).
Padilla v. Kentucky, 130 S.Ct. 1473 (2010).
Vartelas v. Holder, 132 S. Ct. 1479 (2012).

4

Immigration Reform

Will New Political Calculations and New Actors Overcome Enforcement Inertia?

ALI NOORANI, BRITTNEY NYSTROM, AND MAURICE BELANGER

In the wake of the 2012 presidential election, the press focused on the fact that Latinos (and, to an even greater extent, Asians) voted overwhelmingly for Democrats, and the problem for Republicans was their opposition to immigration reform and their harsh tone on the immigration issue. According to the narrative, if Republicans don't broaden their base by attracting Latinos—a fast-growing segment of the voting population—they will face increasing difficulties in winning any future national election. Thus was born an opening for another congressional attempt to tackle the immigration issue. Early in the 113th Congress, a comprehensive immigration reform bill was introduced by Democratic and Republican authors in the Senate. With broad bipartisan support, the bill passed the Senate.

In the years since the last time Congress tried and failed to reform our immigration laws, the immigration system has remained broken, and our nation continues to suffer. Families are devastated when siblings, spouses, parents, and children are caught in endless lines waiting for a visa, or are forced apart by a record-breaking number of annual detentions and deportations. The economy stagnates as the lack of employment visas causes instability or gaps in the workforce. And communities are harmed when the police lose the trust of immigrants who fear their local law enforcement officers are collaborating with federal immigration agents.

While major immigration enforcement legislation was passed in 1996, making even legal immigrants vulnerable to deportation after

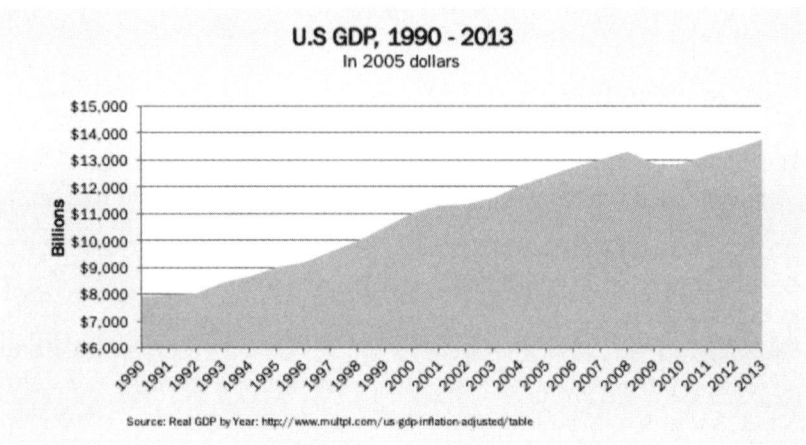

Figure 4.1 Our Broken Immigration System. Source: U.S. GDP, 1990–2013.

committing minor crimes, the last time our *legal* immigration system was adjusted was more than two decades ago, with the 1990 Immigration Act (Leiden and Neal 1990). In that time, our economy nearly doubled, from $7.9 trillion in 1990, to $13.7 trillion at the beginning of 2013 (in 2005 dollars) (U.S. Real GDP n.d.). The need for workers in this larger economy has increased while, at the same time, the native-born workforce has become more educated. It also has been steadily moving toward retirement—between now and the end of the year 2030, an average of 10,000 Americans in the "baby boom" cohort will reach age 65 *each day* (Pew Research Center 2010). An immigration system stuck in the early 1990s cannot match the needs of an economy in the second decade of the twenty-first century.

At the high end of the employment spectrum, foreign professionals, and the U.S. companies looking to hire them, may have to wait several years to obtain a visa. As of September 2014, the second "employment preference" category—for "members of the professions holding advanced degrees or persons of exceptional ability"—is backlogged for immigrants from India and China. Professionals from those countries currently can expect to wait approximately five years for a permanent visa (U.S. Department of State 2014). For the "skilled workers and professionals" in the third employment preference category, the wait for a visa is now a minimum of three and a half years, and for workers from India and China, the wait is longer. For professionals, there are temporary visas available, including the "H-1B" visa for specialty occupations and the "L-1" visa for intracompany transferees. In theory, these are for immigrants who are brought to the United States by an employer on a temporary basis. In practice, given the backlogs in the permanent employment categories, these temporary worker programs for skilled workers have become an avenue for companies to work around the broken permanent immigration system (Batalova 2006).

While worldwide competition for skilled professionals is often the focus of media stories, the American workforce must include a mix of high-skilled individuals and those who can fill jobs that don't require years of schooling or training. According to the U.S. Department of Labor, of the top 20 occupations with the greatest number of new jobs projected between 2012 and 2022, five require nothing more than short-term on-the-job training. These are jobs such as home health aides, construction laborers, and personal care aides (U.S. Department of Labor).

A subcategory of the third employment preference—called "other workers"—allots visas to immigrants coming to fill these jobs. Since 2002, however, only 5,000 visas per year have been available for these immigrants (U.S. Department of State 2014). Meanwhile, in the late 1990s and the early parts of the 2000s, approximately 300,000 to 700,000 immigrants came to the United States without authorization—many to work in jobs that might have made them eligible for a visa in the "other workers" category (Passel and Suro 2005). For example, many jobs in agriculture, where the percentage of workers who are undocumented is estimated to be 25 percent or more, are not seasonal; visas for temporary seasonal workers are not a good match for jobs such as dairy farming. A high percentage of the workforce in construction, building and grounds maintenance, and food preparation and serving is also undocumented (Passel and Cohn 2009). Doing the math, if just 300,000 of those undocumented immigrants came with the intention of working, and they all applied for an "other worker" visa, the backlog that would develop after the first year would be approximately one human lifespan. The disparity between our economy's need for this type of immigrant labor and the number of visas available per year is a major driver of illegal immigration.

Like the employment visa system, the family-based immigration system is also broken. The legal immigration system is weighted toward immigrants coming here with close family connections—spouses and young children of U.S. citizens and permanent residents; parents and brothers and sisters of U.S. citizens. Spouses, minor children, and parents of U.S. citizens are not subject to numerical limitation. However, for most other categories of family immigration, long backlogs are currently the norm. Married sons and daughters of U.S. citizens must wait a minimum of nearly 11 years for a visa to reunite with their family in the United States (more than 20 years for Filipinos and Mexicans). U.S. citizens who are trying to bring in their brothers and sisters from the Philippines must wait more than 23 years for visas to become available (U.S. Department of State 2014). In total, according to the State Department, there are 4.3 million persons waiting for visas to reunite with family members in the United States (U.S. Department of State n.d.). Using the current quota, and assuming there were *no* more applications for family preference immigrants, it will take *19 years* to clear the current backlog in the family preference categories (Bergeron 2013). In sum, the 1990 admission levels that are current law do not nearly accommodate the demand for visas in 2013 and lead to lengthy separation of families.

As the barriers to *legal* immigration have increased, millions of people coming to the United States for employment or to rejoin family members have gone around the legal system by migrating without authorization. The latest official estimate of the undocumented population in the United States is approximately 11.4 million (Baker and Rytina 2013). Undocumented immigrants make up approximately 5.2 percent of the U.S. workforce (Passel and Cohn 2011). For undocumented immigrants living and working here, opportunities to obtain legal status are extremely limited. Even if the immigrant might be eligible to obtain an immigrant visa through family or employer sponsorship, for most immigrants that visa must be picked up abroad, and if the person had been out of status for a year or more, the act of leaving the United States triggers a ten-year bar to reentry. The mandatory bar applies regardless of whether the immigrant has led a productive life and has stayed on the right side of the law.

Why It's Still Broken: An Exclusive Focus on Enforcement

The preceding paragraphs attempt to describe what we mean when we say the current immigration system is broken. Despite the widely acknowledged dysfunction, Congress's approach to the problem until recently has been one-dimensional—more enforcement of laws now on the books.

For proponents of enforcement, the U.S.-Mexican border has been a major focus of get-tough policies. Politicians ceaselessly clamor for more border enforcement along the southern border despite already massive infusions of resources and statistics that show crime in the region is at historic lows, as are the numbers of persons attempting to cross the border illegally.

Even before the "war on terror," sparked by the events of September 11, 2001, border enforcement had been on the rise. In 1996, the budget for Border Patrol was $568 million. By 2003, the year in which border security was transferred from the Immigration and Naturalization Service to the Department of Homeland Security, the budget for the Border Patrol rose 267 percent, from $568 million to $1.5 billion, and between 2003 and 2012, the budget more than doubled again, from $1.5 billion to $3.5 billion (U.S. Border Patrol n.d.(a)). Despite the steady rise in the cost of border enforcement, politicians always seem ready to spend more.

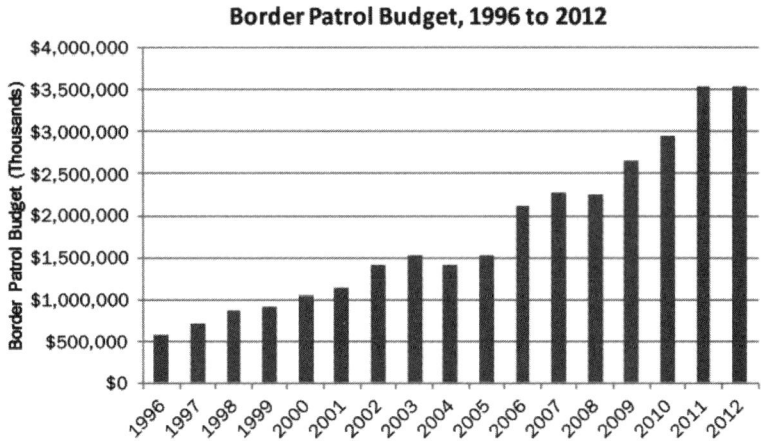

Figure 4.2 Border Patrol Budget, 1996–2012.

For example, in the summer of 2010, Congress passed an *emergency* supplemental appropriations bill for border security. Among other things, this bill provided $179.5 million in additional funding to hire 1,000 additional border patrol agents. $14 million was added to the amount already budgeted for border security fencing, infrastructure, and technology (for "tactical communications"). $32 million was allocated for acquisition and deployment of unmanned aerial vehicles (National Immigration Forum 2010). The bill passed in a special session of Congress during its August recess (Preston 2010). (It is extremely rare that Congress breaks its summer recess to return to Washington to work on legislation.) That "emergency" funding had been requested by the Obama administration, which had earlier announced that it would deploy 1,200 National Guard troops to the U.S.-Mexico border (U.S. Department of Homeland Security 2010).

What was the emergency that Congress and the administration were responding to? At the time the bill passed, there were 21,000 Border Patrol agents (National Immigration Forum 2010). Was there a surge in illegal border crossings? Statistics compiled by the Border Patrol show that, in fiscal year 2010, the number of apprehensions at the border—a proxy for the number of persons attempting to cross illegally—was continuing to decline from a peak in the year 2000. Every Border Patrol sector along the Southwest border showed a decline in apprehensions in 2010 from the year before. The number of apprehensions in 2010— under 447,000—was the lowest since 1973 (U.S. Border Patrol n.d.(b)).

During this time period, there was an escalation of violence on the *Mexican* side of the border, and an *assumption* that there was or would be "spillover" violence on the U.S. side of the border. Speaking of the appropriations bill on the floor of the House, the chairman of the Appropriations Subcommittee on Homeland Security, Rep. David Price of North Carolina (D), said the bill was needed to "address the urgent need for enhanced security on our Southwest border."

> Violence on the Mexican side of the border has intensified because of turf battles among murderous transnational criminal organizations. . . . The bill would . . . enable the Department of Homeland Security, the Department of Justice, and the Judiciary, in cooperation with the National Guard, to counter this threat, building on the current border enforcement

surge. This funding is urgently needed to counter the pressures our law enforcement agencies and our border communities currently face. (Representative Price N.C. 2010)

The spillover violence, however, was more theoretical than real. One law enforcement official in Pima County, Arizona, which borders Mexico, said the talk of border violence was "a media-created event." "I hear politicians on TV saying the border has gotten worse. Well, the fact of the matter is that the border has never been more secure" (Wagner 2010).

A more recent look at the spillover violence phenomenon by the Government Accountability Office concluded that, in general, law enforcement agencies do not separately track spillover violence, but the GAO report noted that, with some exceptions, the violent crime rate and the property crime rate in border counties was lower than in non-border counties, and that in both border and non-border counties, violent crime rates and property crime rates declined between 2004 and 2011 (U.S. Government Accountability Office 2013).

Also at that time, Arizona had recently enacted its controversial immigration enforcement legislation, SB 1070, and Arizona politicians were complaining that the federal government was not doing enough to seal the border. The Obama administration was under pressure to do

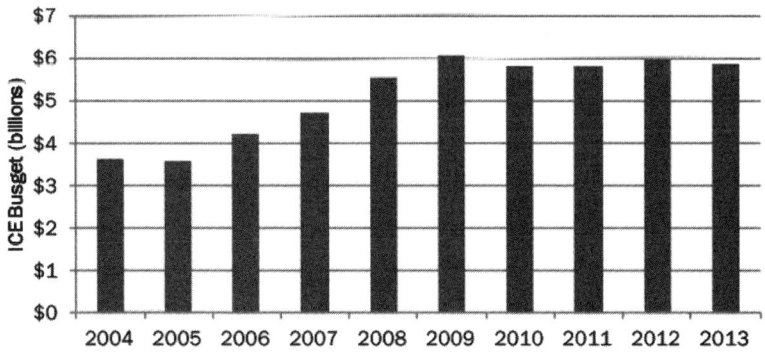

Figure 4.3 Immigration and Customs Enforcement Budget FY 2004–2013. Source: Department of Homeland Security, "Budget in Brief," various years. Numbers are from several fiscal year budget documents.

more, leading to its request to Congress for more border enforcement resources and the deployment of National Guard troops (Preston 2010). The above is an example, and there are others, in which a demand for increased border enforcement is more a reaction to political circumstances than to law enforcement need.

While border enforcement has grabbed the most attention, it is by no means the only aspect of our immigration enforcement apparatus that has received unprecedented levels of resources. From 2004 to 2013, the budget for Immigration and Customs Enforcement (ICE), the component of the Department of Homeland Security charged with enforcing immigration laws in the interior of the country, increased by 62 percent, from $3.6 billion to $5.9 billion (Department of Homeland Security "Budget in Brief," various years). Congress has consistently provided funding over the past several years to increase the number of individuals who are to be detained on a daily basis for immigration purposes. Between 2001 and 2012, the number of funded bed spaces for immigrant detainees rose 73 percent, from 19,700 to 34,000, and by 2012 the government was spending more than $2 billion a year to detain immigrants (Siskin 2012). Today, the U.S. government allocates more for immigration law enforcement agencies than it does for all the other principal criminal law enforcement agencies *combined*. (Those law enforcement agencies include the FBI, Drug Enforcement Agency, Secret Service, ATF, and U.S. Marshal Service.) Our criminal justice resources have also been increasingly diverted to immigration enforcement. Immigration offenders now comprise more than 30 percent of all persons entering the federal prison system, and prosecutions for illegal entry or illegal reentry into the United States now outnumber prosecutions for *all other* federal crimes (Human Rights Watch 2013).

The noise created by immigration restrictionists demanding ever-greater enforcement is magnified in the press, giving the false impression that, as critics of the administration's immigration policies say, the Obama administration is not interested in enforcing the law (Fox News 2012). However, one must consider the context in which these charges are made: On the Southwest border, while there was a slight uptick in fiscal year 2012, the number of apprehensions—a number that is often used as a proxy for the number of people attempting to cross

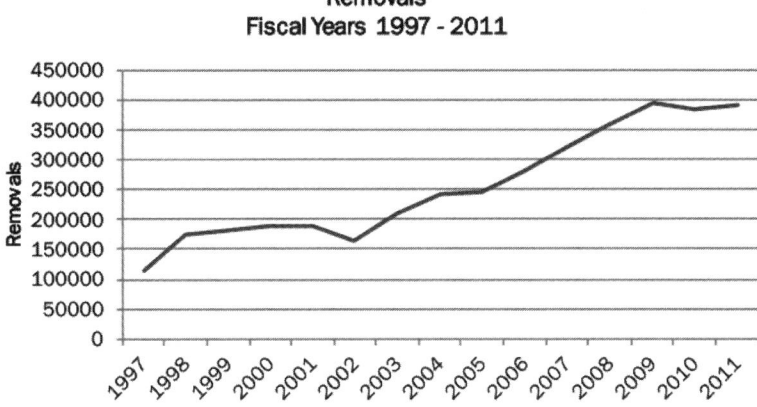

Figure 4.4 Removals, Fiscal Years 1997–2011. Source: 2011 Yearbook of Immigration Statistics.

the border illegally—is now lower than it has been since the 1970s (U.S. Border Patrol n.d.(b)). You have to go back to the Nixon administration (when the populations of the United States and Mexico were much smaller) to find fewer apprehensions. Under the Obama administration, immigrant detention and deportations have been at an all-time high, with almost 441,000 being detained in fiscal year 2013 and more than 438,000 being deported in fiscal year 2013 (Simanski 2014). In fact, President Obama deported more than 1.5 million individuals in his first term (Dade 2012).

Intelligence Sharing Greatly Expanded

There is another aspect of enforcement that is not the focus of much attention, but it is perhaps far more important to national security. Since the terrorist attacks of 2001, there has been an explosion of information collection and sharing among government agencies responsible for screening foreigners entering the United States. A fair accounting of the screening foreigners go through, and of the databases that are now available to a range of law enforcement agencies, is not possible in this space. But a brief summary of the screening process follows, along with a list of major databases now being used by the Department of Homeland Security and Department of State.

With few exceptions, a U.S. consular officer must interview all applicants for immigrant or non-immigrant visas. Information about the individual is checked against immigration, criminal, and terrorist databases containing millions of records. The individual is again screened when he or she arrives at a U.S. port of entry. Homeland Security and State Department officials now have the following databases at their disposal to determine whether an individual is eligible to be admitted to the United States (Meissner et al. 2013).

- *IDENT*, which contains more than 148 million individual fingerprint records from *US-VISIT*, which collects that information when visitors to the United States are inspected at ports of entry.
- *Integrated Automated Fingerprint Identification System*, the FBI's fingerprint screening system, which has access to the FBI's database (National Crime Information Center) containing the fingerprints and criminal histories of 70 million persons.
- *Arrival and Departure Information System*, containing biographic and travel information consolidated from other databases run by Customs and Border Protection, Immigration and Customs Enforcement, U.S. Citizenship and Immigration Services, the Department of State, and cooperating foreign governments.
- The *Terrorist Screening Database*, maintained by the FBI, containing information on hundreds of thousands of individuals believed to be connected to terrorism in some way.
- The State Department's *Consular Consolidated Database*, containing information collected from more than 130 million individuals who have applied for visas or passports at U.S. consular offices.
- The *Consular Lookout and Support System*, another State Department database with more than 25 million records of persons who may be ineligible for admission to the United States.
- The *Student and Exchange Visitor Information System*, a database set up to track foreign students in the United States.
- *TECS*, which contains biographic information on persons entering the United States through a port of entry.
- The *Enforcement Integrated Database*, which contains information about

noncitizens who have been arrested, detained, and removed.
- The *Central Index System*, maintained by U.S. Citizenship and Immigration Services, contains biographic information on individuals who have applied for an immigration benefit.

These and other databases, which are continually expanding with updated information, can be queried by immigration and other law enforcement agencies. Information is now being shared among several government agencies—a departure from pre–9/11 days when agencies would not share information in their databases with personnel outside of their agency and databases could not communicate with each other. The ability to share information among agencies responsible for admitting foreigners has made it much more likely that an individual who should not be admitted to the United States will not be.

Enforcement's Unintended Consequences and Collateral Damage

Despite all of the additional resources devoted to immigration and border enforcement, some in Congress continue to insist that not enough has been done. DHS Secretary Janet Napolitano noted this in her testimony before the Senate Judiciary Committee on the subject of immigration reform in February 2013.

> A constant refrain I have heard as Secretary is that before immigration reform can move forward, border security must come first. Too often, the "border security first" refrain has served as an excuse for failing to address overall immigration reform. The insistence that an overhaul of our immigration laws must wait until the border is secure fails to recognize that immigration reform promotes border security. Moreover, the argument ignores the unprecedented progress we have made. (Napolitano 2013)

As the executive in charge of Homeland Security, then Secretary Napolitano repeatedly said that for enforcement to be more effective, the immigration system had to be fixed. In her State of Homeland Security Address in February 2013, Secretary Napolitano noted, "Our immigration system has been broken for too long, and the time to fix it is now."

> Our communities, workers, and employers are all frustrated by a system that treats a drug smuggler the same as a high-achieving student, undercuts honest employers, and leaves millions in fear of deportation and vulnerable to fraud and other crimes.
>
> This system makes it harder for law enforcement to focus on the greatest threats in their communities, instead spending time and resources on low-priority cases. (Napolitano 2013)

Indeed, in the context of a broken immigration system, immigration enforcement can have harsh and unintended consequences that hurt not just immigrants and their families, but also the communities in which they live.

As part of its border enforcement strategy, the government has been filing criminal charges against individuals apprehended after crossing the border illegally, in a program called "Operation Streamline." The threat of jail time is meant to deter immigrants from crossing illegally (first-time offenders face up to 18 months in prison; the penalty for reentry after removal is much higher). However, as a consequence, there has been a decline in prosecution for more serious crimes. Criminal prosecution for immigration offenses (primarily illegal entry and reentry) make up about half of all federal prosecutions in the nation. The number of criminal immigration cases filed by federal prosecutors in February 2012, for example, was more than the number of filings for all other types of cases combined (National Immigration Forum 2012). In border districts, Assistant U.S. attorneys have less capacity to develop more serious criminal cases due to the number of immigration cases they must handle (Lydgate 2010). As for the deterrent effect, according to a survey conducted of more than 1,100 Mexican deportees during 2010, 2011, and 2012, a large percentage of the deportees considered the United States to be their home or intended to settle permanently in the United States. The majority of those individuals stated their intent to attempt another crossing (Center for Latin American Studies, University of Arizona 2013). So the perspective is not what is usually portrayed. These migrants consider their attempt to cross illegally as an effort to *return home*, rather than to leave their homeland. While strong family ties normally decrease the probability of recidivism in the criminal justice system, for persons who are apprehended while attempting to cross the border illegally, family ties are a *motivator* for recidivism (Human Rights Watch 2013). As long as the immigration system remains broken, their effort to return home will have to be outside of legal channels.

The increase in border enforcement over the past two decades has led to stronger ties to the United States of Mexican migrants who, in the past, arrived in the United States to work and returned to Mexico regularly. Work by Douglas Massey of Princeton University's Mexican Migration Project has shown that, as the United States made it more difficult to cross the border illegally, migrants adjusted to the risk by staying in the United States to avoid risking capture or violence in crossing the border. In 1986, the probability of a Mexican migrant returning home within one year of entering the United States was 60 percent. In 2010, it was 8 percent (Klein 2013). So, migrants who used to alternate between the United States and Mexico have instead made the United States their home.

The children of undocumented immigrants suffer collateral damage from enforcement of our broken immigration laws. In 2011, the Applied Research Center estimated that there were at least 5,100 children in the United States living in foster care because their parents had been detained for immigration purposes or deported—approximately 1.5 percent of the total foster care population (Portillo-Gonzales 2011). There are serious economic consequences when the family's sole breadwinner is deported, including difficulty maintaining housing and food insecurity. Children often develop a range of emotional and behavioral problems when a parent is deported (Chaudry et al. 2010).

Another unintended consequence is the increasing number of migrants who die attempting to cross the U.S.-Mexican border. As tougher border enforcement has been applied in high-traffic areas of the border, migrants utilize increasingly remote and hostile desert terrain to cross into the United States, with often fatal results. In 2012, nearly 500 migrants died attempting to cross the border illegally, according to official statistics (Anderson 2013). With sufficient legal channels to enter the United States, these deaths could be largely avoided.

Setting Priorities in the Absence of Reform

In the first term of the Obama administration, with Congress showing little appetite for fixing the broken immigration system, the administration created a set of policies to strategically deploy enforcement resources. In a memo to "All ICE Employees" dated March 2, 2011, ICE Director John Morton described several categories of immigrants that should be the focus of his agency's enforcement resources. The memo directed ICE agents to focus apprehension, detention, and removal resources on aliens who pose a national security or public safety risk ("Priority 1"); recent illegal entrants ("Priority 2"); and "aliens who are fugitives or otherwise obstruct immigration controls" (Morton 2011a, p. 2). Within the Priority 1 immigrants with criminal convictions, priorities were further divided among those who had committed "aggravated felonies," those who had committed other felonies or three or more misdemeanors; and those who had committed misdemeanors.

Noting that ICE had the resources to remove approximately 4 percent of the undocumented population in a given year, Mr. Morton wrote that "ICE must prioritize the use of its enforcement personnel, detention space, and removal resources to ensure that the removals the agency does conduct promote the agency's highest enforcement priorities, namely national security, public safety, and border security" (Morton 2011a, p. 1).

On June 17, Morton penned another memo to ICE field office directors, special agents, and chief counsel with more instruction on the prioritization of enforcement resources. In this memo, he encourages the use of *prosecutorial discretion* to accomplish the enforcement priorities set out in the March 2011 memo. Morton directs that ICE will not "assert the full scope of the enforcement authority available to the agency" in certain specific cases. The memo contains a list of individual circumstances in which ICE personnel might decide to exercise their prosecutorial discretion. Such circumstances include, among many others, an individual's length of presence in the United States, whether or not the individual was brought to the United States as a child, and whether or not the individual has served in the U.S. military (Morton 2011b).

Another memo, from ICE's Principal Legal Advisor Peter Vincent, issued in November 2011, declared that ICE would review pending and incoming removal cases to see which cases might be administratively closed because they did not fit within the ICE priorities set out in Morton's earlier memos (Vincent 2011). (For individuals offered administrative closure, the immediate threat of deportation would be lifted, but the action does not confer legal status.) The decision to close some cases would, in theory, help reduce the burden on backlogged Immigration Courts.

Despite the promise and excitement of ICE's prosecutorial discretion announcements, by the end of May 2012, ICE had found only 20,648 cases eligible for administrative closure out of more than 288,000 reviewed (Immigration Policy Center 2012). Furthermore, only 55 percent of those deported in fiscal year 2012 were convicted of felonies or misdemeanors (Napolitano 2013).

Meanwhile, the Obama administration was being pressured to provide relief from deportation more broadly, especially for immigrant youth brought to the United States as children by their parents. These "DREAMers" (taking the name from the DREAM Act that had been introduced in several congresses) criticized the Obama administration for deporting more immigrants than any other previous administration. In the spring of 2012, they launched a campaign, "Right to Dream," calling on the administration to grant relief from deportation for all DREAMers (United We Dream 2012). High-profile deportations of young immigrants, and their organizing against the administration, caused a political problem for Obama, who was hoping for a large turnout of Latinos to help his re-election bid (Preston 2012a).

While students were staging sit-ins and hunger strikes at Obama campaign offices across the country, Senator Marco Rubio, a rising star in the Republican Party, seemed on the verge of introducing legislation to give legal status to the DREAMers—legislation the senator had been talking about for months (Preston 2012b). Had he preempted the president and introduced his bill, Senator Rubio would have taken the wind out of the sails of Mr. Obama's efforts to mobilize the Latino vote.

The question remained: Did the administration have the legal authority to grant broad relief? Advocates of relief for the DREAMers were supported by a legal memo signed by dozens of law professors arguing that the administration had the legal authority to grant broad relief from deportation to DREAMers, and laid out several options (Motomura et al. 2012).

In June 2012, Secretary of Homeland Security Janet Napolitano issued a memo directing that immigrants brought to the United States as children who meet certain criteria (specified in the memo and similar to the DREAM Act eligibility criteria) should be considered for an exercise of prosecutorial discretion. The order applied to individuals whether or not they were in removal proceedings. In her memo, she gave U.S. Citizenship and Immigration Services (USCIS) 60 days to develop a "clear and efficient process" for exercising prosecutorial discretion for these individuals, including granting temporary work authorization to those found to be eligible for a grant of discretion (Napolitano 2012). By August 15, USCIS began accepting requests for consideration of deferred action for childhood arrivals in a program known by its acronym, DACA (U.S. Citizenship and Immigration Services 2012). By the program's first anniversary, August 15, 2013, more than 400,000 individuals had their requests for deferred action approved (American Immigration Council 2013).

By the end of his first term, then, even while enforcement was proceeding at record levels, President Obama was grappling with "a system that treats a drug smuggler the same as a high-achieving student" (Napolitano 2013) and had taken some executive actions to make those distinctions without waiting for a resolution from a Congress that had shown no inclination to tackle the problem. In 2014, President Obama once again turned to the promise of executive action to resolve the status of some segments of the immigrant population lacking authorization.

Elections Change the Equation

The presidential election in 2012 changed the immigration debate overnight. Mr. Obama, who promoted immigration reform during his campaign, won 71 percent of the Latino vote and 73 percent of the Asian vote (New York Times 2012). The media wrote extensively of the changing demographics of the country and the problem this posed for a Republican Party that was so dependent on white voters (Shear 2012).

A number of opinion surveys have shown that, for Latino voters, immigration reform is important, and they have been paying close attention to the national debate (Barreto 2013). For Democrats, this demand signaled a political opportunity to press for immigration reform. Republicans, on the other hand, are divided. Leaders in the Republican Party concerned about the long-term viability of the party are very interested in appealing to a broader audience, as the white electorate that has been the party's base is shrinking relative to Latinos, Asians, and African Americans who voted overwhelmingly for Obama. On the other hand, however, the majority of Republicans in the House serve overwhelmingly white districts—nearly half of Republicans in the House represent districts that are more than 80 percent white (Bland 2013). For these Republicans, there is no urgency to appeal to a growing Latino electorate. They can comfortably take a hardline stance against immigration reform without damaging their political career (Ball 2013).

New Voices Speak Out on Immigration Reform

The picture has become more complicated with the addition of new voices in the immigration debate, including some important Republican constituencies. Traditional immigrant rights advocates have been joined by a wide assortment of businesses, labor organizations, law enforcement agencies, religious denominations, high-tech groups, and high-profile pro-reform Republicans.

Among business groups, the U.S. Chamber of Commerce traditionally has been an ally of immigration reformers, and that group continues to support reform (U.S. Chamber of Commerce 2013). In this round of the debate, other groups are devoting significant resources in the push for immigration reform. The Partnership for a New American Economy is a coalition of business leaders and mayors in favor of immigration reform for economic reasons (Partnership for a New American Economy n.d.). In partnership with others, this group organized the "March for Innovation," a "virtual march on Washington" using social media in the spring of 2013 (March for Innovation n.d.). FWD.us is a group of key leaders in the tech community, co-founded by Facebook CEO Mark Zuckerberg, who want Congress to pass immigration reform. This group has paid for cable and broadcast TV ads to support immigration reform (Martinez 2013).

There has traditionally been (and there continues to be) prominent leadership from mainstream faith groups in the immigration reform debate (U.S. Conference of Catholic Bishops n.d.; Lutheran Immigration and Refugee Service n.d.). In the months leading up to the beginning of the 113th Congress, a number of Evangelical Christian denominations came together in a coalition called the Evangelical Immigration Table

(Evangelical Immigration Table, n.d.). This group includes not only groups that minister to Latinos, such as the National Latino Evangelical Coalition, but also groups like the Southern Baptist Convention. Evangelical Christians are an important Republican constituency, and have up to recently tended to view immigration through a rule-of-law lens. But the demographics of the churches are changing, and so are the views of the fellow congregants of the immigrants who are behind the growth in these churches (Preston 2013). These groups are also investing significant resources to press for immigration reform, including purchasing radio ads to persuade Christian audiences to contact Congress about immigration reform (Kelly 2013).

Another set of new voices pressing for immigration reform are the pro-reform Republicans. Not that Republicans have been absent in pro-reform ranks in the past. In the current debate, however, they are devoting more resources to promote reform. One of the most prominent conservative voices in the country, Grover Norquist, has been making appearances around the country, talking to conservatives about why they should support reform (Idaho Statesman 2013). The American Action Network, which promotes itself as a center-right "action tank" and is chaired by former Senator Norm Coleman (R-MN), has been organizing conservatives who support reform and has bought television and digital ads to support reform (American Action Network 2013; Conston 2013). Carlos Gutiérrez, former Secretary of Commerce under President George W. Bush, co-founded the Republican "super-PAC" Republicans for Immigration Reform. The mission of this PAC is to support Republican candidates who support immigration reform (Republicans for Immigration Reform). Americans for a Conservative Direction is another right-of-center organization that is dedicated to immigration reform, and has on its board former Mississippi Governor Haley Barbour, who also is former Chair of the Republican National Committee (Americans for a Conservative Direction). All of these groups help provide political cover for conservative politicians who support reform, and who might otherwise be vulnerable in conservative districts (Peters 2013).

Over the course of 2010 to 2012, key moderate and center-right voices, shepherded by the National Immigration Forum, came together to draft a series of state "compacts" and to meet in a series of regional "immigration summits" in the Mountain West, the Midwest, and the Southeast. These leaders in the faith, business, and law enforcement communities favored an alternative approach to the harsh immigration enforcement laws adopted by states such as Arizona and Alabama.

In the wake of passage of Arizona's SB 1070, leaders in Utah, faced with the prospect of similar legislation being adopted in their state, began to hammer out an immigration statement that would take a more balanced approach, with enforcement balanced by consideration for family unity, the economic importance of immigrants to the state economy, and the humane treatment of immigrants already integrated into communities across the state (Stuart 2010). Thus was born the Utah Compact ("Official text of Utah" 2010). This balanced approach, forged by local leaders, was copied in other states, including Indiana, Texas, Colorado, and Iowa ("A Declaration" n.d.; "Texas Compact" n.d.; "The Colorado Compact" n.d.; Jackson 2011).

Like-minded leaders from the faith, business, and law enforcement communities who worked to forge these state compacts gathered in a series of regional summits beginning in October 2011 ("Forging a New Consensus" n.d.). A Mountain West summit was convened in Salt Lake City, Utah, in October 2011, followed by a Southeast Summit convened in Atlanta, Georgia, in June 2012 and a Midwest Summit in Indianapolis, Indiana, in October 2012 ("Atlanta Gathering" 2012; Hesson 2012; Loftin 2011). These regional summits culminated in a national gathering in which faith, law enforcement, and business leaders urged Congress to pass immigration reform (Wallsten 2012). The constituencies represented at that meeting became what is now Bibles, Badges and Business for Immigration Reform ("Bibles, Badges and Business for Immigration Reform" n.d.). Through events organized throughout the country in the spring and summer of 2013, this network kept the pressure on Congress to pass comprehensive immigration reform, often gaining the ear of Republican members of Congress not ordinarily persuaded by traditional immigrant rights advocates.

Another important centrist network that has become vocal in the immigration debate is the Bipartisan Policy Center, an organization bringing together high-profile former elected and appointed officials, business and labor leaders, and advocates and academics on both sides of the political spectrum. Former Mississippi Governor Haley Barbour, former Housing and Urban Development Secretary Henry Cisneros, former Pennsylvania Governor Edward Rendell, and former Secretary of State Condoleezza Rice lead the Center's Immigration Task Force (Bipartisan Policy Center 2013).

Progressive, or left-of-center voices that traditionally have not engaged with the issue of immigration reform (or indeed might have been suspicious of reform as something to bring cheap labor to business) have also become involved in pressing for broad immigration reform with a path to citizenship. Organizations such as Barack Obama's organizing network, Organizing for Action, have engaged its members (Organizing for Action n.d.). The progressive think tank Center for American Progress publishes research advocating for immigration reform (Center for American Progress n.d.)

The above describes the constellation of constituencies newly engaged in the immigration debate, which have provided an added boost for a push to solve the immigration problem in a way that goes beyond just patching outdated laws with new enforcement. Of course, longtime advocates for immigration reform continue to be very active. Any accounting of the constituencies involved in the immigration reform debate has to include the young undocumented immigrants, brought to the United States as children, known as DREAMers for the legislation that would give them legal status (the DREAM Act). By the hundreds, these courageous young people have stepped into the public eye and demanded that Congress fix the immigration system not only for themselves, but for their families and communities ("United we Dream" n.d.). Despite the support for reform that has blossomed in communities across the country, it has been extremely difficult to break the inertia of congressional inaction.

The Siren Song of Enforcement

Negotiations toward immigration reform in 2013 have revealed that, despite staggering spending on border enforcement and record numbers of apprehensions, detentions, and deportations, members of Congress have been unable to withstand the momentum of a decade spent bolstering immigration enforcement. As the Senate negotiations neared completion on a comprehensive immigration reform bill,

S.744 or the Border Security, Economic Opportunity and Immigration Modernization Act, an extremely expensive amendment to require unprecedented increases in border security was adopted. The amendment was sponsored by Senators Corker (R-TN) and Hoeven (R-ND) and soon became known as the "border surge" amendment. It passed by a vote of 69-29 and was widely speculated to bring along ten to fifteen Republican votes in favor of S.744 (U.S. Senate Roll Call Votes 113th Congress, n.d.). The appeal of the amendment to conservative Republican senators is a political fact. However, the wisdom of the contents of the amendment is far from clear. Senator Corker himself described the amendment as "almost overkill" (Sarlin 2013). As a result of the border surge amendment, the Senate's bill as passed requires an increase of nearly 20,000 Border Patrol agents (nearly doubling the current force), additional surveillance technology, and hundreds more miles of fencing along the U.S.-Mexico border. No corresponding increases in oversight and accountability were included. The amendment would appropriate approximately $40 billion in new security costs along the U.S.-Mexico border (Elmendorf 2013).

The border surge amendment turned traditional political stereotypes upside down. Conservative Republican senators championed an amendment that by all accounts is colossally expensive and results in a significantly larger federal cadre of immigration agents and expands the federal government's ability to conduct surveillance on U.S. territory. The amendment was seemingly fueled by the release of the Congressional Budget Office (CBO) estimate of the overall cost of the bill. Following an announcement from CBO that S.744 would generate $1 trillion in savings, senators immediately approved the costly border surge amendment (Giovagnoli 2013).

For sheriffs in border counties, the prospect of an influx of new agents is being viewed with skepticism. Hudspeth County, Texas, Sheriff Arvin West feels that the 18,500 agents now on the border are already "tripping over themselves." In the view of these sheriffs, what the Border Patrol needs is a new strategy that includes, among other things, more technology, better deployment of existing agents, and beefing up security at ports of entry (Gomez 2013).

Meanwhile, over in the House, one of the harshest pieces of legislation in years focused on expanding interior enforcement of our immigration laws, without addressing the real problems plaguing our immigration system. The Strengthen and Fortify Enforcement Act (SAFE Act), or HR 2278, was introduced by South Carolina Representative Trey Gowdy, Chair of the House Immigration Subcommittee. This bill was considered and passed by the full Judiciary Committee on June 18, 2013, while the Senate was considering comprehensive immigration reform. The SAFE Act took an extreme approach to the enforcement of immigration laws in the interior of the United States. It would create a new crime for the act of being present in the United States without immigration status and for aiding an individual who lacks lawful immigration status. The SAFE Act also would have encouraged state and local law enforcement to participate in immigration enforcement, expanded mandatory and indefinite immigration detention, and limited protection of individuals fleeing persecution (H.R. 2278). While being debated in the House Judiciary Committee, deep divisions emerged along party lines (O'Keefe 2013). Democrats predicted the bill would result in widespread racial profiling and deter crime victims and witnesses from cooperating with police and lamented the bill's approach as one that had been rejected by the American people (Sreeja 2013; O'Keefe 2013). The bill was passed out of the Committee on a 20-15 vote along party lines, with all Republicans in favor and all Democrats opposed (Committee on the Judiciary).

In clinging to outdated notions that our nation's immigration problem can be resolved with tougher laws and more enforcement agents, the SAFE Act harkens back to a time before the 2012 presidential elections or restraints on federal spending. If the SAFE Act had proceeded to the floor and received sufficient votes to pass out of the House, reconciling it with the Senate's reform approach in S.744 would have been extremely difficult. For example, while the Senate provided a pathway toward citizenship for eligible undocumented individuals, the SAFE Act deemed all those in undocumented status to be committing an ongoing crime. Although the human, fiscal, and political costs of the effort to double down on enforcing our broken laws should weigh against its adoption, what ultimately may have halted its progress was the fear by some conservatives that even this harsh enforcement measure, if passed by the House, would be a vehicle for compromise with the Senate's comprehensive bill (Blake 2013).

Conclusion

Political and electoral forces aligned again in 2013 to push immigration reform to the top of the congressional agenda. With the Senate passage of a comprehensive piece of legislation designed to rework the immigration system, pundits, advocates, and voters turned their expectant gaze toward the House of Representatives. The final outcome of the legislative process on immigration reform is still unwritten, but the role of immigration enforcement has again proved to be outsized. Dollars spent or achievements gained toward enforcing the laws already on the books have little sway in the ongoing debate. Cries for more and more types and higher levels of enforcement are persistent. However, enforcement is not the golden key that politicians would like it to be. Reforms to our immigration system must include sufficient legal channels for workers filling open jobs and family members reuniting with loved ones. Reforms must create a system that works for all—migrants, employers, communities, families, and government alike. As history has shown us, shortcomings in our immigration system cannot be solved by more stringent enforcement of the laws. The current flaws are numerous and severe. First, we must devise and implement a system that works for the greatest number of users. Only then should enforcement of the new and improved laws be pursued. The appeal of enforcement is strong, but the appeal of a functioning and efficient immigration system must be stronger.

REFERENCES

"A Declaration of Five Principles to Guide Indiana's Immigration Discussion." Accessed on October 6, 2014. http://www.indianacompact.com/.

American Action Network. 2013. "AAN Launching August Initiative: Conservative Immigration Support Network." Accessed on October 6, 2014. http://americanactionnetwork.org/topic/aan-launching-august-initiative-conservative-immigration-support-network.

Americans for a Conservative Direction. Accessed on October 6, 2014. http://www.americansforaconservativedirection.com/.

American Immigration Council. 2013. "Positive Gains for DACA Recipients Seen at One-Year Anniversary." Accessed on October 6, 2014. http://immigrationimpact.com/2013/08/15/positive-gains-for-daca-recipients-seen-at-one-year-anniversary/.

Anderson, Stuart. 2013. "How Many More Deaths? The Moral Case for a Temporary Worker Program." National Foundation for America Policy. Accessed on October

5, 2014. http://www.nfap.com/pdf/NFAP Policy Brief Moral Case For a Temporary Worker Program March 2013.pdf.

"Atlanta Gathering Aims to Spur Immigration Reform." *Fox News Latino*. 2012. Accessed on October 6, 2014. http://latino.foxnews.com/latino/news/2012/06/12/atlanta-gathering-aims-to-spur-immigration-reform/.

Baker, Bryan and Nancy Rytina. 2013. "Estimates of the Unauthorized Immigrant Population Residing in the United States: 2012." *Population Estimates*, Department of Homeland Security, Office of Immigration Statistics. Accessed on October 5, 2014. http://www.dhs.gov/sites/default/files/publications/ois_ill_pe_2012_2.pdf.

Ball, Molly. 2013. "The Immigration Fight Is the Battle for the Soul of the GOP." *The Atlantic*. Accessed on October 6, 2014. http://www.theatlantic.com/politics/archive/2013/07/the-immigration-fight-is-the-battle-for-the-soul-of-the-gop/277867/.

Barreto, Matt. 2013. "New Poll: Immigration Policy Stance Directly Tied to Winning the Latino Vote." *Latino Decisions*. Accessed on October 6, 2014. http://www.latinodecisions.com/blog/2013/03/05/new-poll-immigration-policy-stance-directly-tied-to-winning-the-latino-vote/.

Batalova, Jeanne. 2006. "The Growing Connection Between Temporary and Permanent Immigration Systems." Migration Policy Institute. Accessed on October 6, 2014. http://www.migrationpolicy.org/ITFIAF/TFI_Batalova.pdf.

Bergeron, Claire. 2013. "Going to the Back of the Line: A Primer on Lines, Visa Categories, and Wait Times." *Issue Brief*, Migration Policy Institute. Accessed on October 6, 2014. http://www.migrationpolicy.org/pubs/CIRbrief-BackofLine.pdf.

Bibles, Badges and Business for Immigration Reform. Accessed on October 6, 2014. http://bbbimmigration.org/.

Bipartisan Policy Center. 2013. "Room for Consensus: A Statement by BPC's Immigration Task Force." Accessed on October 6, 2014. http://bipartisanpolicy.org/library/report/room-consensus-statement-bpc%E2%80%99s-immigration-task-force.

Blake, Aaron. 2013. "Boehner Closes Door on House-Senate Immigration Panel." *Washington Post*. Accessed on October 6, 2014. http://www.washingtonpost.com/politics/boehner-rejects-conference-committee-with-senates-immigration-bill/2013/11/13/5667caf8-4cb1-11e3-ac54-aa84301ced81_story.html.

Bland, Scott. 2013. "Why Immigration Reform Could Die in the House." *National Journal*. Accessed on October 6, 2014. http://www.nationaljournal.com/politics/why-immigration-reform-could-die-in-the-house-20130129.

Center for American Progress. Accessed on October 6, 2014. http://www.americanprogress.org/issues/immigration/view/.

Center for Latin American Studies, University of Arizona. 2013. "In the Shadow of the Wall: Family Separation, Immigration Enforcement and Security. Preliminary Data from the Migrant Border Crossing Study." Accessed on October 6, 2014. http://las.arizona.edu/sites/las.arizona.edu/files/UA_Immigration_Report2013web.pdf.

Chaudry, Ajay et al. 2010. "Facing our Future: Children in the Aftermath of Immigration Enforcement." Urban Institute. Accessed on October 5, 2014. http://carnegie.org/fileadmin/Media/Publications/facing_our_future.pdf.

Committee on the Judiciary, U.S. House of Representatives. June 18, 2013. "Roll Call No. 12, Final Passage of H.R. 2278." Accessed on October 6, 2014. http://judiciary.house.gov/_files/hearings/Markups%202013/mark_06182013/HR%202278/Votes/061813%20RC12%20Final%20Passage%20HR2278.pdf.

Conston, Dan. 2013. American Action Network, "AAN Releases Pro-House Immigration Reform Ad in CA-23: 'Fighting.'" Accessed on October 6, 2014. https://americanactionnetwork.org/press/aan-releases-pro-house-immigration-reform-ad-in-ca-23-fighting.

Dade, Corey. 2012. "Obama Administration Deported Record 1.5 Million People." *National Public Radio.* Accessed on October 6, 2014. http://www.npr.org/blogs/itsallpolitics/2012/12/24/167970002/obama-administration-deported-record-1-5-million-people.

Elmendorf, Douglas W. 2013. Director, Congressional Budget Office, Letter to Senator Patrick Leahy. 2013. Accessed on October 6, 2014. http://www.corker.senate.gov/public/_cache/files/acecdcfa-acc9-428e-bb98-4088ef3e6203/CBO%20Report%20on%20Hoeven-Corker%20Amendment%20to%20Immigration%20Bill.pdf.

Evangelical Immigration Table. Website. Accessed on October 6, 2014. http://evangelicalimmigrationtable.com/.

Forging a New Consensus. Accessed on October 6, 2014. http://www.forgingconsensus.org.

Fox News. 2012. "Study Accuses Obama Administration of 'Dismantling' Immigration Enforcement." 2012, July 24. Accessed on October 6, 2014. http://www.foxnews.com/politics/2012/07/24/study-accuses-obama-administration-gutting-immigration-enforcement/.

Giovagnoli, Mary. 2013. "Is a Border Surge the Only Way to Pass Immigration Reform and Ensure Legalization?" *Immigration Impact.* American Immigration Council. Accessed on October 6, 2014. http://immigrationimpact.com/2013/06/21/is-a-border-surge-the-only-way-to-pass-immigration-reform-and-ensure-legalization/.

Gomez, Alan. 2013. "Congress's Border Efforts Are Bunk, Say Border Sheriffs." *USA Today.* Accessed on October 6, 2014. http://www.usatoday.com/story/news/nation/2013/09/11/immigration-sheriffs-border-security-congress/2770807/.

Hesson, Ted. 2012. "Conservative Grover Norquist Talks Immigration Reform." ABC News. Accessed on October 6, 2014. http://abcnews.go.com/ABC_Univision/Politics/grover-norquist-immigration-reform/story?id=17471517.

H.R. 2278. Accessed on October 6, 2014. http://www.gpo.gov/fdsys/pkg/BILLS-113hr2278ih/pdf/BILLS-113hr2278ih.pdf.

Human Rights Watch. 2013. "Turning Migrants into Criminals: The Harmful Impact of US Border Prosecutions." Accessed on October 6, 2014. http://www.hrw.org/reports/2013/05/22/turning-migrants-criminals.

Idaho Statesman. 2013. "Norquist in Boise: Conservatives Should Embrace Immigration Reform." (No longer available.) http://www.idahostatesman.com/2013/06/25/2631218/norquist-in-boise-conservatives.html.

Immigration Policy Center. 2012. "Prosecutorial Discretion: A Statistical Assessment." Accessed on October 6, 2014. http://www.immigrationpolicy.org/sites/default/files/docs/pd_-_a_stastical_assessment_061112.pdf.

Jackson, Geena. 2011. "As Iowa Caucuses Approach, Signatories of Iowa Compact Hope to Reframe 'Immigration Debate.'" *Immigration Impact*, American Immigration Council. Accessed on October 6, 2014. http://immigrationimpact.com/2011/12/19/as-iowa-caucuses-approach-signatories-of-iowa-compact-hope-to-reframe-immigration-debate/.

Kelly, Erin. 2013. "Evangelical Group to Back Immigration Bill." *USA Today*. Accessed on October 6, 2014. http://www.usatoday.com/story/news/politics/2013/08/21/evangelicals-immigration-support/2681041/.

Klein, Ezra. 2013. "Who're You Going to Believe on Immigration? Mark Krikorian or Your Lying Eyes?" *Washington Post*. Accessed on October 6, 2014. http://www.washingtonpost.com/blogs/wonkblog/wp/2013/08/14/whore-you-going-to-believe-on-immigration-mark-krikorian-or-your-lying-eyes/.

Leiden, Warren R. and David L. Neal. 1990. "Highlights of the Immigration Act of 1990." *Fordham International Law Journal* 14, no. 1. Accessed on October 5, 2014. http://ir.lawnet.fordham.edu/cgi/viewcontent.cgi?article=1270&context=ilj.

Loftin, Josh. 2011. "States Talk Immigration Economics at Utah Summit." *Associated Press* Deseret News. Accessed on October 6, 2014. http://www.deseretnews.com/article/700191777/States-talk-immigration-economics-at-Utah-summit.html.

Lutheran Immigration and Refugee Service, n.d. Website. Accessed on October 16, 2014. http://lirs.org/.

Lydgate, Joanna. 2010. "Assembly-Line Justice: A Review of Operation Streamline." *Policy Brief*, The Chief Justice Earl Warren Institute on Race, Ethnicity & Diversity, University of California, Berkeley Law School. Accessed on October 5, 2014. http://www.law.berkeley.edu/files/Operation_Streamline_Policy_Brief.pdf.

March for Innovation. 2013. "The Top 10 #iMarch Highlights." Accessed on October 6, 2014. http://www.marchforinnovation.com/highlights.

Martinez, Jennifer. 2013. "Zuckerberg's FWD.us Blankets Country with Immigration Reform Ad." *The Hill*. Accessed on October 6, 2014. http://thehill.com/blogs/hillicon-valley/technology/316145-zuckerbergs-fwdus-unveils-new-pro-immigration-ad-.

Meissner, Doris K., Donald M. Kerwin, Muzaffar Chishti, and Claire Bergeron. 2013. "Immigration Enforcement in the United States: The Rise of a Formidable Machinery." Migration Policy Institute. Accessed on October 6, 2014. http://www.migrationpolicy.org/pubs/enforcementpillars.pdf.

Morton, John. 2011a. "Civil Immigration Enforcement: Priorities for the Apprehension, Detention, and Removal of Aliens." *Memorandum for All ICE Employees*, U.S. Immigrations and Customs Enforcement. Accessed on October 5, 2014. https://www.ice.gov/doclib/news/releases/2011/110302washingtondc.pdf.

Morton, John. 2011b. "Exercising Prosecutorial Discretion Consistent with the Civil Immigration Enforcement Priorities of the Agency for the Apprehension, Detention, and Removal of Aliens." *Memorandum for All Field Office Directors, All Special Agents in Charge, All Chief Counsel*, U.S. Immigration and Customs Enforcement. Accessed on October 5, 2014. http://www.ice.gov/doclib/secure-communities/pdf/prosecutorial-discretion-memo.pdf.

Motomura, Hiroshi et al. 2012. "Executive Authority to Grant Administrative Relief to DREAM Act Beneficiaries." Accessed on October 6, 2014. http://www.law.uh.edu/ihelg/documents/ExecutiveAuthorityForDREAMRelief28May2012with-Signatures.pdf.

Napolitano, Janet. 2012. "Exercising Prosecutorial Discretion with Respect to Individuals Who Came to the United States as Children." *Memorandum for David V. Aguilar, Acting Commissioner, U.S. Customs and Border Protection; Alejandro Mayorkas, Director, U.S. Citizenship and Immigration Services; John Morton, Director, U.S. Immigration and Customs Enforcement*, Department of Homeland Security. Accessed on October 6, 2014. http://www.immigrationpolicy.org/sites/default/files/docs/Napolitano-memo-6-15-2012.pdf.

Napolitano, Janet. 2013. "Secretary of Homeland Security Janet Napolitano's Third Annual Address on the State of Homeland Security: 'The Evolution and Future of Homeland Security.'" Department of Homeland Security. Accessed on October 6, 2014. http://www.dhs.gov/news/2013/02/26/secretary-homeland-security-janet-napolitano%E2%80%99s-third-annual-address-state-homeland.

National Immigration Forum. 2010. "Evaluating Supplemental Border Appropriations (HR 6080)." Accessed on October 6, 2014. http://immigrationforum.org/images/uploads/2010/HR6080_Summary.pdf.

National Immigration Forum. 2012. "Operation Streamline: Unproven Benefits Outweighed by Cost to Taxpayers." Accessed on May 14, 2015. http://immigrationforum.org/blog/operation-streamline-unproven-benefits-outweighed-by-cost-to-taxpayers/.

New York Times. 2012. "President Exit Polls." Accessed on October 6, 2014. http://elections.nytimes.com/2012/results/president/exit-polls.

"Official Text of Utah Compact Declaration on Immigration Reform." *Deseret News*. 2010. Accessed on October 6, 2014. http://www.deseretnews.com/article/700080758/Official-text-of-Utah-Compact-declaration-on-immigration-reform.html.

O'Keefe, Ed. 2013. "House Panel Approves Controversial Immigration Bill." *Washington Post*. Accessed on October 6, 2014. http://www.washingtonpost.com/blogs/post-politics/wp/2013/06/19/house-panel-approves-controversial-immigration-bill/.

Organizing for Action. "We need to fix America's broken immigration system, to grow our economy and give undocumented youth and their families the chance to earn their citizenship." Accessed on October 6, 2014. http://ofa.barackobama.com/immigration/.

Partnership for a New American Economy. Accessed on October 6, 2014. http://www.renewoureconomy.org/. http://www.renewoureconomy.org/wp-content/uploads/2012/05/pnae-members.pdf.

Passel, Jefferey S. and D'Vera Cohn. 2009. "A Portrait of Unauthorized Immigrants in the United States." Washington, DC: Pew Research Center. Accessed on October 6, 2014. http://pewhispanic.org/files/reports/107.pdf.

Passel, Jefferey S. and D'Vera Cohn. 2011. "Unauthorized Immigration Population: National and State Trends, 2010." Washington, DC: Pew Research Center. Accessed on October 5, 2014. http://www.pewhispanic.org/files/reports/133.pdf.

Passel, Jefferey S. and Roberto Suro. 2005. "Rise, Peak, and Decline: Trends in U.S. Immigration 1992–2004." Pew Research Center. Accessed October 5, 2014. http://pewhispanic.org/files/reports/53.pdf.

Peters, Jeremy W. 2013. "G.O.P. Groups Offering Cover for Lawmakers on Immigration." *New York Times* (July 1). Accessed on October 6, 2014. http://www.nytimes.com/2013/07/02/us/politics/gop-groups-offering-cover-for-lawmakers-on-immigration.html?hp&_r=0.

Pew Research Center. 2010. *Daily Numbers*. Accessed on October 6, 2014. http://www.pewresearch.org/daily-number/baby-boomers-retire/.

Portillo-Gonzales, Esther. 2011. "Shattered Families: The Perilous Intersection of Immigration Enforcement and the Child Welfare System." Applied Research Center. Accessed on October 6, 2014. http://act.colorlines.com/acton/attachment/1069/f-0079/0/-/-/l-sf-cl-70140000000T6DHAA0-000f/l-sf-cl-70140000000T6DHAA0-000f:caa2/file.pdf.

Preston, Julia. 2010. "Obama Signs Border Bill to Increase Surveillance." *New York Times*. Accessed on October 6, 2014. http://www.nytimes.com/2010/08/14/us/politics/14immig.html?src=me&_r=1&.

Preston, Julia. 2012a. "Students Press for Action on Immigration." *New York Times*. Accessed on October 5, 2014. http://www.nytimes.com/2012/05/31/us/students-press-for-action-on-immigration.html?_r=0.

Preston, Julia. 2013. "For Evangelicals, a Shift in Views on Immigration." *New York Times*. Accessed on October 6, 2014. http://www.nytimes.com/2013/04/14/us/evangelical-christians-increasingly-favor-pathway-to-legal-status-for-immigrants.html?ref=juliapreston&_r=1&.

Preston, Julia, and Helene Cooper 2012. "After Chorus of Protest, New Tune on Deportations." *New York Times*. Accessed on May 14, 2015. http://www.nytimes.com/2012/06/18/us/politics/deportation-policy-change-came-after-protests.html.

Representative Price (N.C.). "Emergency Border Security, Supplemental Appropriations, Fiscal Year 2010." *Congressional Record* 156 (2010) p. H6584. Accessed on October 6, 2014. http://www.gpo.gov/fdsys/pkg/CREC-2010-08-10/pdf/CREC-2010-08-10-pt1-PgH6584-2.pdf.

Republicans for Immigration Reform. Accessed on October 6, 2014. http://www.republicansforimmigrationreform.org/.

Sarlin, Benjy. 2013. "Democrats Let GOP Name Their Price on Immigration." MSNBC. Accessed on October 6, 2014. http://tv.msnbc.com/2013/06/20/democrats-let-gop-name-their-price-on-immigration/.

Shear, Michael. 2012. "Demographic Shift Brings New Worry for Republicans." *New York Times*. Accessed on October 6, 2014. http://www.nytimes.com/2012/11/08/us/politics/obamas-victory-presents-gop-with-demographic-test.html?pagewanted=all.

Simanski, John. 2014. Department of Homeland Security Office of Immigration Statistics, "Immigration Enforcement Actions: 2013." *Annual Report*. Accessed on October 22, 2014. http://www.dhs.gov/sites/default/files/publications/ois_enforcement_ar_2013.pdf.

Siskin, Alison. 2012. "Immigration-Related Detention: Current Legislative Issues." Congressional Research Service. Accessed on October 6, 2014. http://www.fas.org/sgp/crs/homesec/RL32369.pdf.

Sreeja, V. N. 2013. "House Panel Approves U.S. Rep. Trey Gowdy's SAFE Act Immigration Bill, Which Makes Staying in the Country Unlawfully a Federal Crime." *International Business Times*. Accessed on October 6, 2014. http://www.ibtimes.com/house-panel-approves-us-rep-trey-gowdys-safe-act-immigration-bill-which-makes-staying-country.

"Statement for the Record 'Commonsense Immigration Reform.'" Secretary Janet Napolitano, U.S. Department of Homeland Security, Before the United States Senate Committee on the Judiciary (February 13, 2013). Accessed on October 5, 2014. http://www.judiciary.senate.gov/imo/media/doc/2-13-13NapolitanoTestimony.pdf.

Stuart, Elizabeth. 2010. "Community Leaders Urge Moderate Approach to Immigration Reform." *Deseret News*. Accessed on October 6, 2014. http://www.deseretnews.com/article/700080754/Community-leaders-urge-moderate-approach-to-immigration-reform.html.

"Texas Compact." Accessed on October 6, 2014. http://texascompact.org/.

"The Colorado Compact: Bringing Colorado Together for Immigration Reform." Accessed on October 6, 2014. http://coloradocompact.com/.

U. S. Border Patrol. n.d.(a). "Enacted Border Patrol Program Budget by Fiscal Year." Accessed on May 13, 2015. http://www.cbp.gov/sites/default/files/documents/BP%20Budget%20History%201990-2014_0.pdf

U. S. Border Patrol. n.d. (b). "Southwest Border Sectors Total Illegal Alien Apprehensions by Fiscal Year." Accessed on May 13, 2015. http://www.cbp.gov/sites/default/files/documents/BP%20Southwest%20Border%20Sector%20Apps%20FY1960%20-%20FY2014_0.pdf.

U.S. Chamber of Commerce. 2013. "Infographic: Immigration Reform Makes Sense for Our Economy." Accessed on October 6, 2014. http://www.freeenterprise.com/immigration/infographic-immigration-reform-makes-sense-our-economy.

U.S. Citizenship and Immigration Services 2012. "USCIS Begins Accepting Requests for Consideration of Deferred Action for Childhood Arrivals. Press Release. Accessed on May 14, 2015. http://www.uscis.gov/news/uscis-begins-accepting-requests-consideration-deferred-action-childhood-arrivals

U.S. Conference of Catholic Bishops. n.d. "Justice for Immigrants." Accessed on October 6, 2014. http://www.justiceforimmigrants.org/index.shtml.

U.S. Department of Homeland Security. 2010. "Obama Administration Announces Aug. 1 National Guard Deployment to Support Federal Law Enforcement Along the Southwest Border." Accessed on October 6, 2014. http://www.dhs.gov/news/2010/07/19/obama-administration-announces-aug-1-national-guard-deployment-support-federal-law.

U.S. Department of Homeland Security. Various dates. "Budget in Brief," various years. Available at "DHS Budget." Accessed on October 6, 2014. http://www.dhs.gov/dhs-budget. This page contains links to "Budget in Brief" documents going back to 2004.U.S. Department of Labor. 2014. "Fastest Growing Occupations." *Occupational Outlook Handbook.* Accessed on October 6, 2014. http://www.bls.gov/ooh/fastest-growing.htm.U.S. Department of Labor. 2014. "Fastest Growing Occupations." *Occupational Outlook Handbook.* Accessed on October 6, 2014. http://www.bls.gov/ooh/fastest-growing.htmU.S. Department of State. 2014. "Visa Bulletin for September 2014." Accessed on October 6, 2014. http://travel.state.gov/content/visas/english/law-and-policy/bulletin/2014/visa-bulletin-for-september-2014.html.

U.S. Department of State. n.d. "Annual Report of Immigrant Visa Applicants in the Family-sponsored and Employment-based Preferences Registered at the National Visa Center as of November 1, 2013." Accessed on October 6, 2014. http://travel.state.gov/content/dam/visas/Statistics/Immigrant-Statistics/WaitingListItem.pdf.

U.S. Government Accountability Office. 2013. "Southwest Border Security: Data Are Limited and Concerns Vary about Spillover Crime along the Southwest Border." Accessed on October 6, 2014. http://www.gao.gov/assets/660/652320.pdf.

U.S. Real GDP by Year. Accessed on October 5, 2014. http://www.multpl.com/us-gdp-inflation-adjusted/table.

U.S. Senate Roll Call Votes 113th Congress—1st Session. Accessed October 6, 2014. http://www.senate.gov/legislative/LIS/roll_call_lists/roll_call_vote_cfm.cfm?congress=113&session=1&vote=00163.

United We Dream. 2012. "Immigrant Youth Launch National 'Right to Dream' Campaign Calling on Obama to Provide Relief for All DREAMers." Press Release. Accessed on October 6, 2014. http://unitedwedream.org/press-releases/immigrant-youth-launch-national-right-to-dream-campaign-calling-on-obama-to-provide-relief-for-all-dreamers/.

United We Dream. n.d. "United We Dream Pledges to Fight for Fair Treatment and Citizenship for DREAMers, Families and Communities," *Press Release.* Accessed on October 6, 2014. http://unitedwedream.org/press-releases/united-we-dream-pledges-to-fight-for-fair-treatment-and-citizenship-for-dreamers-families-and-communities/.

Vincent, Peter S. 2011. "Case-by-Case Review of Incoming and Certain Pending Cases." *Memorandum for All Chief Counsel, Office of the Principle Legal Advisor*, U.S. Immigration and Customs Enforcement. Accessed on October 6, 2014. http://www.ice.gov/doclib/foia/prosecutorial-discretion/case-by-case-review-incoming-certain-pending-cases-memorandum.pdf.

Wagner, Dennis. 2010. "Violence Is Not Up on Arizona Border Despite Mexican Drug War," *Arizona Republic*. Accessed on October 6, 2014. http://www.azcentral.com/news/articles/2010/05/02/20100502arizona-border-violence-mexico.html.

Wallsten, Peter. 2012. "Conservative Activists Plan Strategy on Immigration Issue." *Washington Post*. Accessed on October 6, 2014. http://www.washingtonpost.com/politics/conservative-activists-plan-strategy-on-immigration-issue/2012/12/03/b558a136-3d6c-11e2-a2d9-822f58ac9fd5_story.html.

PART II

Interdisciplinary Research, Advocacy, and Actions for and with Migrants Affected by Detention and Deportation

5

Legal and Social Work Responses to the Detained and Deported

Interdisciplinary Reflections and Actions

JESSICA CHICCO AND ELAINE P. CONGRESS

Attorneys and social workers both act as advocates for their clients and share the common goal of ameliorating the lives of those they serve. Drawing on previously articulated models for interdisciplinary work, we delineate and reflect on two examples of how social workers and lawyers interact and collaborate in responding to challenges that arise frequently in work with immigrants. We explore the immense potential for gaining greater insight, developing integrated knowledge, and enriching the quality of the services provided to the clients. Specifically, we review how social workers and lawyers approach case assessments within each of our professions. Next, we examine a series of issues including ethical norms and some of the tensions arising from the differing professional responsibilities of social workers and attorneys and the systems in which they operate. We then explore two models for interdisciplinary work through the lens of two vignettes: one in which the lawyer and social worker each provide services to a shared client, and where they lean on each other to achieve their independent but overlapping goals; and one in which the social worker is understood to be a member of the legal team in a truly collaborative interdisciplinary setting. We conclude with some suggestions of how we can work to minimize existing barriers to interdisciplinary work toward better serving immigrant communities, and how internalizing values and skills from each other's professions may shed new light on our professional roles.

Deportation by the Numbers

More than 430,000 people were deported in 2013—a near-record number, and nearly double the number of individuals deported in the year 2000 (DHS 2014). This number does not account for the hundreds of thousands of "voluntary returns" of individuals turned back at the border, or the estimated thousands of *de facto* deportations of family members—including documented and undocumented immigrants as well as U.S. citizens—who accompany their loved one to the country of deportation (ibid.).

There is no doubt that such a massive deportation system creates extraordinary familial hardship. A Human Rights Watch report estimated that 1.6 million family members have suffered as a result of the deportation of a loved one between 1997 and 2007. An analysis of the data shows that of the nearly 1 million individuals—both lawfully and unlawfully present—who were deported based on criminal grounds between 1997 and 2007, nearly 400,000 had at least one U.S. citizen or legally present child or spouse (Human Rights Watch 2009). The Pew Research Center estimates that there are 4 million U.S. citizen children who live in "mixed-status" homes with one or both parents undocumented and therefore at risk of deportation (Passel and Cohn 2009). According to data released by Immigration & Customs Enforcement, more than 200,000 parents of U.S. citizens were removed in the two years ending in 2012. Further, a report by the Applied Research Center revealed that at least 5,100 children are in foster care at any given time as a result of a parent having been placed in immigration detention or having been deported (ARC 2011).

It is on this backdrop that immigration attorneys and social workers serve immigrants and their families and interact with immigrant communities through the course of their work. Settings in which a social worker may encounter immigrant clients include social services agencies, health facilities, schools, and legal offices wherein they counsel immigrant children and adults, provide information and referral services, advocate for the rights of immigrants, and collaborate with other professionals, including lawyers. Immigration attorneys, by the very nature of their work, are in constant interaction with immigrant communities, clients, and their families. Though doing so from the perspectives of their own professional fields and governed by their professions' differing codes of ethics and responsibility, they are increasingly called upon to collaborate with each other in developing integrated responses to immigrants and their families. Given the intense specialization within a wide range of professions, it has remained challenging to develop interdisciplinary collaborations despite widespread recognition that such collaboration is in the best interest of the client.

Assessing Needs, Conceptualizing Cases

In many instances, immigrant families may first come into contact with a social worker, for example through a school or a medical clinic, and that social worker may then make a referral for legal services. In other cases, an attorney may refer her client to a social worker or a social services agency for assistance with any number of matters, such as housing, benefits, or mental health counseling. Yet in other cases, an individual may separately seek out the assistance of either a social worker or an immigration lawyer, or both. In this section, we briefly examine how lawyers and social workers independently conduct assessments of their clients within the boundaries of their professions. Whereas lawyers are trained to focus "on analysis of statutory and case law," social workers are trained to focus on "empowering disadvantaged populations in society," and this difference in training and orientation can lead to "a profound difference in thinking" (Faller and Vandervort 2007). A better understanding of the professional approaches will contextualize the challenges that arise when social workers and lawyers work together.

Legal case assessments. Lawyers are often perceived as focused on the complex and highly technical aspects of the law, yielding a narrow view of obstacles faced by a client and corresponding solutions. In reality, few issues are purely legal, and this is particularly true in the immigration context, where an individual's immigration status is intimately linked to his or her financial well-being, family unity, and ability to access services and justice, among myriad other things. Nonetheless, the primary task of an immigration attorney is to address the client's immigration concerns, a task that becomes significantly more pressing when the client lacks lawful immigration status or is being threatened with deportation.

In exploring legal avenues of relief, basic information on the client's manner of entry, the status if any he or she held after entry, and the acts or facts that may make the client deportable, are all relevant. Equally relevant to the inquiry, however, is gathering information on additional details, perhaps not thought to be as closely connected to potential immigration relief. This includes whether the client has been or is being abused or has ever been the victim of a crime, whether the client is fearful of returning to his or her country, how long he or she has been in the United States, the existence and immigration status of spouses, parents, and children in the United States, and the list goes on. Several of these factors—though many, including the authors, would argue not enough and not with sufficient weight—might become relevant in determining both whether the client will have an avenue to seek legal status, and whether he or she will be granted that status at the discretion of the decision-maker. They will also impact how a lawyer crafts a theory of the case that will in turn provide the framework for the relevant facts and law.

Social workers' case assessments. An overarching theme in social work practice is "person in environment." Using a systems approach, a social worker conducts an assessment that includes identification of the biological, psychological, and social issues affecting each family member, as well as the internal family interactions and the family's interactions with outside resource systems. Specific attention is directed to resources in the community that are supportive or challenging to the well-being of clients, including but not limited to current immigration policies and laws that present particular challenges for noncitizen clients and their families.

Social workers are committed to identifying and promoting the strengths of their clients. This important theory in social work proposes that clients have much intrinsic capability within themselves to cope with problems in their environments (Saleeby 2012). This is very true of immigrants and refugees who often demonstrate an ability to cope and thrive despite very difficult past and present experiences. Many immigrants and refugees have endured traumatic events at every stage of immigration. Separation from home and familiar environment is every immigrant's experience, but many immigrants, especially refugees, have endured violent loss of relatives and sudden dislocation from their homelands, and fears for their own safety and well-being. After immigration, many struggle with constant fear of deportation, as well as diminished ability to provide for basic needs and discrimination in education and employment. Mental health symptoms of anxiety and depression often are suggestive of post-traumatic stress disorder in which immigrants relive their traumatic pre-immigration experiences.

Further, social workers would find it helpful in understanding the immigrant's experience to take a three-stage approach—pre-migration, transition, and current situation (Pine and Drachman 2004). Stage 1 refers to immigrants in their countries of origin. What push and pull factors contributed to their decisions to immigrate? What were the political, economic, social, and personal factors that influenced their migration? Stage 2 looks at their transition experience. For many it is a long plane ride; for others, a long, dangerous water or desert crossing. Finally, Stage 3 involves assessing immigrants in their current environments. What social economic issues do they encounter? How has the process of migrating and immigration enforcement policies affected their physical and emotional well-being?

Contextualizing the Challenges of Interdisciplinarity

Interdisciplinary collaboration between social workers and lawyers is not a novel concept. Mary Richmond (1917) spoke about connecting social casework with a legal framework as early as the beginning of the twentieth century. The National Association of Social Workers Code of Ethics (2008a) acknowledges both the benefits and challenges of interdisciplinary collaborations and provides some limited guidance. More recently, authors from the social work perspective, including Cole (2012) and Forgey and Colarossi (2003), have addressed advantages and challenges of collaborative work, especially in the areas of domestic violence and child abuse. (*See also* Aiken and Wizner 2003.) Helping clients by providing expertise from the two professions, as well as increased social support for both lawyers and social workers handling difficult cases (Cole 2012) have been easily identified as benefits of interdisciplinary collaborations. Legal scholars have also been evaluating the benefits and challenges of interdisciplinary work between lawyers and social workers, especially within the context of law school clinics (Aiken and Wizner 2003; Anderson, Barenberg, and Tremblay 2007).

Both social workers and lawyers are guided by a set of professional standards of ethics in their work with immigrants. Lawyers are bound by their states' codes of professional responsibility. Although these vary by state, most are based on the Model Rules of Professional Conduct issued by the American Bar Association. The Model Rules explain that a lawyer acts in various capacities as a representative of clients—as an advisor, an advocate, a negotiator, and an evaluator. Specifically, the Rules state that as an advocate, "a lawyer zealously asserts the client's position under the rules of the adversary system" and as a negotiator the lawyer "seeks a result advantageous to the client but consistent with requirements of honest dealings with others" (ABA 2014).

Social workers follow the International Federation of Social Workers Statement of Ethical Principles (IFSW 2012a) and the National Association of Social Workers Code of Ethics (NASW 2008a). The former stresses a human rights approach to protecting and advocating for individuals, especially those who are most vulnerable. Important principles include promoting the right to self-determination and participation, as well as identifying and developing strengths. Both IFSW and NASW have developed several policies and provisions that focus on protecting the rights of immigrants and refugees (IFSW 1998, 2012b; NASW 2008b, 2011). Social workers are expected to avoid discrimination based on immigration status, advocate to eliminate discrimination based on immigration status, and receive specific education to this end (NASW 2008a).

Taylor (2006) and Congress (2007), building on an early article (Stein 1991), identified three difficulties that arise in the context of interdisciplinary work: (1) definition of the client, (2) task delineations, and (3) confidentiality responsibilities. We will discuss them here as they are particularly challenging in interdisciplinary work between social workers and lawyers.

Lawyers and social workers are likely to identify the client served differently. Lawyers generally are understood to have a responsibility to serve one client or individual. The lawyer's duty to the client may demand a narrow focus on the individual client's interests, disregarding—and certainly not prioritizing—the broader impact of the law on the community or society at large. This in turn may lead to situations in which a lawyer's duty to the client may come into conflict with a lawyer's sense of what is in the best interests of the community or the advancement of justice, and the lawyer must weigh these in deciding whether and how to continue representing an individual client. In contrast, social workers have been trained to take a more comprehensive approach and take into account the needs and strengths of all family members or the relevant community without focusing on the legal rights of one individual above all else (Aiken and Wizner 2003). In the vignettes discussed below, for example, an immigration lawyer would see her role as primarily advocating for the cases of Maria and Dith. A social worker would instead define her client as including their families as well, or assess the case from a more comprehensive and multi-faceted perspective. Thus, a case in which clients may have disparate interests may be particularly challenging in interdisciplinary work.

Further, problems may emerge in task delineation when each profession strays from its area of competence. This may be difficult to avoid, however, especially when clients are seen separately by the lawyer and by the social worker rather than as part of a team. For example, a client may express suicidal feelings after learning that his immigration appeal has been denied and he is facing prolonged detention. The lawyer may, by necessity, be in a position of offering personal counseling. On the other hand, a social worker working with an immigrant navigating deportation proceedings may find herself explaining steps in the appeal process, information that is clearly within the legal arena. A model in which social workers and lawyers work together as part of one team will often be more effective at minimizing such blurring of roles than a side-by-side model where the two professionals are working independently with no or little communication (St. Joan 2001).

Despite some similarities, the two sets of professional codes of ethics diverge in the obligations of confidentiality and, in particular, a social worker's duty to act as a mandatory reporter. For example, when there is risk of harm to others, such as suspicion of child abuse, social workers are typically expected to report this to protective services within their state (McLeod and Polowy 2013; Lau, Krase, and Morse 2009). In contrast, ABA Model Rule 1.6(b) allows—but does not mandate—disclosure of confidential information in very limited enumerated circumstances, including "to prevent reasonably certain death or substantial bodily harm." Rule 3.3(b), which is concerned with candor to the tribunal, states that a lawyer "who represents a client in an adjudicative proceeding and who knows that a person intends to engage, is engaging or has engaged in criminal or fraudulent conduct related to the proceeding shall take reasonable remedial measures, including, if necessary, disclosure to the tribunal" (ABA 2014). But this mandated disclosure is significantly more narrow than a social worker's ethical duty as a mandated reporter, which in 48 states includes the duty to report suspected child abuse (Child Welfare Information Gateway 2012).[1]

A Closer Look: Integrative Approaches to Immigrants and Their Families

Having set forth some of the challenges to interdisciplinary collaborations stemming from different and at times divergent professional roles and responsibilities, we now turn to the application of two of the possible models of collaboration by reference to the two vignettes, including one presented in full in the introduction and excerpted below. The discussion that follows provides some practical insight into the many challenges that social workers and lawyers encounter in their work with immigrant clients. The examples raise questions on the setting and role in which the two professions collaborate as well as the needs of the individual client, family members, and the broader community. Both sets of professionals must grapple with weighing the influence of a wide range of contextual factors affecting the immigrants' life options. As importantly, both face complex questions that challenge each to weigh the value of family unity and that of the best interests of the children involved. The discussion offers insight into the multiple and complex settings in which social workers, immigration lawyers, and immigrants encounter each other and how each may respond. Moreover, it explores opportunities for increased interdisciplinary collaboration and discusses some of the benefits that can result from such collaboration. Finally, we argue herein that the advantages to be gained—both in expanding professional horizons and in enriching the type and quality of services provided to immigrant clients—far outweigh the difficulties that may be encountered.

Model #1: When Professional Lines Intersect

> Maria and Felipe are Maya from the Quiché region of Guatemala. In 1998 Felipe entered the United States illegally from Guatemala, to rejoin Maria,

his wife, who had gone to the United States in 1997 on a visitor visa in order to get heart surgery, a procedure donated by a major Boston hospital. After a long recovery, Maria "overstayed" and has been in the United States without documentation ever since. Felipe and Maria had to sell much of their land in Guatemala in order to pay for Maria's medical care. After Felipe's arrival in the United States in 1998 he found work as a laborer.

In 2001, while in the United States, Felipe and Maria had another child, Camila, who is a U.S. citizen. Three years later, in 2004, Maria was stopped by police for a traffic violation. Following an appearance in criminal court, Maria was turned over to immigration authorities. She posted a bond, however, and was released from their custody. She received a Notice to Appear in immigration court, but never followed up or heard anything further about her case. She and Felipe had changed their address soon after her criminal court appearance, and did not report the change to any governmental authority.

In late 2007 Felipe was picked up by ICE agents in a workplace raid and detained. Felipe was detained for several months and ultimately was deported in early 2008. Maria has been anxious ever since, worried that ICE agents will find her again and deport her. She is especially worried about Camila. In early 2009, Camila was diagnosed with leukemia. Felipe has been very distressed about Camila and Maria. He wanted to return to the United States to help care for his sick child and to comfort Maria, but he knew that he could not obtain a visa. Seeing no other options, Felipe decided to return to the United States by hiring a coyote and crossing over the Mexican border on foot. He has recently arrived in Massachusetts and been reunited with Maria and Camila. Felipe's mother has just called to say that Sergio, the couple's 15-year-old son, has also left their village to follow his father north.

Drawing on the story of Maria and Felipe's family, this section will explore the setting in which individuals may be seeking the services of an immigration lawyer and a social worker independently of one another, but in which communication between the two may be mutually beneficial and in the best interests of the client. The story of Maria and Felipe's family underscores the reality many mixed-status families face—in this case a family in which the parents are undocumented and both in precarious situations, and in which one of the two children is a U.S. citizen.

Each member of the family has distinct legal challenges tied to their immigration status, or lack thereof, but they are inevitably interlinked (*see* Brabeck, Porterfield, and Loughry, this volume). Further, there are at least three settings in which Maria may have had interaction with social workers independent of seeking immigration legal advice—the hospitals/outpatient clinics where Maria and her U.S. citizen daughter Camila received and may still receive medical treatment, social service agencies, and the children's school.

On a separate track—or perhaps as a result of a referral made by a social worker or other "helping professional"—members of this family may seek out the assistance of an immigration lawyer. Though each member of the family has a set of distinct legal questions when it comes to their immigration status, an immigration lawyer meeting with any member of the family would gather facts relevant not only to the individual's status, but also to the immigration status of all members of the family, as relatives' ability to obtain lawful status is often intertwined. Both Maria and Felipe could face deportation at any moment. Maria's failure to attend her Immigration Court hearing likely resulted in an order of deportation being issued in her absence. Felipe's illegal reentry following his deportation makes him subject to a fast-track deportation procedure which would lead to his deportation without the opportunity of seeing an Immigration Judge. The fact that Maria and Felipe have a U.S. citizen daughter who is seriously ill would not by itself stop their deportations, or even guarantee them a chance to present their equities to an Immigration Judge. If her parents are deported, Camila could be left behind or follow her parents to Guatemala. Both choices have implications for Camila's health, family unity, and government intervention. Finally, Sergio, who is only about 15 years old as he makes the dangerous journey across the border, may become eligible for a special form of protection for minors who are deemed to have been abandoned, neglected, or abused by one or both parents.

In a scenario in which the social worker (or social workers) and the immigration lawyer are both providing services to the family but are doing so independently of one another, social workers and lawyers might benefit from connecting. For example, though Felipe may not have any path to lawful status, the unique circumstances related to his daughter's medical condition could support a request that immigration enforcement exercise discretion not to deport him and to grant him "deferred action status" that would allow him to remain in the United States and obtain work authorization. In support of such a request, the lawyer would greatly benefit from the insight and supporting documentation the social worker could provide to document the numerous and severe hardships the family would face if Felipe were to be deported, such as Camila's medical and school records. Or a social worker may be better connected in the immigrant community she serves and more familiar with services that may be available to the family despite their immigration status. For example, she may be able to help the family identify an interpreter who can also assist the family in their communications with the immigration lawyer. Or she can help the parents get set up for mental health counseling, evidence of which may again assist their requests for immigration relief.

In turn, a social worker providing services to the family may benefit from learning more about the possible implications of Maria and Felipe's tenuous status and the limitations and risks that it poses. For example, a better understanding of the family's immigration status may assist her in sorting through what social services or health benefits may be available. Knowing more about the family's immigration situation may also help the social worker understand that the family may be living under constant fear of deportation and may not trust government officials. Such an understanding may in turn assist the social worker in contextualizing the clients' reluctance to provide personal identifying information or to seek needed health care or social services.

Collaborations across disciplines in this sense—working together with a shared client and having an open line of communication (with the client's consent)—will therefore inevitably enrich the quality of services that each professional can provide.

Model #2: Social Workers as Members of the Legal Team

The case of Dith and his family, as summarized in the introduction to this volume, presents additional challenges for interdisciplinary teams. Briefly, Dith arrived in the United States in 1980 at the age of 4, became a lawful permanent resident but never naturalized. Arrested for drug-related gang activities, he served a prison sentence, then married a U.S.

citizen, and had one child. He was re-arrested in 2004 following a repatriation agreement between the United States and Cambodia signed in 2002 and was deported. Melissa was killed by a drunk driver in 2009, but Dith was unable to return for the funeral nor to care for his child (*see* Introduction, this volume, for full details).

Let us now instead assume a setting in which a legal office also employs a social worker—a truly collaborative and integrated interdisciplinary setting. When Dith is placed in deportation proceedings, the family seeks legal advice and representation. The lawyer on the team is trained to immediately begin processing the "facts" as they are legally relevant. The social worker, on the other hand, will take a broader approach and assess the well-being of the client as well as the family members. In such a setting, the social worker is understood to be a member of the legal team, and thereby bound by the same duties of confidentiality and obligations as the legal professionals (Anderson, Barenberg, and Tremblay 2007). The social worker's training and perspective would enable her to provide context for the clients' priorities and decision-making and enrich the quality of services the team is able to provide to their clients.

As a long-term lawful permanent resident, Dith could have avoided the risk of deportation if he had naturalized promptly upon turning 18 and obtained U.S. citizenship years before the criminal conviction that led to his deportation. Dith's story highlights the importance—too often overlooked in immigrant communities—of naturalizing to secure one's status and eliminate the risk of deportation. Studies and surveys have explored the reasons why green card holders do not naturalize, and they range from practical difficulties—the cost of the application, the requirement of passing an English test—to more complex personal reasons (Gonzalez-Barrera, Lopez, Passel, and Taylor 2013). Though a moot point in Dith's current predicament, a psychosocial evaluation by a social worker may provide insight into the reasons underlying Dith's decision not to naturalize, which may in turn assist the lawyer and the social worker in counseling future clients who may be eligible for naturalization. Though a lawyer could provide clients information regarding the process of naturalization, a social worker on the same team may be better positioned to counsel clients about confronting the financial, emotional, and social barriers to applying for citizenship.

In conducting the legal assessment of Dith's case, an immigration lawyer will examine the legal reasons for Dith's deportation and look for any potential challenges. The tightening of immigration laws in 1996 significantly curtailed the availability of discretionary relief. For example, the laws repealed a form of discretionary relief that had been available to lawful permanent residents found to be deportable if they could show certain periods of residence and that a balancing of the equities weighed in their favor. The laws also drastically expanded the categories of individuals, including long-term lawful permanent residents, who are subject to mandatory detention and deportation for having been convicted of "aggravated felonies"—which, in spite of the name, need be neither aggravated nor felonies. In so doing, Congress effectively foreclosed even the possibility of favorable discretion to stop the deportation of such individuals. In Dith's case, he was ordered removed based on an interpretation of "aggravated felony" that was overturned by the Supreme Court in a nearly unanimous decision just a year after Dith's deportation (*Lopez v. Gonzales* 2006). Had the correct interpretation of the law been applied, Dith would have been eligible to apply for discretionary relief to avoid deportation, and an Immigration Judge would have been able to consider factors such as his long-term residence in the United States since childhood, his rehabilitation, and his family ties, including his young U.S. citizen son.

Having looked at the frameworks that allowed Dith's deportation, the legal team would now ask: What happens next? Dith's deportation, based on an interpretation of the law that was later deemed erroneous by the Supreme Court, squarely raises the issue of whether individuals should be able to seek review of their immigration cases after deportation. Because he has already been deported, under current law it will be extremely difficult for Dith to get an Immigration Court to revisit its finding. Currently, immigration regulations preclude the filing of "motions to reopen" after the individual's deportation, though nearly all federal courts around the country have found this regulation to be invalid in certain circumstances. However, because more than a year has passed since Dith's deportation, he would nonetheless face significant obstacles in seeking to have his case revisited. In requesting that the case be reopened, Dith would also have to present evidence that he would merit discretionary relief from deportation. A standard biopsychosocial assessment undertaken by a social worker, therefore, may provide crucial information that an immigration lawyer would want to have to more effectively represent the client, for example in the context of an application for relief that requires a showing of rehabilitation and community ties.

A social worker is trained and has special expertise in working with clients around emotional issues. Though immigration attorneys are often thrust into such conversations, having the support and guidance of a social worker with such expertise can be clearly beneficial. A social worker would be concerned about Dith's welfare since his return to Cambodia, especially since his aunt was very fearful about his deportation to Cambodia and his wife Melissa and son Chris experienced much emotional and financial loss because of his departure. There may be resources such as the Returnee Integration Support Center (RISC in Phnom Penh) that could work with Dith to help him reintegrate in Cambodia. Such reintegration assistance organizations, however, are not always available. To add to the earlier stress in regard to the violent deaths of Dith's parents when he was preschool age and his deportation, there were more recent stresses such as Melissa's death in an accident.

Chris has lost both parents, one by deportation and the other by sudden death within a short period of time. It is not surprising if he manifests depressive symptoms or acting out behavior. He could definitely benefit from counseling, which a social worker experienced in working with children and adolescents after childhood traumas could provide. After a thorough diagnostic assessment, a psychiatric referral might be necessary to provide medication for acute symptoms. Chris is an adolescent, a time during which identity formation occurs. As with many immigrant adolescents there may be challenges in developing a bicultural identity. He has been raised in the United States, his mother is an American citizen, and as an adolescent he may be more comfortable in identifying with mainstream American adolescent culture. Yet he is keenly aware that his father is Cambodian and now he is being raised by a Cambodian aunt, Arunny, which certainly may have an effect on his cultural identity. The social worker might also be involved in making a referral to Big Brothers or a similar type of organization to provide Chris with additional male support after the forced departure of his father. Arunny herself may be experiencing post-traumatic symptoms from the trauma she experienced in Cambodia, the loss of her nephew Dith who was deported, and Melissa's death. In terms of intervention, both Chris and Arunny could probably benefit from individual counseling to help them work through feelings of loss and subsequent depression. Since young children often act out their feelings through play rather than putting them into words, the social worker may want to use play therapy techniques to elicit details about the quality of the relationship between Chris and Dith. The social worker would share information learned with the lawyer —such as Dith's positive work and education involvement since his incarceration as a youth, the quality of his relationship with Melissa and Chris, and finally the negative impact his departure would have on the family's well-being—in an attempt to provide information that may assist in efforts to challenge Dith's deportation.

A "conundrum of confidentiality," as coined by Corbin (2007), occurs in terms of mandated reporting when a social worker works for a legal agency. As discussed above, social workers are generally bound by professional obligations and laws regarding mandated reporting of child abuse. As a member of the legal team, however, many commentators have concluded that the social worker would not be bound by mandated reporting obligations, but would instead be subject to the rules of professional conduct governing attorneys (Anderson et al. 2007; Tencer Block and Soprych 2011; Conti 2011). According to the American Bar Association's *Model Rules of Professional Conduct*, Rule 5.3 (2013), as well as similar rules adopted by states, lawyers that employ nonlawyer professionals are required to "make reasonable efforts to ensure that the person's conduct is compatible with the professional obligations of the lawyer." In addition, the social worker would be bound by a different set of confidentiality rules and would be able to share information gained through his assessment with the rest of the legal team.

Thus, while the immigration lawyer may be primarily occupied with analyzing whether Dith's deportation can still be challenged and what the appropriate legal vehicle for such a challenge may be, a social worker might be more attuned to other complexities faced by Dith and his family. Among the most troubling consequences of the deportation is the seemingly permanent separation of Dith from his son, Chris. There is a significant lack of coordination between the immigration enforcement and deportation systems and the family court and child welfare systems, with at times devastating consequences for the families involved (Rabin

2011; Thronson 2008; Thronson, this volume). Whereas in some instances family and immigration law appear to work hand in hand—as is the case for special immigrant juvenile status available to children who have been neglected, abused, or abandoned and special relief for victims of domestic abuse—in other cases immigration law disregards or is even in conflict with the interests recognized by family law. For example, Immigration Judges are not encouraged—and in most instances not even permitted—to consider the best interests of the child, even when the child is a U.S. citizen, in deciding whether to order the deportation of a parent or family member of the child. The Inter-American Commission for Human Rights most recently reiterated that the American Declaration mandates that deportation proceedings "duly consider the best interests of the child," and that a flexible balancing approach, specific to the facts of each individual case, should be employed in making deportation decisions (IACHR 2010). The U.S. government, however, does not consider itself bound by decisions of the Inter-American Commission, and has not altered its policies as a result. Further, when there is a question of custody, social workers and family court judges try to make a decision guided by the best interests of the child. This principle has been adopted by all states in their domestic relations law and is widely considered to be the gold standard for custody determinations. (See, for example, Mass. Gen. Laws Ann. Ch. 119, § 1.) However, as set forth above, this standard has not been adopted by the immigration and deportation system. Custody decisions are already often complicated by the varying capacities and desires of different family members to raise a child as well as the child's own wishes. A parent's deportation and at times opposing interests of immigration enforcement add yet another layer of complexity.

A social worker would be trained and well positioned to make a holistic assessment and arrive at a recommendation regarding the best interests of the child, and in this instance may well arrive at the conclusion that reunification of Chris with his father in the United States is in the best interests of the child. However, as we have seen, Dith's permanent return to the United States is an unlikely outcome. Even Dith's return for purposes of attending a custody hearing poses at times insurmountable challenges (Rabin 2011). Though legal avenues to return exist in theory—an individual needing to be present for a judicial proceeding could seek a temporary visitor's visa or temporary entry on humanitarian parole—in practice obtaining the necessary documents can be difficult. In this scenario, a social worker would likely be more familiar with the child welfare system, as well as any relevant local policies or procedures, than an immigration lawyer. She may also be in contact with the child welfare worker. In an interdisciplinary collaborative setting, in addition to drawing on the existing knowledge and expertise of a social worker, the immigration lawyer can educate herself about the child welfare system or lean on the expertise of her colleague to more effectively represent her client's interests.

Concluding Reflections

Despite some significant differences in professional approaches, the benefits of interdisciplinary collaboration at any level are evident, with benefits generally increasing with closer and more integrated collaboration. Further, divisions among professional boundaries delineate somewhat of a false dichotomy. Though trained in different professional paths, both immigration lawyers and social workers relate to clients as individuals. It is nearly impossible—and indeed often detrimental—to compartmentalize a client's problems as being purely legal and therefore only appropriate for a lawyer, or nonlegal and therefore only to be tackled by a social worker or other helping professional. In reality, an individual's situation is more complex and questions of legal immigration status are often inextricably linked with a myriad other obstacles an individual may be facing. In other words, the interests of lawyers and social workers will—more often than not—converge.

Increasing interdisciplinary collaboration between lawyers and social workers could mean a gradual internalization of the values and skills of each other's profession into one's own, leading to a professional "reacculturation." It is not just in assisting one's client that interdisciplinary collaboration can be valuable, but also in expanding the understanding of an individual's and a profession's role in effecting change, not only on the client's behalf but for the community of which the client is a member. Much has been written about this in the context of "community lawyering," in which lawyers look beyond the immediate scope of their work and engage more holistically and effectively with the systemic issues their clients face, thereby becoming better advocates. (See, e.g., Tokarz et al. 2008.) Community lawyering will, by definition, require interdisciplinary collaboration, and interdisciplinary collaborations as described above may in turn evolve into community lawyering settings in some cases.

The examples set forth above provide an opportunity to examine some of the benefits and challenges presented by interdisciplinary collaboration between immigration lawyers and social workers, both from a theoretical and a practical perspective. It is important that social workers arm themselves with basic knowledge on immigration in order to understand the added complexities created by immigration status or lack thereof. In turn, the perspective of social workers, with their understanding of psychosocial theory and environmental impacts, should inform not only the work of individual lawyers but also the legal framework, and whenever feasible social workers and attorneys should work together in a variety of collaborative settings to more effectively address the multi-layered problems their clients face. In this chapter, we have set forth two potential models for varying levels of interdisciplinary collaboration between lawyers and social workers. Though increased and intense collaboration is generally positive and advantageous, one model of collaboration may be better suited than another to a particular situation or client. Therefore, it is important for lawyers and social workers to consider the goals of the collaboration, the potential obstacles that such collaboration is likely to pose, and the value added of working together in varying capacities.

NOTE

1 As an example, Rhode Island has a broad mandatory reporting law, mandating that "[a]ny person who has reasonable cause to know or suspect that any child has been abused or neglected . . . shall, within twenty-four (24) hours, transfer that information to the department of children, youth and families." R.I. Gen. Laws § 40-11-3. However, the attorney-client privilege is recognized as a ground for failure to report. R.I. Gen. Laws § 401-11-11.

REFERENCES

Aiken, Jane and Stephen Wizner. 2003. "Promoting Justice Through Interdisciplinary Teaching, Practice, and Scholarship: Law as Social Work." *Washington University Journal of Law and Policy* 11: 63–81.

American Bar Association (ABA). 2014. *Model Rules of Professional Conduct.* Chicago: American Bar Association Book Publishing.

Anderson, Alexis, Lynn Barenberg, and Paul R. Tremblay. 2007. "Professional Ethics in Interdisciplinary Collaboratives: Zeal, Paternalism and Mandated Reporting." *Clinical Law Review* 13: 659–718.

Applied Research Center (ARC). 2011. Shattered Families: The Perilous Intersection of Immigration Enforcement and the Child Welfare System. Accessed on October 21, 2014. Available at https://www.raceforward.org/research/reports/shattered-families.

Child Welfare Information Gateway. 2012. Mandatory Reporters of Child Abuse and Neglect. Accessed on September 26, 2014. Available at https://www.childwelfare.gov/systemwide/laws_policies/statutes/manda.pdf.

Cole, Portia L. 2012. "You Want Me to Do What?: Ethical Practice Within Interdisciplinary Collaborations." *Journal of Social Work Values and Ethics* 9(1): 26–39.

Congress, Elaine. 2007. "Ethical Practice in Forensic Social Work." In Albert R. Roberts and David W. Springer, eds., 75–86. *Social Work in Juvenile and Criminal Justice Settings*. Springfield, IL: Charles C. Thomas.

Conti, Stephanie. 2011. "Lawyers and Mental Health Professionals Working Together: Reconciling the Duties of Confidentiality and Mandatory Child Abuse Reporting." *Family Court Review* 49: 388–396.

Corbin, James R. 2007. "Confidentiality and the Duty to Warn: Ethical and Legal Implications for the Therapeutic Relationship." *The New Social Worker* 14(4). Retrieved May 13, 2015 from http://www.socialworker.com.

Faller, Kathleen Coulborn, and Frank E. Vandervort. 2007. "Interdisciplinary Clinical Teaching of Child Welfare Practice to Law and Social Work Students: When World Views Collide." *University of Michigan Journal of Law Reform* 41: 121–164.

Forgey, Mary Ann, and Lisa Colarossi. 2003. "Interdisciplinary Social Work and Law: A Model Domestic Violence Curriculum." *Journal of Social Work Education* 39(3): 459–476.

Gonzalez-Barrera, Ana, Mark H. Lopez, Jeffrey S. Passel, and Paul Taylor. 2013. *The Path Not Taken: Two-thirds of Legal Mexican Immigrants Are not U.S. Citizens*. Washington, DC: Pew Research Center. Accessed October 21, 2014. http://www.pewhispanic.org/2013/02/04/the-path-not-taken/.

Human Rights Watch (HRW). 2009. "Forced Apart (By the Numbers): Noncitizens Deported for Mostly Nonviolent Offenses." New York, NY: Author.

Inter-American Commission on Human Rights, Report No. 81/10. 2010. *Wayne Smith, Hugo Amerndariz, et al. v. United States* (July 12, 2010).

International Federation of Social Workers (IFSW). 1998. *Policy on Refugees*. Berne, Switzerland: IFSW.

International Federation of Social Workers (IFSW). 2012a. *Social Work: Statement of Ethical Principles*. Berne, Switzerland: IFSW.

International Federation of Social Workers (IFSW). 2012b. *Policy on Migrants*. Berne, Switzerland: IFSW.

Lau, Kenneth, Kathryn Krase, and Richard H. Morse. 2009. *Mandated Reporting of Child Abuse and Neglect: A Practical Guide for Social Workers*. New York: Springer.

McLeod, Peter and Carolyn I. Polowy. 2013. *National Association of Social Workers (NASW) Law Note Social Workers and Child Abuse Reporting, A Review of State Mandatory Reporting Requirements.* Washington, DC: NASW Press.

National Association of Social Workers (NASW). 2008a. *Code of Ethics.* Washington, DC: NASW Press.

National Association of Social Workers (NASW). 2008b. *Immigration Policy Toolkit.* Washington, DC: NASW Press.

National Association of Social Workers (NASW). 2011. *Impact of Immigration Detention on Children and Families.* Washington, DC: NASW Press.

Passel, Jeffrey S., and D'Vera Cohn. 2009. A Portrait of Unauthorized Immigrants in the United States. Washington, DC: Pew Research Center. Accessed October 21, 2014. http://www.pewhispanic.org/2009/04/14/a-portrait-of-unauthorized-immigrants-in-the-united-states/.

Pine, Barbara A., and Diane Drachman. 2004. "Effective Child Welfare Practice with Immigrant and Refugee Children and their Families." *Child Welfare* 84(5): 537–562.

Rabin, Nina. 2011. "Disappearing Parents: Immigration Enforcement and the Child Welfare System." *Connecticut Law Review* 44: 99–160.

Richmond, Mary. 1917. *Social Diagnosis.* New York: Russell Sage Foundation.

Saleeby, Dennis. 2012. *The Strengths Perspective in Social Work Practice*, 6th ed. New York: Pearson.

St. Joan, Jacqueline. 2001. "Building Bridges, Building Walls: Collaboration Between Lawyers and Social Workers in a Domestic Violence Clinic and Issues of Client Confidentiality." *Clinical Law Review* 7: 403–466.

Stein, Theodore J. 1991. *Child Welfare and the Law.* New York: Longman.

Taylor, Sarah. 2006. "Educating Future Practitioners of Social Work and Law: Exploring the Origins of Inter-Professional Misunderstanding." *Children and Youth Services Review* 28(6): 638–653.

Tencer Block, Mara, and Andrya Soprych. 2011. "Beyond Advocacy Alone: Incorporating Social Work into Legal Aid Practice." *Clearinghouse Review Journal of Poverty Law and Policy* Jan–Feb 2011: 465–470.

Thronson, David B. 2008. "Custody and Contradictions: Exploring Immigration Law as Federal Family Law in the Context of Child Custody." *Hastings Law Journal* 49: 453–513.

Tokarz, Karen, Nancy L. Cook, Susan Brooks, and Brenda Bratton Blom. 2008. "Conversations on 'Community Lawyering': The Newest (Oldest) Wave in Clinical Legal Education." *Washington University Journal of Law and Policy* 28: 359–402.

United States Department of Homeland Security (DHS). 2014. "2013 Yearbook of Immigration Statistics: Enforcement Actions." Table 39. Accessed May 13, 2015. http://www.dhs.gov/yearbook-immigration-statistics-2013-enforcement-actions.

CASE CITATION

Lopez v. Gonzales, 549 U.S. 47 (2006).

6

Immigrants Facing Detention and Deportation

Psychosocial and Mental Health Issues, Assessment, and Intervention for Individuals and Families

KALINA M. BRABECK, KATHERINE PORTERFIELD, AND MARYANNE LOUGHRY

This chapter will discuss psychosocial issues related to the impact of detention and deportation on migrants and their families. Specifically, the chapter: (1) describes some of the unique characteristics of migrant families; (2) reviews the impact of unauthorized status, detention, and deportation on migrants' mental health; and (3) outlines basic principles for mental health assessments and interventions with this population. The vignette presented in the introductory chapter of this book and the second vignette, summarized in the Chicco and Congress chapter, have been used to illustrate the issues raised.

The Constellations of Migrant Families: Transnational and Mixed Status

Many migrant families living in the United States challenge traditional Western conceptions of the "family unit." Many are transnational, that is, physically divided by borders and yet relationally attached through regular communication and financial interdependence between the migrated family member and the family back home (Orellana et al. 2001). Scholars (e.g., Schmalzbauer 2004) point out that families become transnational in the context of country conditions and events, such as poverty and war, which lead family members to migrate in search of economic betterment and physical safety. In many cases, as illustrated in the case of Felipe and Maria (see Chicco and Congress chapter, this volume, for details on the family), both parents migrate and leave children in the care of extended family members or friends who become "other mothers" (Moran-Taylor 2008). These migrant parents maintain communication with children in the country of origin (Abrego 2009). They remit money home to pay for children's care and to support extended family members (Orellana et al. 2001). While maintaining long-distance intimacy over time is challenging, and children "left behind" often report feeling abandoned (Suarez-Orozco, Bang, and Kim 2010), parents and children frequently maintain ties and many children recognize and appreciate parents' sacrifices that result in remittances (Hershberg and Lykes 2012). Transnational families' lives are complicated by U.S immigration policies that preclude family members from obtaining legal residency and diminish the possibility for family reunification (Menjivar and Abrego 2012).

Many migrant families are "mixed status," i.e., at least one family member is unauthorized, while others are authorized to reside in the United States (Capps and Fortuny 2006). Current estimates indicate that 82% of the children born to the United States's 11.7 unauthorized migrants are U.S.-born citizen children (Passel, Cohn, and Gonzalez-Barrera 2013). These numbers are likely underestimates because it is difficult to accurately count a population that is "living in the shadows" out of fear of deportation.[1] "Marie's" family demonstrates one such mixed legal status family structure: Her partner is a Legal Permanent Resident (LPR), she is unauthorized, their son is a U.S.-born citizen, and her son from a previous marriage is unauthorized.[2]

The mixed-status family confronts a heart-wrenching decision when faced with the deportation of an unauthorized parent: (1) The entire family may leave the United States., uprooting the individual from the familiar cultural, social, and linguistic environment, and often depriving access to healthcare, educational opportunities, and social service programs (Hagan, Rodriguez, and Castro 2011); (2) the unauthorized parent may leave, creating a single-parent family in the United States or leaving the child with other caregivers; or (3) the intact family may remain in the United States and face the chronic risk of being caught and deported (Dreby 2012; Zayas 2010). Following her husband's deportation, Marie, for example, struggles with whether to remove her daughter from her familiar environment, which provides medical treatment for her leukemia; leave Camila with LPR friends in the United States who are not members of her family or cultural/ethnic group; or continue to live with

Camila, separated from their father/husband, and with the constant anxiety of discovery. Chris's relatives must weigh whether reunion with his father is worth displacement to a country that the family fled as refugees. Like Felipe, reunification with U.S.-citizen children is a motivation for some deportees to reenter the United States (Brabeck, Lykes, and Hershberg 2011). These decisions are driven, not only by emotional/social ties and practical/financial considerations, but also by complex legal implications and constraints.

Migrant families are also characterized by remarkable resourcefulness. Research has demonstrated that first-generation migrants may actually experience better psychological health (Alegria et al. 2006), physical health (Morales et al. 2002), and educational outcomes (Garcia Coll and Marks 2009) than subsequent generations. Migrant families appear to benefit from protective extended family networks, lower substance abuse, strong spirituality, and better diet and exercise habits, when compared with U.S.-born members (American Psychological Association 2012). Many migrants learn to successfully navigate two cultures, two languages, and family obligations on both sides of the U.S. border. Although many work low-paying jobs, they manage their incomes so that they cover multiple costs in the United States as well as back home (Brabeck, Lykes, and Hershberg 2011). Such strengths are evident, despite the numerous challenges experienced, in the case vignettes: Felipe exhibits strong determination to care for his family and Arunny assumes the role of stable caretaker for her orphaned great-nephew, even after surviving the Khmer Rouge and migrating to the United States (see Introduction, this volume).

Challenges for Unauthorized Migrants and Their Mental Health Consequences

Unauthorized status. Living without authorization to reside and work in the United States has profound consequences for migrants' physical, emotional, and financial health. Specifically, although the majority of unauthorized adults (especially men) are employed, unauthorized families are typically low-income or poor, with 32% of adult parents and 51% of children in 2011 living below the federal poverty level (FPL) (Capps et al. 2013). Only 30% of unauthorized adults are English proficient, and the vast majority (71%) lack health insurance. Unauthorized migrant adults (compared to authorized) are more likely to experience economic hardship (Kalil and Chen 2008), occupational stress, social isolation (Yoshikawa 2011), decreased access to social service programs (Cleveland and Ihara 2013), psychological distress (Furman et al. 2013; Human Impact Partners 2013), and acculturative stress (Arbona et al. 2011). They are also less willing to report a crime (Hacker et al. 2011) and more likely to avoid public spaces and experience discrimination and racial profiling (Human Impact Partners 2013).

Research consistently finds that parental psychological and economic stress impacts parenting and child outcomes (Garcia, Manongdo, and Ozechoswki 2013; Lee, Wickrama, and Simons 2013). Thus, it is not surprising, given the multiple stressors unauthorized parents experience, that parent legal status is a predictor of multiple adverse outcomes for children, including emotional well-being, academic performance, and health status (American Psychological Association 2012; Brabeck and Xu 2010; Dreby 2012; Human Impact Partners 2013). Children of unauthorized migrants are more likely to report anxiety, fear, sadness, posttraumatic stress symptoms, anger, and withdrawal (Human Impact Partners 2013; Potochnick and Perreria 2010). Yoshikawa (2011) followed children of low-income mothers from birth to age six and found that the unauthorized parents experienced greater levels of occupational and psychological distress, lower social support, and lower access to center-based childcare, when compared to other groups of low-income mothers of color. For the children of unauthorized parents, delays were found in their cognitive development at 24 and 36 months. Other researchers have found that children of unauthorized parents are at greater risk for developmental delay (Ortega et al. 2009) and lower school readiness (Crosnoe 2006; Fuller et al. 2009). U.S. citizen children with two unauthorized parents or an unauthorized mother are estimated to have 1.18 fewer years of education (Bean et al. 2011). Children of unauthorized parents are also less likely to be medically insured (Capps et al. 2013; Ku and Jewers 2013), less likely to have seen a physician in the past year (Human Impact Partners 2013) and more likely to have poor eating, sleep, and exercise habits (Human Impact Partners 2013). Even when children are eligible for services, unauthorized parents may be reluctant to apply for public assistance or seek medical care for them (Ku and Jewers 2013).

Migrant children's identity formation and beliefs about themselves and their communities can be affected by experiences regarding their and their family members' status. Romero (2008) argues that immigration enforcements aimed at unauthorized parents put pressure on migrant youth to assimilate. Research has found that children in migrant families begin to associate all migrants with illegal status, and to associate being "illegal" with being a criminal (Dreby 2012). As a result, these youth may reject or carry negative attributions about their own migrant heritage. Moreover, children may conflate police with ICE officials, thereby growing up seeing the police as a threat and not a resource (Hacker et al. 2011). Lykes and colleagues (2013) identified strategies that migrant parents reported using to help their children with their understanding and management of identity issues around being a migrant. These parents described strategies to help children, ranging from educating them about their country of origin and the family's decision to migrate, to clarifying the important difference between being unauthorized and being a criminal (Lykes et al. 2013)

Migrants in detention. The nature of immigration detention, compounded by the uncertainty of its length, is regarded as a major contributing factor to mental deterioration, despondency, suicidality, anger, and frustration (Newman, Dudley, and Steel 2008). A systematic review of the mental health implications of detaining asylum seekers found that studies consistently supported an association between the experience of immigration detention practices and poor mental health (Robjant, Hassan, and Katona 2009). This population may have had a greater risk of mental health problems due to their reported histories of persecution and maltreatment in their home countries. Among more general migrant samples, Amnesty International (2009), the investigative branch of Department of Homeland Security (DHS) (2006), and Philips, Hagan, and Rodriguez (2006) found instances of mistreatment and neglect of detainees, e.g., inadequate healthcare, physical abuse, and lack of due process for reporting human rights violations.

Children who are detained experience psychological and physical difficulties, which appear to be related to the detention experience (Lorek et al. 2009). A report issued by the Center for Public Policy Priorities on workplace raids found that noncitizen children in deportation proceedings have experienced maltreatment by ICE officials, lack of access to

Child Protective Services and/or to a lawyer, lack of access to country of origin consulates, lengthy detentions, and removal to unsafe conditions (Benjet et al. 2009).

Consequences of deportation. When deported migrants are eventually released into the community, many are still found to have significantly elevated levels of anxiety and depression. They may face employment difficulties and feel demoralized (Barrios and Brotherton 2011). Research has also found that deportation is associated with more frequent drug use in deported individuals and less frequent utilization of medical or treatment services (Brouwer et al. 2009). For female deportees, deportation increases the risk for physical and sexual assaults, and involvement in prostitution (Robertson et al. 2012). In the case vignettes, Dith (see Introduction, this volume) demonstrates the stress of post-deportation adaptation. Not only has Dith had to struggle with integrating into a country and community with which he is no longer familiar, he is also isolated from key social supports and prevented from interacting in significant family events, all factors known to erode an individual's well-being. On the other hand, some research has found that deportees report feeling positively toward and "at home" in their communities of origin (McMillan 2011).

Impact of detention and deportation for families and communities. Not only is there detrimental impact on the mental health of the migrant individuals as they either anticipate or experience detention or deportation, there is also a negative impact on family members and the family environment of those either left behind or in fear of being left behind. Maria and Camila exemplify this: Felipe has been detained and deported. In the meantime Maria remains increasingly anxious that she will be deported and is considering how best to address Camila's pressing needs (see Chicco and Congress, this volume)..

Detained migrants who have children face additional stressors, as they must manage the custodial and daily needs of their children, often with no preparation or forewarning (Androff et al. 2011). Sometimes detained individuals are transferred to a facility far from their family members (McLeigh 2010). A study following workplace raids in three communities found that approximately 500 children were left in the care of others with little to no information on the whereabouts or conditions of the children's parents (Capps et al. 2007). This type of sudden "disappearance" of a family member can be particularly traumatic for migrants who experienced state-sponsored kidnapping and murders in their countries of origin (Brabeck, Lykes, and Hershberg 2011). Compounding the lack of information and resources available to these families, many parents are reluctant to disclose that they have children when they are detained, for fear that the children will be permanently removed from their custody (Capps et al. 2007).

Deportations involve multiple potential traumas for children, who may witness the forcible removal of the parent, and be thrust into the subsequent changes in their family constellations and environments (Dreby 2012; McLeigh 2010). When a child is placed in the child welfare system, reunifications are complicated by legal status, increasing the likelihood that the child will remain in the system (Wessler 2011). From the attachment perspective (Bowlby 1969), a child's sense of security is rooted in relationships with familiar caregivers; this secure base is a necessary foundation for developing social, cognitive, and emotional regulation skills that are fundamental throughout life. The physical separation of parent and child, particularly when unexpected, as in the case of deportation, can disrupt this essential secure base, thereby increasing the risk of internalizing symptoms (depression, anxiety), externalizing behaviors (withdrawal, aggression), and social and cognitive difficulties (Makariev and Shaver 2010).

In a study of the short- and long-term impact of worksite raids on three communities where a total of 500 children, mostly U.S.-born citizens, temporarily or permanently lost parents, the most common short-term effects to children's psychological well-being following a parent's arrest included disruptions in eating and sleeping (Capps et al. 2007; Chaudry et al. 2010). Additionally, children were reported to demonstrate crying and feeling afraid. Additional symptoms reported included anxiety, withdrawal, anger/aggression, clinginess, developmental difficulties (e.g., speech delay), and behavioral and academic decline at school. These negative outcomes were more prevalent among children whose household structure and primary caregiving relationships changed after a parent's arrest (Chaudry et al. 2010). These social/emotional/behavioral presentations are reflected in the reactions of Camila and Chris, who live under the threat of, or in the immediate aftermath of, a parent's deportation.

Dreby (2012) notes that, unlike separations involved in voluntary migration decisions, which may hold the promise of economic benefits in spite of social/emotional costs, forced separations due to deportation incur social/emotional costs without the accompanying economic benefits. Families experience difficulties paying bills, increasing debts, housing instability, food insecurity, inability to send remittance money, and apprehension about applying for public assistance (Chaudry et al. 2010; Dreby 2012). Dreby (2012) draws on a model from public health, the injury pyramid, to illustrate how the worst cases can sometimes obscure the less severe but much more numerous incidents. Drawing on her interviews with 80 immigrant households, Dreby (2012) provides evidence that while the most obvious and detrimental effects of deportation occur at the level of the individual and her family, there are numerous other, less severe and yet much more prevalent impacts on the broader community. Such impacts include decreased trust of law enforcement, declining participation in community and school events, diminished use of social service programs, and a generalized environment of hypervigilance, silence, and fear. Thus, while smaller numbers of individuals are directly impacted and suffer the worst consequences of deportation, the entire community suffers adverse effects (Dreby 2012). Importantly, this fear extends beyond the unauthorized population, to include authorized Latino immigrants who still fear deportation, experience discrimination, and as a result feel less optimistic about the future for their children and more mistrusting of their government (Becerra et al. 2013). Additionally, the psychological and financial sequelae of detention and deportation extend to family members living in the country of origin, who also experience the sudden panic of losing contact with their family member, and often go for weeks or months with no information regarding loved ones' whereabouts (Brabeck et al. 2011).

Trauma Exposure before, during, and after Migration and Deportation

Many migrants, including those who are not formally afforded refugee status by the U.S. government, migrate because of war, state-sponsored violence, trauma, and related poverty in their countries of origin (Brabeck et al. 2011). Migration journeys can be highly dangerous and frightening, involving inhumane conditions of travel and border crossings, as well as threats and actual victimization by smugglers (Pumariega and Roth 2010). Recovery from experiences of trauma, human rights violations, and displacement takes place within an ongoing process of adaptation to the new environment and its demands, cultural norms, and values (Silove and Steel 2006). Individuals who have suffered trauma can usually stabilize only once they are afforded a safe and secure environment in which to recover. For some, this adaptation process is compromised by ongoing experiences of stress, trauma, and insecurity in resettlement countries. The pervasive threat of uncertainty and the knowledge that neighbors and co-workers have been detained are additional burdens as individuals strive to adapt. The threat that government agents might "take away" family members is expounded when considered against the backdrop of historical disappearances and state-sponsored kidnappings (Brabeck et al. 2011).

Other potentially traumatic stressors some migrant families experience include discrimination, xenophobia, and racism, and, in some cases, community and domestic violence. Many unauthorized migrants live within conditions of severe poverty, including lack of access to healthcare and social services and inadequate housing in unsafe communities (Dettlaff and Rycraft 2010). These daily stressors exacerbate past trauma, and have been found to partially mediate the impact of prior trauma on mental health and the development of mental illness (Miller and Rasmussen 2009). Compounding their lack of security, unauthorized migrants may be hesitant to call upon police, for fear of being deported or due to fears about abusive authorities stemming from country of origin traumas. Additionally, unauthorized migrants may be wary of seeking help from physical and mental health services, compounding the emotional distress and isolation that they endure (Sullivan and Rehm 2005). In the absence of safe communities and viable educational and economic opportunities, and in the context of previous losses and traumas, some youth, like Dith, may become involved in gangs, drugs, and crime (see Introduction, this volume).

Mental Health Issues for Migrants Facing Detention and Deportation

Not all persons subjected to stressful and even traumatic events go on to develop psychiatric symptoms and disorders. Most people, in fact, demonstrate resilience in the face of aversive events (Bonnano 2004). Researchers have identified protective factors, such as social support at home and school, parental closeness, and the absence of parent-child conflict, which can ameliorate the risk of emotional disturbance for unauthorized migrants (Perreira and Ornelas 2011; Potochnick and Perreira 2010). In spite of the traumatic experiences described in the case vignettes, we see individuals forming new and meaningful relationships, parenting, working in demanding jobs, and providing emotional support to family members. These adaptive activities take place in a context of the constant threat of detention and deportation. While the strengths of migrant individuals and families abound, this section reviews potential psychological difficulties.

Research on the psychological functioning of unauthorized migrants has predominantly used Western constructs of disorder and well-being to assess and describe their mental health and adaptation (Rasmussen et al. 2007). Posttraumatic Stress Disorder (PTSD) is one of the most widely studied and documented diagnoses examined in studies of migrant mental health (Jaycox et al. 2002; Rasmussen et al. 2007). PTSD is a condition that may develop following an individual's exposure to life-threatening events, either directly or indirectly. Characterized by disruptions in an individual's arousal and memory functioning, PTSD symptoms include intrusive re-experiencing of the traumatic event(s), negative alterations in thoughts and mood, alterations in arousal and reactivity, and avoidance of reminders of the trauma (American Psychiatric Association 2013). PTSD may be more practically understood as an expression of the human reaction to feelings of terror and horror. Rasmussen et al. (2007) report prevalence rates of PTSD of 11% in the unauthorized migrants assessed. Jaycox et al. (2002) found a PTSD prevalence rate of 32% among poor Latino migrant youth. While these rates are high, they also reveal resilience, given that a majority do not meet the clinical criteria for a diagnosis. PTSD rates climb to 50% in detained asylum seekers (PHR and Bellevue/NYU 2003). Studies have found that 50% (Steele et al. 2004) and up to 100% (Mares and Jureidini 2004) of children in detention centers met criteria for PTSD.

Depression has also been examined as a clinical condition in unauthorized immigrants. Depression is characterized by pervasive sadness, sleep and appetite disturbance, low energy, irritability, and in some cases suicidality. Rates of depression in migrant adult populations are highly variable, with studies finding prevalence rates ranging from 10% (Ethiopian refugees; Fenta, Hyman, and Noh 2004), 12% (Latina immigrants; Miranda et al. 2005), 38% (Mexican immigrants; Hovey and Magana 2000), and 40% (Asian immigrants; Mui and Kang 2006). Detained asylum seekers have been found to manifest rates of depression up to 86% (PHR and Bellevue/NYU 2003) and 95% (Steele et al. 2004). Being separated from one's children increases the risk of depression (Miranda et al. 2005). Moving beyond diagnostic categories, depression may be more meaningfully conceptualized as a manifestation of and reaction to pervasive and overwhelming experiences of loss and powerlessness. The experience of grief and mourning may be more relevant than a mental health diagnosis to an immigrant family. For Dith, multiple losses shape his experience of migration and resettlement, including the death of his parents in Cambodia through state-sponsored violence, his experience of deportation back to Cambodia, and the death of his wife in the United States. Dith's son, Chris, manifests the stress of his family's multiple losses, in his disturbed sleep, defiant behaviors, and low mood.

While PTSD, depression, and other DSM-V diagnoses are frequently used in the assessment and treatment of immigrants presenting for mental health care, there are limitations to their descriptive and clinical usefulness. As the Western mental health field has expanded its focus to international populations, there has been a call to identify and explore cultural variations in conceptions and manifestations of well-being and distress in underrepresented ethno-cultural populations (Betancourt and Williams 2008; American Psychological Association 2010). For example, exploration of what is "normal" and "abnormal" in a cultural community may help uncover how community members appear to be functioning in the face of migration stressors, acculturation, and threat of deportation or detention. Betancourt et al. (2009) argue for qualitative exploration of communities' concepts of healthy or distressed functioning, rather than reliance on Western symptoms and syndromes as descriptors of functioning (Betancourt et al. 2009).

Mental Health Assessment and Intervention

Clinical assessment. Assessment of individuals facing detention and deportation should be thorough, focusing on the individual's life history pre- and post-migration, including stressors, social support and positive resources, past coping strategies, cultural values and priorities, as well as the current functioning and primary concerns (Bemak, Chung, and Pedersen 2003; Chicco and Congress, this volume). If a mental health diagnosis is relevant, practitioners are encouraged to utilize a culturally competent approach in which symptoms and their explanations are understood within the client's cultural context, as well as within standard diagnostic categories such as those found in the DSM-V (Michultka 2009; American Psychiatric Association 2013). Failure to consider sociocultural context may result in "clinician bias," which can include a tendency to emphasize Western models of illness, to pathologize, and to underestimate strengths and culturally salient coping strategies (American Psychological Association 2012). Standardized assessment measures must be used cautiously given that there is a lack of standardized translations of assessment instruments and a lack of appropriate normative studies of the reliability of test scores with different immigrant groups (Park-Taylor, Ventura, and Ng 2010).

Mental health services. Referral for mental health services should be framed in normalizing, goal-focused ways. Mental health interventions that are culturally competent, strengths-focused, and community-based are more likely to be successful (Dettlaff and Rycraft 2010; APA 2010). Providing services in community-based settings, such as schools or community centers, may alleviate some barriers to seeking treatment (Adleman and Taylor 1999; American Psychological Association 2012) and connect the family with additional resources (Xu and Brabeck 2012).

Developing a relationship. The development of a strong therapeutic alliance between practitioner and client is essential for any therapeutic success (Castonguay, Constantino, and Holtforth 2006). Establishing a strong relationship may be particularly challenging and especially important in working with immigrant families facing detention and deportation, due to the multiple power differentials between practitioner and client and the generalized fear that may be transferred onto the clinician (Michultka 2009). As noted, immigrant families, including those impacted by detention and deportation, demonstrate considerable strength and resilience in the face of the multiple obstacles and challenges described above. Maintaining a resiliency perspective is crucial in identifying strengths that can be built upon in therapeutic work, countering xenophobic and racist attitudes, and building a therapeutic relationship (American Psychological Association 2012).

Collaborative goal-setting. To build trust and establish credibility, mental health interventions cannot be delivered in isolation of the reality of the client's current life situation. Thus it is recommended that clinical interventions with this population involve a shared process of setting clinical goals. The immigrant client's very real concerns about immigration status, safe housing, employment, child care, medical care, and transportation may overshadow their feeling that they need to address psychological trauma or emotional distress (Michultka 2009; Miller and Rasumussen 2009). Similarly, the practical considerations a family must deal with in the aftermath of a family member's detention or deportation, e.g., knowledge of the family member's whereabouts, referral to legal services, coordination with social services, and needs for interpretation services, are essential to the family members' emotional well-being and thus should be part of the pragmatic process of setting goals that will decrease stress. This also suggests the importance of mental health professionals working on these goals in interdisciplinary ways with advocates, lawyers, case managers, and other professionals.

Treatment of mental health symptoms. As previous described, immigrants and refugees are at an increased risk for mental health problems, notably anxiety, post-traumatic stress, and depression, as a result of the stresses of migration, acculturation, and trauma (Birman and Chan 2008; Kataoka et al. 2003). These stressors can be exacerbated by unauthorized status and the detention or deportation of a family member (Brabeck et al. 2011). The American Psychological Association (2010; 2012) recommends utilizing evidence-based approaches to decrease symptoms, while integrating "practice-based evidence" that has emerged from practitioners on the "front lines" of working with refugee families.

Such practice-based evidence includes adaptations made to treatment protocols by adding culturally relevant components to the treatment. For example, practitioners are advised to explore culturally syntonic systems of help and healing for immigrant clients, such as community ceremonies, storytelling, and indigenous healing practices, as additions to Western treatment methods (Michultka 2009).

Researchers have found that evidenced-based treatments for depression, anxiety, and PTSD, e.g., cognitive behavioral therapy (CBT) that includes *in vivo* and imaginal exposure, can be effective in treating these symptoms in immigrants and refugees (Kataoka et al. 2003). Narrative Exposure Therapy (NET), a treatment in which an individual tells his life story to a trained clinician who documents it and shares it with the client, has been shown to be particularly effective in decreasing PTSD in adult and child refugees and survivors of war trauma (Neuner et al. 2004; Schauer, Neuner, and Elbert 2005). For chronic trauma survivors, developing skills (e.g., in emotional regulation, interpersonal effectiveness, self-soothing) may be a necessary precursor to focused trauma work (Cloitre et al. 2010). Issues of trust, safety, and appropriate boundaries are important antecedents to integrating traumatic memories and desensitization of the intense negative affect associated with these memories (Luxenberg et al. 2001). Assessment of the relationships between past and present trauma is important in working with immigrants facing detention and deportation.

Clinical work with children and families. Children affected by detention and deportation may respond to clinical techniques that are creative or expressive in nature, such as storytelling, movement therapy, or art therapies. Creative expression techniques have been demonstrated to be effective in helping children in immigrant families construct meaning and identity (Elbedour, Bastien, and Center 1997) and in assisting children work through losses, process trauma, and establish social ties (Rousseau et al. 2005). Additionally, solution-focused group therapy (i.e., a strengths-based approach that encourages clients to develop future-oriented, positively worded goals) has also been demonstrated to be effective in helping Latino children of incarcerated parents; this may have implications for children whose parents have been detained (Springer, Lynch, and Rubin 2000). Work with children should incorporate developmental theory and foster children's innate resiliency; the

Immigrant Children's Affirmative Network (ICAN), a program for unaccompanied migrant youth, is an example of one such approach (see http://www.education.miami.edu/ppsc/ICAN.htm).

Family therapy techniques. Family therapy interventions can assist migrant families who face detention and deportation by enhancing healthy communication and information-sharing between family members. Although they live with daily fear and stress related to their status and fears of deportation, many migrant parents do not directly communicate with their children about immigration status and policies and the possibility of detention and deportation (Lykes et al. 2013). Lykes and colleagues (2013) point out that while direct communication among family members may serve practical purposes, the avoidance of such conversations may serve psychological functions, i.e., (temporarily) protecting family members from directly acknowledging, and thereby having to confront, the vulnerability and possibility of family separation. Mental health practitioners may help caregivers process *what makes it difficult* to engage in these conversations and make plans, which may be a necessary precursor to encouraging direct parent-child communication (ibid.). Mental health practitioners may further facilitate the transfer of knowledge among family members, e.g., help parents confront the reality that children often understand much more than parents presumed; create a safe space for processing feelings and thoughts related to status and its implications; and assist families to develop a concrete plan for who will care for a child in case of a caregiver's deportation.

Goals and techniques used in grief counseling, including Trauma-focused CBT for Traumatic Grief (Cohen, Mannarino, and Deblinbger 2006), may assist family members in coping with the losses associated with deportation and detention. Grief counseling aims to help individuals confront the reality of the loss, cope with emotional pain (anger, guilt, anxiety, helplessness, and sadness), and find ways to maintain a bond with the absent member (Worden 2008).

Mental Health Workers in Forensic Contexts

Mental health professionals may also interface with migrant populations facing detention and deportation in forensic contexts, e.g., asylum proceedings; U-visa applicants; Violence Against Women Act (VAWA) applicants; unaccompanied migrant minors; or U.S.-citizen family members seeking a cancellation of removal. In addition to evaluating and testifying, the mental health professional may act as consultant to the legal team regarding mental health issues that potentially impact the client and the legal team (*see* Chicco and Congress, this volume).

Mental health professionals may help the legal team and the court understand how trauma can impact memory and result in inconsistent testimonies. As Meffert and colleagues (2010) note, the hallmarks of credibility in the legal system don't take into consideration the ways in which trauma disrupts the ability to provide "believable" testimony; for example, the absence of a "normal" emotional response (e.g., crying) while discussing painful events may be evidence of the dissociative aspect of trauma. Similarly, as suggested by the dual-representation model (Brewin 2007), while involuntary memories of trauma (e.g., flashbacks, intrusive thoughts) may appear spontaneously, verbally accessible and voluntary memories of the event are much harder to retrieve; thus, trauma may impact an individual's ability to consistently and accurately recall the detail of the trauma (Herlihy, Scragg, and Turner 2002). The mental health professional might explain to judges and lawyers the nature of traumatic memory: fragmented, difficult to chronologically arrange, and sometimes entirely suppressed (Meffert et al. 2010). Mental health professionals might assist legal professionals in understanding how avoidance trauma symptoms may account for individuals missing the one-year deadline for asylum application. Finally, mental health professionals may be useful in explaining the role that culture plays in emotional expression and norms of mental health and pathology (Meffert et al. 2010).

Mental health professionals can also teach lawyers who work with immigrants different strategies for maintaining safety while interviewing the client, for example, by emotionally preparing the client; checking in periodically about the client's emotional welfare; rallying social, spiritual, and other community supports; and knowing and identifying early warning signs of emotional distress (Meffert et al. 2010). They can similarly aid lawyers who may experience vicarious victimization that can lead to burnout and deteriorating mental health (Levin and Greisberg 2003).

Conclusion

Frequently absent from the debates about the role of migrants in the United States's past and present are the lived realities of migrants themselves. This chapter offers a perspective on how social, cultural, and political forces affect the psychological lives of individuals and families. A mounting research confirms both the detrimental impact of immigration policies and practices on migrants' psychosocial well-being, and the creative, adaptive, and resourceful ways in which migrants survive and thrive in the context of these forces. This chapter further summarizes ideas for mental health professionals who are increasingly seeing in their clinics, schools, hospitals, and practices how legal vulnerability, detention, and deportation impact individuals and families. It is imperative for mental health professionals to understand how systemic forces shape individual lives and to acknowledge the limits of individually based solutions for socially rooted problems. It is equally necessary for those involved in the development of systemic policies, programs, and social movements to consider the individual unit of analysis and to reflect on how broad policies and programs play out within unique families, households, and psyches.

NOTE

1 Research with unauthorized, detained, and deported immigrants is complicated by the understandable mistrust and secrecy that many employ for protection. Some researchers (e.g., Brabeck and Xu 2010; Perreira and Ornelas 2011) have asked forthrightly about immigrant status; responses are likely underestimates due to fear of disclosure. Other researchers (e.g., Yoshikawa 2011) avoid the issue, and instead use a proxy for legal status (e.g., lack of driver's license, financial credit, checking account) in their estimates. Demographers (e.g., Passel, Cohn, and Gonzalez-Barrera 2013) draw on large data sets from the Current Population Survey and use the "residual method": subtracting a demographic estimate of the legal foreign-born population from the total foreign-born population; the "residual" is assumed to be unauthorized.
2 *See* Case Study/Vignette #1, available at http://www.bc.edu/centers/humanrights/book

REFERENCES

Abrego, Leisy. 2009. "Economic well-being in Salvadoran transnational families: How gender affects remittance practices." *Journal of Marriage and Family* 71:1070–1085.

Adleman, Howard S., and Linda Taylor. 1999. "Mental health in schools and system restructuring." *Clinical Psychology Review* 19:137–163.

Alegría, Margarita, Glorisa Canino, Frederick S. Stinson, and Bridget F. Grant. 2006. "Nativity and DSM-IV psychiatric disorders among Puerto Ricans, Cuban Americans, and non-Latino Whites in the United States: Results from the national epidemiologic survey on alcohol and related conditions." *Journal of Clinical Psychiatry* 67:56–65.

American Psychiatric Association. 2013. *Diagnostic Statistical Manual– Fifth Edition*. Washington, DC: Author.

American Psychological Association. 2010. *Resilience of Refugee Children After War*. Washington, DC: Author.

American Psychological Association, Presidential Task Force on Immigration. 2012. *Crossroads: The Psychology of Immigration in the New Century*. Accessed May 10, 2014. http://www.apa.org/topics/immigration/report.aspx.

Amnesty International, USA. 2009. *Jailed Without Justice: Immigration Detention in the USA*. Washington, DC: Amnesty International USA. Accessed May 10, 2014. http://www.amnestyusa.org/pdfs/JailedWithoutJustice.pdf.

Androff, David K., Cecilia Ayon, David Becerra, Maria Gurrola, Lorraine Salas, Judy Krysik, Karen Gerdes, and Elizabeth Segal. 2011. "U.S. immigration policy and immigrant children's well-being: The impact of policy shifts." *Journal of Sociology and Social Welfare* 38 (1):77–98. Accessed October 19, 2014. http://www.law.asu.edu/Portals/25/Files/Facutly%20Scholarship/Androff_US%20immigration%20and%20children.pdf.

Arbona, Consuelo, Norma Olvera, Nestor Rodriguez, Jacqueline Hagan, Adriana Linares, and Margit Wisener. 2011. "Acculturative stress among documented and unauthorized Latino immigrants in the United States." *Hispanic Journal of Behavioral Sciences* 32:362–384.

Barrios, Luis, and David C. Brotherton. 2011. *Banished to the Homeland: Dominican Deportees and Their Stories of Exile*. New York: Columbia University Press.

Bean, Frank D., Mark A. Leach, Susan K. Brown, James D. Bachmeier, and John R. Hipp. 2011. "The educational legacy of unauthorized migration: Comparisons across US-immigrant groups in how parents' status affects their offspring." *International Migration Review* 45(2):348–385.

Becerra, David, David Androff, Andrew Cimino, M. Alex Wagman, and Kelly Blanchard. 2013. "The impact of perceived discrimination and immigration policies upon perceptions of quality of life among Latinos in the United States." *Race and Social Problems* 5:65–78. doi:10.1007/s12552-012-9084-4.

Bemak, Fred, Rita C. Chung, and Paul B. Pedersen. 2003. *Counseling Refugees: A Psychosocial Approach to Innovative Multicultural Interventions*. Westport, CT: Greenwood Press.

Benjet, Corina, Guilherme Borges, Maria Elena Medina-Mora, Joaquin Zambrano, and Sergio Aguilar-Gaxiola. 2009. "Youth mental health in a populous city of the developing world: Results from the Mexican Adolescent Mental Health Survey." *Journal of Child Psychology and Psychiatry* 50(4):386–395. doi: 10.1111/j.1469-7610.2008.01962.x.

Betancourt, Theresa Stichick, Liesbeth Speelman, Grace Onyango, and Paul Bolton. 2009. "A qualitative study of mental health problems among children displaced by war in Northern Uganda." *Transcultural Psychiatry* 46:238–256.

Betancourt, Theresa Stichick, and Timothy Williams. 2008. "Building an evidence base on mental health interventions for children affected by armed conflict." *International Journal of Mental Health* 6:39–56.

Birman, Dina, and Wing Yi Chan. 2008. *Screening and Assessing Immigrant and Refugee Youth in School-based Mental Health Programs*. Center for Health and Health Care in Schools. Accessed May 10, 2014. http://www.healthinschools.org/~/media/Images/IssueBrief1.ashx.

Bonnano, George A. 2004. "Loss, trauma, and human resilience: Have we underestimated the human capacity to thrive after extremely aversive events?" *American Psychologist* 59:20–28.

Bowlby, John. 1969. *Attachment and Loss: Vol. 1. Loss*. New York: Basic Books.

Brabeck, Kalina M., M. Brinton Lykes, and Rachel Hershberg. 2011. "Framing immigration to and deportation from the United States: Central American immigrants make meaning of their experiences." *Community, Work & Family*: 275–296. doi.org/10.1080/13668803.2010.520840.

Brabeck, Kalina M., and Qingwen Xu. 2010. "The impact of detention and deportation on Latino immigrant children and families: A quantitative exploration." *Hispanic Journal of Behavioural Sciences* 32:341–361. doi: 10.1177/0739986310374053.

Brewin, Chris R. 2007. "Autobiographical memory for trauma: Update on four controversies." *Memory* 15:227–248.

Brouwer, Kimberly C., Remedios Lozada, Wayne A. Cornelius, Michelle F. Cruz, Carlos Magis-Rodriguez, Maria L. Zuniga de Nuncio, and Steffanie A. Strathdee. 2009. "Deportation along the U.S.-Mexico border: Its relation to drug use patterns and accessing care." *Journal of Immigrant Minority Health* 11:1–6. doi: 0.1007/s10903-008-9119-5.

Capps, Randy, James Bachmeier, Michael Fix, and Jennifer VanHook. 2013. *A Demographic, Socioeconomic, and Health Coverage Profile of Unauthorized Immigrants in the United States*. Washington, DC: Migration Policy Institute. Accessed May 10, 2014. http://www.migrationpolicy.org/research/demographic-socioeconomic-and-health-coverage-profile-unauthorized-immigrants-united-states.

Capps, Randy, Rosa Marie Castaneda, Ajay Chaudry, and Robert Santos. 2007. *Paying the Price: The Impact of Immigration Raids on America's Children*. Washington, DC: Urban Institute. Accessed October 19, 2014. http://www.urban.org/uploaded-PDF/411566_immigration_raids.pdf.

Capps, Randy, and Karina Fortuny. 2006. *Immigration and Child and Family Policy*. Washington, DC: Urban Institute. Accessed October 19, 2014. http://www.urban.org/publications/311362.html.

Castonguay, Louis G., Michael J. Constantino, and Martin Grosse Holtforth. 2006. "The working alliance: Where are we and where should we go?" *Psychotherapy: Theory, Research, Practice, Training* 3:271–279.

Chaudry, Ajay, Randy Capps, Juan Pedroza, Rosa Marie Castaneda, Robert Santos, and Molly M. Scott. 2010. *Facing Our Future: Children in the Aftermath of Immigration Enforcement*. Washington, DC: Urban Institute. Accessed October 19, 2014. http://www.urban.org/publications/412020.html.

Cleveland, Carol, and Emily S. Ihara. 2013. "'They treat us like pests': Undocumented immigrant experiences obtaining health care in the wake of a 'crackdown' ordinance." *Journal of Human Behavior in the Social Environment* 22(7):771–788. doi: 10.1080/10911359.2012.704781.

Cloitre, Marylene, Chase Stovall-McClough, Kate Nooner, Patty Zorbas, Stephanie Cherry, Christine L. Jackson, Weijin Gan, and Eva Petkova. 2010. "Treatment for PTSD related to childhood abuse: A randomized control trial." *American Journal of Psychiatry* 167:915–924.

Cohen, Judith, Anthony P. Mannarino, and Esther Deblinbger. 2006. *Treating Trauma and Traumatic Grief in Children and Adolescents*. New York: Guilford Press.

Crosnoe, Robert. 2006. *Mexican Roots, American Schools: Helping Mexican Immigrant Children Succeed*. Palo Alto, CA: Stanford University Press.

Dettlaff, Alan J., and Joan R. Rycraft. 2010. "Adapting systems of care for child welfare practice with immigrant Latino children and families." *Evaluation and Program Planning* 33:303–310. doi:10.1016/j.evalprogplan.2009.07.003.

Dreby, Joanna. 2012. "The burden of deportation on children in Mexican immigrant families." *Journal of Marriage and Family* 74:829–845. doi: 10.1111/j.1741-3737.2012.00989.x.

Elbedour, Salman, David T. Bastien, and Bruce A. Center. 1997. "Identity formation in the shadow of conflict: Projective drawings by Palestinian and Israeli Arab children from the West Bank and Gaza." *Journal of Peace Research* 34:217–231. doi: 10.1177/0022343397034002007.

Fenta, Haile Ilene Hyman, and Samuel Noh. 2004. "Determinants of depression among Ethiopian refugees in Toronto." *Journal of Nervous & Mental Disease* 192:363–372. doi: 10.1097/01.nmd.0000126729.08179.07.

Fuller, Bruce, Margaret Bridges, Edward Bein, Heeju Jang, Sunyoung Jung, Sophia Rabe-Hesketh, Neal Halfon, and Alice Kuo. 2009. "The health and cognitive growth of Latino toddlers: At risk or immigrant paradox?" *Maternal and Child Health Journal* 13:755–768. Accessed October 14, 2014. http://www.ncbi.nlm.nih.gov/pmc/articles/PMC2759448/.

Furman, Rich, Alissa R. Ackerman, Derek Iwamoto, Nalini Negi, and Gladys Mondragon. 2013. "Undocumented Latino immigrant men at risk." *Social Developmental Issues* 35(1)1–12. doi: 10.1177/0020872812450729.

Garcia Coll, Cynthia T., and Amy K. Marks. 2009. *Immigrant Stories: Ethnicity and Academics in Middle Childhood*. New York: Oxford University Press.

Garcia, Jorge I. Ramirez, Jennifer A. Manongdo, and Timothy J. Ozechoswki. 2013. "Depression symptoms among Mexican American youth: Parental parenting in the context of maternal parenting, economic stress, and youth gender." *Cultural Diversity and Ethnic Minority Psychology* 20(1):27–36. doi: 10.1037/a0033350.

Hacker, Karen, Jocelyn Chu, Carolyn Leung, Robert Marra, Alex Pirie, Mohamed Brahimi, Margaret English, Joshua Beckmann, Dolores Acevedo-Garcia, and Robert P. Marlin. 2011. "The impact of immigration and customs enforcement on immigrant health: Perceptions of immigrants in Everett, Massachusetts, USA." *Social Science Medicine* 73(4):586–594. doi: 10.1016/j.socscimed.2011.06.007.

Hagan, Jacqueline, Nestor Rodriguez, and Brianna Castro. 2011. "The social effects of mass deportations by the United States government 2000–10." *Ethnic and Racial Studies* 34(8):1374–1391. Accessed May 10, 2014. http://www.actionresearch.illinois.edu/courses/FAA391_Spring12/Hagan_2011.pdf.

Herlihy, Jane, Peter Scragg, and Stuart Turner. 2002. "Discrepancies in autobiographical memories: Implications for asylum-seekers—Repeated interviews study." *British Medical Journal* 324:324–327.

Hershberg, Rachel, and M. Brinton Lykes. 2012. "Redefining family: Transnational girls narrate experiences of parental migration, detention, and deportation." *FQS: Forum Qualitative Sozialforschung/Forum: Qualitative Research* 14(1). http://nbn-resolving.de/urn:nbn:de:0114-fqs130157.

Hovey, Joseph D., and Christina Magana. 2000. "Acculturative stress, anxiety, and depression among Mexican immigrant farmworkers in the Midwestern United States." *Journal of Immigrant Health* 2:119–131. doi: 10.1023/A:1009556802759.

Human Impact Partners. 2013. *Family Unity, Family Health: How Family-focused Immigration Reform Will Mean Better Health for Children and Families.* Oakland, CA: Author. Accessed May 10, 2014. http://www.familyunityfamilyhealth.org/uploads/images/FamilyUnityFamilyHealth.pdf.

Jaycox, Lisa H., Bradley D. Stein, Sheryl Kataoka, Marleen Wong, Arlene Fink, Pia Escudera, and Catalina Zaragoza. 2002. "Violence exposure, PTSD, and depressive symptoms among recent immigrant school children." *Journal of the American Academy of Child and Adolescent Psychiatry* 31:1104–1110. http://dx.doi.org/10.1097/00004583-200209000-00011.

Kalil, Ariel, and Jen-Hao Chen. 2008. "Mothers' citizenship status and household food insecurity among low-income children of immigrants." *New Directions in Child and Adolescent Research* 121:43–62.

Kataoka, Sheryl H., Bradley D. Stein, Lisa H. Jaycox, Marleen Wong, Pia Escudera, Wenli Tu, Catalina Zaragoza, and Arlene Fink. 2003. "A school-based mental health program for traumatized Latino immigrant children." *Journal of American Academy of Child & Adolescent Psychiatry* 42:311–318. doi: 10.1097/01.CHI.0000037038.04952.8E.

Ku, Leighton, and Mariellen Jewers. 2013. *Health Care for Immigrant Families.* Washington, DC: Migration Policy Institute. Accessed May 10, 2014. http://www.migrationpolicy.org/pubs/COI-HealthCare.pdf.

Lee, Tae Kyoung, Kandauda A. S. Wickrama, and Leslie G. Simons. 2013. "Chronic Family Economic Hardship, Family Processes and Progression of Mental and Physical Health Symptoms in Adolescence." *Journal of Youth Adolescence* 42:821–836. doi: 10.1007/s10964-012-9808-1.

Levin, Andrew, and Scott Greisberg. 2003. "Vicarious trauma in attorneys." *Pace Law Review* 24. Accessed May 10, 2014. http://digitalcommons.pace.edu/cgi/viewcontent.cgi?article=1189&context=plr&sei-redir=1#search=%22Levin,+A.+&+G reisberg,+S.+%282003%29.+Vicarious+trauma+in+attorneys.+Pace+Law+Rev iew,+24,%22.

Lorek, Ann, Kimberly Ehntholtc, Anne Nesbitt, Emmanuel Wey, Chipo Githinji, Eve Rossor, and Rush Wickramasinghe. 2009. "The mental health and physical health difficulties of children held within a British immigration center: A pilot study." *Child Abuse and Neglect* 33:573–585.

Luxenberg, Toni, Joseph Spinazzola, Jose Hidalgo, Cheryl Hunt, and Bessel A. Van der Kolk. 2001. "Complex trauma and disorders of extreme stress (DESNOS): Treatment." *Directions in Psychiatry* 21:395–414.

Lykes, M. Brinton, Kalina M. Brabeck, and Cristina Hunter. 2013. "Exploring parent-child communication in the context of threat: Mixed-status families facing detention and deportation in post 9/11 USA." *Community, Work & Family* 16(2):123–146. doi: 10.1080/13668803.2012.752997.

Makariev, Drika W., and Phillip R. Shaver. 2010. "Attachment, parental incarceration, and possibilities for intervention." *Attachment & Human Development* 12(4):311–331. doi: 10.1080/ 14751790903416939.

Mares, Sarah, and Jureidini, Jon. 2004. "Psychiatric assessment of children and families in immigration detention: Clinical, administrative & ethical issues." *Australia & New Zealand Journal of Public Health* 28:520–526.

McLeigh, Jill D. 2010. "How do immigration and customs enforcement (ICE) practices affect the mental health of children?" *American Journal of Orthopsychiatry* 80(1):96–100. doi: 10.1111/j.1939-0025.2010.01011.x.

McMillan, Anita S. 2011. *"They are waiting in the middle of the desert": Experiences of Guatemalan migrants deported from the US: Pilot study.* Coventry, UK: Warwick Medical School, University of Warwick.

Meffert, Susan M., Karen Musalo, Dale E. McNiel, and Renee L. Binder. 2010. "The role of mental health professionals in political asylum processing." *Journal of the American Academy of Psychiatry and the Law* 38:479–489.

Menjivar, Cecilia, and Leisy J. Abrego. 2012. "Legal violence: Immigration law and the lives of Central American immigrants." *American Journal of Sociology* 117(5):1380–1421. Accessed May 10, 2014. http://www.jstor.org/stable/10.1086/663575.

Michultka, Denise. 2009. "Mental health issues in new immigrant communities." In F. Chang-Muy and E. P. Congress, eds., *Social Work with Immigrants and Refugees: Legal Issues, Clinical Skills, and Advocacy* (pp. 135–172). New York: Springer.

Miller, Kenneth E., and Andrew Rasmussen. 2009. "War exposure, daily stressors, and mental health in conflict and post-conflict settings: Bridging the divide between trauma-focused and psychosocial frameworks." *Social Science & Medicine* 70:7–16.

Miranda, Jeanne, Juned Siddique, Claudia DerMartirosian, and Thomas Belin. 2005. "Depression among Latina immigrant mothers separated from their children." *Psychiatric Services* 56:717–720.

Morales, Leos S., Marielena Lara, Raynard S. Kington, Robert O. Valdez, and Jose J. Escarce. 2002. "Socioeconomic, cultural, and behavioral factors affecting Hispanic health outcomes." *Journal of Health Care for the Poor and Underserved* 13(4):477–503.

Moran-Taylor, Michelle J. 2008. "When mothers and fathers migrate North: Caretakers, children, and child rearing in Guatemala." *Latin American Perspectives* 35:79–95.

Mui, Ada C., and Suk-Young Kang. 2006. "Acculturation stress and depression among Asian immigrant elders." *Social Work* 51:243–255.

Newman, Louise, Michael Dudley, and Zachary Steel. 2008. "Asylum, detention, and mental health in Australia." *Refugee Survey Quarterly* 27(3):110–127.

Neuner, Frank, Maggie Schauer, Unni Karunakara, Christine Klaschik, and Thomas Elbert. 2004. "A comparison of narrative exposure therapy, supportive counseling and psychoeducation for treating PTSD in an African refugee settlement." *Journal of Consulting and Clinical Psychology* 72:579–587.

Orellana, Marjorie F., Barrie Thorne, Anna Chee, and Wan Shun Eva Lam. 2001. "Transnational childhoods: The participation of children in processes of family migration." *Social Problems* 48:572–591.

Ortega Alex N., Sarah M. Horwitz, Hai Fang, Alice A. Kuo, Steven P. Wallace, and Moira Inkelas. 2009. "Documentation status and parental concerns about development in young U.S. children of Mexican origin." *Academic Pediatrics* 9:278–282. doi: 10.1016/j.acap.2009.02.007.

Park-Taylor, Jennie, Allison Ventura, and Vicky Ng. 2010. "Multicultural counseling and assessment with children." In J. Ponterrotto, J. M. Casas, L. A. Suzuki, and C. M. Alexander, eds., *Handbook of Multicultural Counseling* (3rd ed., pp. 621–631). Los Angeles: Sage.

Passel, Jeffrey S., D'Vera Cohn, and Ana Gonzalez-Barrera. 2013. *Population Decline of Unauthorized Immigrants Stalls, May Have Reversed.* Washington, DC: Pew Research Center. Accessed May 10, 2014. http://www.pewhispanic.org/files/2013/09/Unauthorized-Sept-2013-FINAL.pdf.

Perreira, Krista M., and India J. Ornelas. 2011. "The physical and psychological wellbeing of immigrant children." *Future of Children* 21:195–218.

Phillips, Scott, Jacqueline Hagan, and Nestor Rodriguez. 2006. "Brutal borders: Examining the treatment of deportees during arrest and detention." *Social Forces* 85(1):93–110. doi: 0.1353/sof.2006.0137.

Physicians for Human Rights and Bellevue/NYU Program for Survivors of Torture. 2003. *From persecution to prison: The health consequences of detention for asylum seekers.* Accessed October 19, 2014. https://s3.amazonaws.com/PHR_Reports/persecution-to-prison-US-2003.pdf.

Potochnick, Stephanie, and Krista M. Perreira. 2010. "Depression and anxiety among first-generation immigrant youth." *Journal of Nervous and Mental Disease* 198:470–477.

Pumariega, Andres J., and Eugenio Roth. 2010. "Leaving no children or families outside: The challenges of immigration." *American Journal of Orthopsychiatry* 80:505–515.

Rasmussen, Andrew, Barry Rosenfeld, Kim Reeves, and Allen S. Keller. 2007. "The subjective experience of trauma and subsequent PTSD in a sample of unauthorized immigrants." *Journal of Nervous and Mental Disease* 195:137–143.

Robertson, Angela M., Remedios Lozada, Alicia Vera, Lawrence A Palinkas, Jose L. Burgos, Carlos Magis-Rodriguez, Gudelia Rangel, and Victoria D. Ojeda. 2012. "Deportation experiences of women who inject drugs in Tijuana, Mexico." *Qualitative Health Research* 22(4):499–510. doi: 10.1177/1049732311422238.

Robjant, Katy, Rita Hassan, and Cornelius Katona. 2009. "Mental Health implications of detaining asylum seekers: Systematic review." *British Journal of Psychiatry* 194:306–312. doi: 10.1102/bjp.bp.108.053223.

Romero, Mary. 2008. "The inclusion of citizenship status in intersectionality: What immigrant raids tell us about mixed-status families, the state and assimilation." *International Journal of Sociology of the Family* 34:131–152. http://www.jstor.org/stable/23070749.

Rousseau, Cecile, Aline Drapeau, Louise Locroix, Deogratias Bagilishya, and Nicole Heusch. 2005. "Evaluation of a classroom program of creative expression workshops for refugee and immigrant children." *Journal of Child Psychology and Psychiatry* 46:180–185.doi: 10.1111/j.1469-7610.2004.00344.x.

Schauer, Maggie, Frank Neuner, and Thomas Elbert. 2005. *Narrative Exposure Therapy: A Short-term Intervention for Traumatic Stress Disorders After War, Terror, or Torture*. Cambridge, MA: Hogrefe & Huber.

Schmalzbauer, Leah. 2004. "Searching for wages and mothering from afar: The case of Honduran transnational families." *Journal of Marriage and Family* 66:1317–1331. doi: 10.1111/j.0022-2445.2004.00095.x.

Silove, Derek, and Zachary Steel. 2006. "Understanding community psychosocial needs after disasters: Implications for mental health services." *Journal of Postgraduate Medicine* 52:121–125.

Springer, David W., Courtney Lynch, and Allen Rubin. 2000. "Effects of a solution-focused mutual aid group for Hispanic children of incarcerated parents." *Child & Adolescent Social Work Journal* 17:431–442. doi: 10.1023/A:1026479727159.

Steele, Zachary, Shakeh Momartin, Catherine Bateman, Atena Hafshejani, Derek Silove, Naleya Everson, Konya Roy, Michael Dudley, Louise Newman, Bijou Blick, and Sarah Mares. 2004. "Psychiatric status of asylum seeker families held for a protracted period in a remote detention centre in Australia." *Australia & New Zealand Journal of Public Health* 28:527–536.

Suarez-Orozco, Carola, Hee Jin Bang, and Ha Yeon Kim. 2010. "I felt like my heart was staying behind: Psychological implications of family separations and reunifications for immigrant youth." *Journal of Adolescent Research* 26:222–257. doi: 10.1177/0743558410376830.

Sullivan, Margaret M., and Roberta Rehm. 2005. "Mental health of unauthorized Mexican immigrants: A review of the literature." *Association of Advances in Nursing Science* 28:240–251.

U.S. Department of Homeland Security (DHS). 2006. *Treatment of Immigration Detention at Enforcement Facilities.* Washington, DC: U.S. Department of Homeland Security, Office of the Inspector General. Accessed May 10, 2014. www.oig.dhs.gov/assets/Mgmt/OIG_07-01_Dec06.pdf.

Wessler, Seth. 2011. *Shattered Families: The Perilous Intersection of Immigration Enforcement and the Child Welfare System.* New York: Applied Research Center. Accessed May 10, 2014. http://www.atlanticphilanthropies.org/sites/default/files/uploads/ARC_Report_Shattered_Families_FULL_REPORT_Nov2011Release.pdf.

Worden, J. William. 2008. *Grief Counseling and Grief Therapy: A Handbook for the Mental Health Practitioner.* New York: Springer.

Xu, Qingwen, and Kalina M. Brabeck. 2012. "Service utilization among unauthorized Latino immigrant families." *Social Work Research* 32(3):341–361. doi: 10.1093/swr/svs015.

Yoshikawa, Hirokazu. 2011. *Immigrants Raising Citizens: Undocumented Parents and Their Young Children.* New York: Russell Sage Foundation.

Zayas, Luis. 2010. "Protecting citizen-children safeguards our children." *Journal of Health Care for the Poor and Underserved* 21(3):809–814. doi: 10.1353/hpu.0.0325.

7

Participatory Action Research with Transnational and Mixed-Status Families

Understanding and Responding to Post–9/11 Threats in Guatemala and the United States

M. BRINTON LYKES, ERIN SIBLEY, KALINA M. BRABECK,
CRISTINA HUNTER, AND YLIANA JOHANSEN-MÉNDEZ

Recent estimates by the Pew Research Center suggest that in 2013 there were approximately 11.2 million unauthorized migrants[1] (28% of the foreign-born population) living in the United States (Passel et al. 2014). As of 2012, an estimated 82% of children of unauthorized migrants were U.S.-born citizens living in mixed-status families, amounting to 4.5 million children. In 2010, over 80% of these children were born after their parents resided in the United States. for more than two years, and over 50% were born after their parents lived in the United States for at least five years (Passel and Taylor 2010). The majority of these families are also transnational, that is, they include family members (including children) to whom they have obligations, attachments, and communication, residing in their countries of origin.

This chapter draws on findings from seven years of an ongoing interdisciplinary participatory action research (PAR) with unauthorized Central American migrants and their families. Participants are members of both mixed-status families, which include U.S.-born children, and transnational families, which include children "left behind" in the country of origin. We argue that the experiences of Central American mixed-status families are best understood within a historical and transnational framework. These participatory action research processes are sponsored by the Center for Human Rights & International Justice (CHRIJ) at Boston College, and explore experiences and threats of detention and deportation among migrant families. Participants included predominantly mixed-status families based in New England and sending family members and deportees in the Southern Quiché region of Guatemala. All co-authors have been involved in various facets of this work over the years discussed in this chapter. Through collaboration with these families, their communities, and community-based organizations, university-based project participants advocate for fundamental changes that will introduce proportionality, compassion, and respect for family unity into U.S. immigration laws and bring these laws into compliance with international human rights standards. Furthermore, in light of the transnational nature of these families and their experiences, researchers seek to better understand and respond to the effects of U.S. policies and practices beyond U.S. borders. To achieve these goals, the CHRIJ affiliates engage in direct legal representation of deported migrants, participatory and action research projects intended to systematically document the effects of Immigration and Customs Enforcement (ICE) policies and practices on migrant families in New England, and community organizing and advocacy. Through ongoing collaborative research and educational programs in Zacualpa, Quiché, Guatemala (the place of origin of many of the participating U.S.-based families), researchers seek to better understand the factors that push many parents to migrate, the mixed consequences of transnational family relations for children and families, and the impact of deportation from the United States on family members abroad.

This chapter focuses on mixed-status and transnational Central American families' experiences and the meanings they make of migration, detention, and deportation on both sides of the U.S. border. Such experiences and meanings are situated within their histories and current realities, including previous armed conflicts (e.g., civil war and state-sponsored violence) and ongoing extreme violence in migrants' countries of origin (e.g., femicide, drug and human trafficking, gang violence) (Internal Displacement Monitoring Centre & Norwegian Refugee Council 2011; Stone 2011); recent iterations and intensification of U.S. immigration policies and practices (see below); and other global social structural factors (e.g., extreme poverty in countries of origin as well as the North American Free Trade Agreement (NAFTA), the Central American Free Trade Agreement (CAFTA), and other International

Figure 7.1 PAR in 2014

Monetary Fund (IMF) and World Bank policies (Cohen 2006; Washington Office on Latin America [WOLA] 2003). The chapter then examines the psychosocial effects of migration, detention, and deportation on U.S.-based migrants living in mixed-status families and on transnational families in Guatemala and argues the importance of understanding U.S.-based mixed-status families within a transnational framework.

Data were drawn from interviews, ethnographic research, community surveys, and community-based participatory educational and reflection processes that were part of participatory and action research processes in New England and in Zacualpa (see figure 7.1). Each of these participatory research activities was designed collaboratively with local organizations. Each effort aimed to enhance leadership development and to design strategies to educate the wider U.S. and Guatemalan publics through systematic research based in migrants' own stories and participatory workshops.

Below we summarize and bridge the knowledge generated within and across selected data-gathering processes. We begin by situating our work within the literature on the political environment for unauthorized migrants in the United States and the socio-historical context for migrants' families and children "left behind" in the sending country of Guatemala where our transnational project is based. While scholarship on the effects of parental legal vulnerability on U.S.-based children is extremely relevant to our work, we do not include it in this chapter as it is summarized elsewhere in this volume (see Brabeck, Porterfield, and Loughry, this volume). We next discuss participatory action research as a resource for fostering the project's goals. We then present findings which argue: (1) that unauthorized migrants, including those in mixed-status families, situate themselves historically and are deeply affected by ongoing violence and poverty in their countries of origin; and (2) that threats to these mixed-status families are experienced transnationally, that is, actions that occur in the United States have profound implications for children "left behind" in migrants' country of origin and for their caretakers. Together these data reveal the challenges for service providers and U.S. policy makers who promote an ideology of the United States as a family-oriented society that values and supports family unification. We conclude with recommendations for those who seek to transform repressive practices and support mixed-status and transnational migrant families.

Situating Unauthorized Migrants in 2014: Changing Legal Context

The political and social climate for migrants in the United States has undergone many changes during the past decades, with significant implications for mixed-status families and their family members abroad (see also Kantroom and Lykes, this volume). In the mid-1990s, under the Clinton administration, the U.S. government passed laws that amplified the authority of the federal government to arrest, detain, and deport noncitizens (Hagan, Eschbach, and Rodriguez 2008). The Illegal Immigration Reform and Immigrant Responsibility Act (IIRIRA) (1996) and the Anti-terrorism Effective Death Penalty Act (AEDPA) (1996) expanded the offenses for which a noncitizen could be deported, allowed for retroactive deportation, increased the categories of persons subject to "removal," and eliminated the range of judicial review and due process rights formerly available to immigrants. Additionally, the 2001 USA PATRIOT Act, signed into law under the George W. Bush administration, expanded the ability of the government to deport persons who were deemed as "threats to national security" and allowed for use of "secret evidence" in such cases.

Due in large part to the aforementioned legislation, between 2001 and 2012 approximately 3.6 million immigrants were deported from the United States, a vast majority of whom were from Mexico and Central America (DHS Office of Immigration Statistics 2012a). Immigration Customs Enforcement's (ICE) Office of Enforcement and Removal Operations (2013) reports that the number of removals reached an all-time high of 419,384 in 2012, but declined by 12% to 368,644 removed in 2013 (DHS Office of Immigration Statistics 2013). These numbers do not reflect the immigrants who were "returned" by a means other than a removal order, such as an order of "voluntary departure," which accounts for an additional 9.9 million from 2001 through 2012 (DHS Office of Immigration Statistics 2012a). The Department of Homeland Security (DHS) has also neglected to take into account the many more "*de facto* deportees" (Argueta 2010)—including U.S. citizen spouses and children—who were forced to leave the United States when a family member was deported (Lykes and Chicco 2011).

More deportations have occurred under the Obama administration than in any previous administration (DHS Office of Immigration Statistics 2012b; Slevin 2010). In many of these cases, deported parents are separated from their U.S.-born children. For example, Baum, Jones, and Barry (2010) found that between 1997 and 2007, 88,000 U.S. citizen children (44,000 of whom were under the age of 5) lost a legal permanent resident parent to deportation. A more recent report by Wessler et al. (2011) from the Applied Research Center (ARC) reported that at least 5,100 children whose parents were detained or deported currently live in U.S. foster care and face significant barriers to reunification with parents. Extrapolating from the 205,000 deportees between July 2010 and September 2012 who reported having at least one U.S.-citizen child, these figures suggest an estimated annual average of 90,000 parental deportations (Wessler 2012). Moreover, the Immigrant Rights Clinic at the New York University School of Law found that, between 2005 and 2010, 87% of processed immigration cases of noncitizens with citizen children resulted in deportation (NYU School of Law Immigrant Rights Clinic 2012). Overall, these statistics suggest that between 2005 and 2012, persons detained and deported were typically parents and workers, with no criminal records, who migrated from Latin American countries.

Federal and local collaborative and independent initiatives. Although the number of worksite raids has decreased under the Obama administration, these raids and arrests have been largely replaced by home and street arrests in addition to "silent raids" that entail federal auditing of employer records (Bacon and Hing 2010). A hallmark of the Obama administration's approach to immigration enforcement, Secure Communities (SC) (implemented in 2008), further threatens noncitizens in the United States. SC calls for checking fingerprints of every person booked by local law enforcement against DHS databases for immigration violations. While it was purportedly designed to identify and deport unauthorized migrants convicted of serious crimes, in practice, the majority of those deported under SC have committed no serious offense: ICE records reveal that 70% of those removed or returned under SC had no criminal records or had been picked up for low-level offenses (e.g., misdemeanors and traffic violations), while only 30% had been charged with or convicted of serious "Level 1" crimes (e.g., aggravated felonies) (National Day Labor Organizing Network (NDLON) and Center for Constitutional Rights (CCR) 2010).

Some states and localities have voiced their opposition to mandatory participation in the SC program (Foley 2011) and others have initiated a grassroots response to counter this federal effort (e.g., Just Communities/ Comunidades Justas in Massachusetts). Despite this, many other states and local authorities have sought opportunities to enforce immigration laws themselves (Friedland, Johnson-Firth, and Garnett-McKenzie 2009). This push to enforce immigration laws is evident in the dramatic increase in the number of Memoranda of Agreement (MOAs) between ICE and state and local governments under 287(g) since 2007 (287(g) Program 2008; Friedland et al. 2009). The 287(g) MOAs essentially delegate the federal function of enforcement of immigration laws to state law enforcement agencies. This means that local police departments that enter into a 287(g) agreement with federal immigration authorities can legally investigate individuals' immigration status and detain those persons suspected of being in violation of immigration laws until federal immigration authorities can verify their status or initiate removal proceedings. Further, state laws related to immigration have dramatically increased in recent years. In 2005, there were 300 immigration-related bills introduced in state legislatures. In the years 2007–2013, that number increased to an estimated average of 1,300 immigration-related bills per year (National Conference of State Legislatures 2014).

In these ways, U.S. immigration policies function increasingly as mechanisms of internal social control, constraining unauthorized migrants' daily lives and pushing them further into "the shadows." They have consequences for the mental and physical health, social, economic, and acculturative experiences for families, parents, and children in the U.S. These experiences are summarized elsewhere in this volume (see Brabeck, Porterfield, and Loughry). We complement this information with a brief description of some of the multiple challenges facing Guatemala-based sending families with transnational ties.

Transnational Families: Migration Pushes and Children and Youth "Left Behind"

Researchers have documented the migration experiences of Central Americans and Mexicans and the value of remittances to the gross domestic product of sending countries, as well as local improvements in housing, education, and healthcare for children "left behind" and their caretakers (Smith 2006; UNICEF and IOM 2011). Children and youth are often described as *beneficiaries* of their parents' sacrifices (Dreby 2007; Frank and Wildsmith 2005). Other more recent scholarship focuses on indebtedness of sending families (see, e.g., Brabeck, Lykes, and Hershberg 2011; Barrett, Gibbons, and Peláez Ponce 2014) and the many consequences for children "left behind," particularly within the current political environment for migrants in the United States. These are among the pushes and pulls experienced by the Salvadoran and Guatemalan migrants with whom we have worked. The experiences of Salvadorans—and a brutal history of armed conflict—are summarized briefly in another chapter in this volume (see Dingeman-Cerda and Rumbaut). We describe below some of the migratory antecedents to current experiences of the transnational Guatemalan Mayan families with whom we have worked.

During an economic boom in agriculture exports in Guatemala in the 1960s and '70s more than 300,000 indigenous people each year began to migrate to coastal farmlands for seasonal agricultural work. Salaries were low and working conditions were grueling and unsanitary, but the economic need was so great that many either left their families at home or took their children out of school for months at a time to join them on the journey (Davis 1988). Other Guatemalans migrated beyond formal nation-state borders to work on Mexican coffee plantations, having begun that journey in the 1800s. The U.S. government's economic and political interests in Guatemala have been widely documented, e.g., the United Fruit Company's vast land holdings and the U.S. Central Intelligence Agency's involvement in directing the overthrow of the democratically elected government of Jacobo Arbenz in 1954 (Schlesinger and Kinzer 1999). This history situates current migrations into an older history of exclusion and forced labor fueled by U.S. interests in Guatemala over many decades.

The history of the U.S. government's continued involvements in Guatemala is lengthy, culminating in its support for the Guatemalan military's campaign against Mayan communities during the 36-year armed conflict (Grandin, Levenson, and Oglesby 2011, among others). By the mid-twentieth century, Guatemalans organizing in search of economic equality and political, social, and cultural change became more militant (Chamarbagwala and Morán 2011). They protested increases in the cost of living, low wages, lack of sufficient land, cultural oppression, and racism (Grandin et al. 2011). These movements coalesced and insurgent groups, including, for example, the Guerrilla Army of the Poor (EGP, by its Spanish acronym), became increasingly violent in the 1980s. The Guatemalan army, with support from the U.S. government, destroyed villages in the highlands and displaced many peasants. Then President Efraín Ríos Montt instituted social control in the form of a new army tactic that armed civilian villagers with rifles (Civil Self-Defense Patrols, PACs by its Spanish acronym) to fight off the EGP and other militant groups (Stewart 2012). The municipality of Zacualpa, the center of work described below, was bombed by military planes and occupied by the Guatemalan army during the early 1980s, while PACs controlled many of the surrounding villages (Remijnse 2002).

The Guatemalan government, the guerrilla forces, and a UN commission established to seek truth and justice in the wake of nearly 36 years of armed conflict signed a Peace Accord in December 1996 (Comisión para el Esclarecimiento Histórico [CEH] 1999). The Commission for Historical Clarification (CEH for its Spanish acronym) report estimated that 200,000 individuals had been murdered or "disappeared" during the conflict, with 93% of the crimes linked to the Guatemalan state. Eighty-three percent of the victims were classified as indigenous Maya, contributing to the report's conclusion that genocide had been committed against the Maya. According to the CEH, "racism nourished an attitude toward Indians [the Maya] as different, separate, inferior, almost less than human and outside of the universe of moral obligations, making their elimination less problematic" (Commission for Historical Clarification 2011:390). Moreover, large numbers of Maya were displaced from their communities, fleeing bombings, massacres, and military occupations. Approximately one million people were "internal refugees" within the country, out of an estimated population of 8.5 million. Many working with the displaced estimated another 150,000 Guatemalans sought refuge in Mexico, 6,000 in Belize, 1,000 in Honduras, and between 100,000 and 200,000 in the United States (Melville and Lykes 1992). Some estimates at the time put the number of children who had lost one or both parents at 200,000; the Guatemalan press suggested that there were as many as 500,000 (Carmack 1988; Salvadó 1988).

Thus, migration predated but was deeply exacerbated by nearly four decades of armed conflict (e.g., Hamilton and Stoltz Chinchilla 1991). Moreover, despite the horrors that populations displaced by the war experienced, estimates are that only about 2–3% of Guatemalans who sought refuge in the United States during this period were granted political asylum (González 2000). Despite cessation of the armed conflict, current economic conditions, drug trafficking, ongoing gang violence, and impunity continue to create conditions in the twenty-first century that push an ever-increasing number of Guatemalans and Salvadorans north (see Dingeman-Cerda and Rumbaut, this volume, for estimates of Salvadorans; Grandin et al. 2011 on Guatemala).

Research with more recent Central American migrants has found that many choose to migrate and separate from their family to be able to find work and earn a living wage in order to support those back home (Andrade-Eekhof and Silva-Avalos 2003). They are motivated by a combination of health, education, and/or monetary needs of the family members who remain in origin countries (Schmalzbauer 2004).

Thus, despite an ever-more harrowing journey to the U.S.-Mexico border, challenging socioeconomic conditions and ongoing gang violence facing families in origin countries push some members, most typically males, north (De Genova 2002; Schmalzbauer 2005; Zentgraf and Stolz Chinchilla 2012). Moreover, increased militarization of the U.S.-Mexican border and the increasingly difficult legal constraints facing twenty-first-century migrants contribute to unauthorized migrants' decisions to stay in the United States for longer durations than in past years (Dreby 2010; Dreby and Stutz 2012). It is estimated that more than 1 million Guatemalans (of a total population of approximately 14 million) live in the United States today (Smith 2006), with a large percentage of them being unauthorized. Many of these are also transnational, having left family members behind in Guatemala.

Interdisciplinary Participatory Action Research with Unauthorized Migrants, Mixed-Status, and Transnational Families

Given the realities confronting the growing number of Central American migrants "living in the shadows" in New England and others struggling in their countries of origin as well as the increasingly hostile public discourse about unauthorized migrants in the United States, the CHRIJ directors initiated relationships with several New England community-based organizations working mainly with Salvadoran and Guatemalan migrants. This initiative was under way in March 2007, when approximately 300 federal immigration agents raided a New Bedford, Massachusetts leather factory, arresting more than 360 unauthorized migrants, many of whom were Maya K'iche' from the southern Quiché area of Guatemala. Our initial partnerships shifted to better respond to those families most directly affected by the raid, a move that fortified and focused both the community engagement and the participatory research aspects of the project. As project priorities shifted, we sought collaborations with organizations seeking to support mixed-status and transnational families with everyday life problems "living in the shadows."

Our selection of participatory and action research as a methodology reflects our recognition that the policies, enforcements, and public attitudes reviewed above as well as a longer colonial history punctuated by racism against Mayan communities generated distrust between unauthorized migrants and their families and outsiders, including members of the CHRIJ. As significantly, it reflects our prioritizing the development of collaborative relationships and generative spaces in which unauthorized migrants and their mixed-status, transnational families could engage in educational, advocacy, and organizing activities that contribute to generating knowledge about their lived experiences "in their own words." The participatory methodology and activist stance of PAR (Fals Borda 1985; 1998; 2000) facilitates the development of "just enough trust" (Maguire 1987) between community members and outsiders (e.g., CHRIJ researchers, lawyers, and activists) to risk emerging from the shadows. Through "pragmatic solidarity" (Farmer 2003) we engage together in action-reflection processes through which we (1) identify a problem focus or injustice, (2) gather information about it, (3) critically analyze its root causes, and (4) generate collaborative strategies toward redressing the injustice (Reason and Bradbury 2008). The participatory processes are teaching-learning contexts through which unauthorized migrants deepen their analyses about the causes of their current threats and strengthen their voices and local protagonism. These local understandings and the development of solidarity across communities contribute to collaborative generation of pragmatic responses to migrant families' ongoing marginalization in the United States and in their countries of origin.

PAR processes with transnational and mixed-status families. In the multi-year interdisciplinary PAR project herein described (see figure 7.1), we developed three initial goals: (1) to document how Guatemalan and Salvadoran mixed-status and transnational families experience and respond to detention and deportation; (2) to contextualize current risks to families within a socio-historical, sociopolitical, and transnational framework; and (3) to collaboratively respond to the current realities through community-based actions, policy development, advocacy, and organizing. The work in Central America was initiated in partnership with Ricardo Falla, S.J., a Guatemalan anthropologist conducting research with returning migrants and sending families in Zacualpa in the Southern Quiché region, and with the social programs of the local Catholic church.

The participatory action research initiatives discussed in this chapter include: (1) in-depth interviews with 18 Central American migrant families in the United States, a majority of whom are mixed-status and all of whom had at least one unauthorized member; (2) community-based educational and organizational activities with migrant families in the United States; and (3) in-depth interviews, community-based survey research, and educational programming with sending families and children in Guatemala. Much of our community-based participatory work with migrant communities in New England has been in the form of community-led *Know Your Rights* (KYR) workshops and the development of educational curriculum resources about migrants' rights. Similar workshops with adults in Guatemala included a focus on the local community's questions about migrating family members' experiences in the United States. In response to the request from the local community, educational workshops with children and youth were designed to educate them about life in the United States and to elicit, through creative activities, their experiences regarding family members' migration north. Additional goals of the participatory educational workshops in both sites were to foster leadership development from within participating communities and to inform families about how U.S.-based migrants can best protect themselves in the face of the shifting U.S. immigration policies and practices (see Lykes, McDonald, and Boc 2012; and Migration and Human Rights Project, Center for Human Rights and International Justice 2012, 2013; formerly, Post-Deportation Human Rights Project 2009; 2010; 2011, for more details).

These initiatives complement additional work by the project's legal team that supports individual deportees with U.S.-based family members who have been denied the right to appeal for reentry once they have been deported beyond U.S. borders. The Boston-based team also consults with families in Guatemala who are searching for U.S.-based family members who have been detained or who face deportation. U.S. educational initiatives that expand knowledge on post-deportation issues include the publication of practice advisories on post-departure motions to reopen, as well as a self-help manual for deportees.

These PAR processes aim to develop a critical body of scholarship "from the bottom up" that will influence social and political change. Most of the qualitative data have been transcribed and analyzed using a range of qualitative methods including content analysis and thematic narrative analysis. NVivo 8 was used to consolidate initially coded data facilitating the enumeration and analysis of themes and their interrelationships in the first phase of the analyses. Analyses of community survey data were performed using SPSS 19. Meetings with participants and other community members were opportunities to review preliminary findings and explore alternative interpretations. These research and action processes are iterative and facilitate strengthening relationships between collaborating community and university groups. They were tape recorded, with data analyses of meeting transcripts following similar strategies as those articulated above. The Human Subjects Review Board of Boston College, one of the host institutions, has approved all phases of the PAR processes described herein. To protect the anonymity of participants, all names in this text are pseudonyms. We next report U.S.-based parents' historically rooted narratives of current detention and deportation threats and experiences and explore children and youths' stories based on experiences in the United States and in Guatemala. We thereby aim to provide a thicker description of mixed-status and transnational families.

Narrating the Present through Past Experiences

As discussed in this volume, researchers (e.g., Capps et al. 2007; Chaudry et al. 2010) have increasingly documented the negative impact of U.S. immigration policies and their enforcement on migrant families' emotional, social, relational, and financial well-being in the United States. We conducted interviews with 18 Salvadoran and Guatemalan parents residing in New England whose families had been impacted directly by detention and deportation; 93% of these families had U.S.-born children and 39% had children residing in the country of origin. Parents reported several psychological consequences of detention and deportation, including sadness, loss of energy, feelings of hopelessness, crying, anxiety, lost sleep, weight loss and gain, anger, fear, hypervigilance, distrust, nightmares, and worry, as well as economic hardship. Negative effects on children identified by their parents included academic problems, depressive symptoms, anxiety symptoms, developmental regression, and behavioral difficulties (Brabeck et al. 2011).

Violence and violations in the U.S. and Central America. An important theme that emerged from interview data was that current threats posed by the detention and deportation system are experienced by Salvadoran and Guatemalan participants as deeply connected to previous threats including poverty, histories of state-sponsored violence in countries of origin, ongoing violence in sending countries, and related migrations and resulting family separations. Our research confirms that the current atmosphere of vulnerability and anxiety caused by immigration policies and enforcements is especially poignant when considered against the historical backdrop of state-sponsored violence during which families were divided, family members "disappeared," self-silencing was a means of survival, and people feared that the government would "take away" a loved one. Nine of the 18 interviewed families (50%) spontaneously discussed the fear, silence, and displacement of family members that took place during *la violencia* (e.g., the twentieth-century civil wars in El Salvador and Guatemala (Betancur, Planchart, and Buergenthal 1993; CEH 1999)). Eight of the interviewed families (44%) reported the murder of an immediate family member during the years of armed conflict in El Salvador and Guatemala. Two male participants reported that they migrated to the United States specifically to avoid being forcibly "recruited" into the armed forces. Four participants (22%) described decisions to migrate to the United States as related to loss of family, security, land, and community that followed from *la violencia*; Arturo recounts,

> I left [Guatemala] approximately in the '80s, as a result of the war. The army came knocking on the door . . . to the home of my father. . . . They said that we belonged to the mafia or to the guerrillas. . . . This was not right, and as a result of this we could not live in peace in that community, instead simply every day we lived in fear.

Following this assault on his family, Arturo fled to Mexico and later migrated to the United States.

Participants in the United States drew connections between the atmosphere during these years of armed conflict in their countries of origin and the current U.S. atmosphere for migrants—one characterized by suspicion, distrust, and fear. For example, Mario, whose wife was detained in a large workplace raid, described how previous traumas were retriggered in the current atmosphere: "What happened last year [raid] . . . It starts to open up the wound, or the fear, that you have held, because these things are not easy to erase. Because the wound is always there and when you open it, it burns anew." Julia, who was detained in the workplace raid described above and separated from her 2-year-old son, described the current assault on immigrants as a "second war": "If they are taking children away and everything, then for me, that's a second war." Marta, whose father was kidnapped and "disappeared" during Guatemala's civil war, had a husband detained at the time of our interview. Understanding that her own unauthorized status made her vulnerable, Marta recounted being unable to investigate where he was held, thus re-experiencing the "disappearance" of a family member. Her options were further complicated by having two U.S.-born children, who would experience significant repercussions should their mother also be detained and possibly deported. Marta's example demonstrates the importance of understanding mixed-status families within their transnational and historical contexts.

Poverty and racism precede and follow armed conflict. Although Peace Accords in El Salvador in 1992 and in Guatemala in 1996 brought an end to armed conflicts, the wars had decimated local economies; the gross social inequalities that lay at the roots of these earlier conflicts remain unaddressed (Smith 2006). Salvadoran and Guatemalan participants described poverty as both preceding and resulting from these wars. Moreover, poverty resulting from violence and ongoing racism motivated participants' migrations; this was underscored in the survey work completed in Guatemala which we discuss next. For example, soldiers in Guatemala robbed and killed Mario's father and left his family without means of support, prompting his migration to the United States: "We endured hunger, poverty; we hardly had clothing for the babies to use each week. Then coming here [U.S.], seeing the blessings, you want to grab hold of that to be able to give your children a life, a future, what you yourself never had." Similarly, Jorge, another U.S. participant, recounted how fear during *la violencia*, and the resulting poverty and destruction, led many Guatemalans to flee to the south coast, where they worked on *fincas* (plantations), a foreshadowing of the later migrations "*al norte*" (northward):

> The war started. . . . Soldiers came, entered homes, there was fear. They fired guns, threw bombs. The people left running; they [soldiers] grabbed them all of a sudden. They started killing them, without [the people] having done anything. This is the fear. . . . We left; we went as far as the south coast. . . . the south coast where they plant sugar cane, cotton, cardamom, vegetables.

Histories of poverty, racism, and violence in countries of origin also complicated participants' current efforts to organize and speak out against the policies that threaten their families in the United States, thereby curtailing efforts toward collective action. Julia, for example, is a mother of two U.S.-born children and three children in Guatemala. Having been detained in a large workplace raid in 2007, she was applying for defensive asylum at the time of this interview. Julia described how indigenous Guatemalans were conditioned to believe that speaking out would result in death for their families, communities, and themselves:

> We are all afraid, because I know our [indigenous/Mayan] race; we all walk with fear like this. Because in our country we were threatened, the indigenous race was threatened in many ways. If one speaks, if you say something, they [government] say we have no right to do so, and so we never did.

Her statement reflects how transnational, historical experiences influence current responses of unauthorized migrants in mixed-status families. In contrast, Julian describes a similar fear in Guatemala but re-vindicates his rights to speak out in the United States, despite his unauthorized status: "I work for an organization because all of our people are afraid of speaking out, but here in this country [the U.S.] we don't have to be afraid of speaking out, whereas in other countries, like Guatemala, if you speak out you are killed."

Repeated family separations. Poverty in countries of origin motivates migration northward, which allows families to potentially thrive financially, but also separates family members. These previous experiences of migration-related family separation also exacerbate and texture current risks to the integrity of mixed-status families posed by deportation policies and practices. When participants decided to migrate northward, disconnection from family in countries of origin produced feelings of isolation, loneliness, and sadness. Thirteen of the interviewed families (72%) discussed migration-related separation. Seven of the 18 parents (39%) interviewed in the United States had left a total of 22 children in their country of origin and most had not seen them for many years. Clara, who has both U.S.-born children and children residing in El Salvador, explained her decision to leave four children behind in El Salvador:

> Still today I sometimes regret that I came [to the U.S.] because there is nothing more important than your children. But at the same time, I know I'm achieving something. In my view, here [in the U.S.] things are possible. There are people who say, well, the laws say that a person who crosses [the border] is a criminal. It's more criminal to let your children starve to death. If I have to lose my life, at least I wanted to try rather than let my children die of hunger.

The seven parents (39%) interviewed in the United States who had children both "*allá*" (over there) and "*acá*" (right here), described watching their U.S.-born children thrive and succeed in the United States; learn English and study; have access to needed services like healthcare, physical and speech therapy; and experience opportunities that do not seem possible "*allá*" (i.e., in their countries of origin). In Clara's words: "My heart is divided; I have three [children] in my country and three here. I'm here because I want my kids to study and speak English, and not go through life cleaning bathrooms like I did." Again, the experiences of these mixed-status families are often best understood within the context of their relationships being structured, ruptured, and sustained transnationally. These experiences are similar to the ones described in the vignette in the fifth chapter of this volume in which Maria and Felipe struggle with similar transnational and mixed-status challenges (*see* Chicco and Congress, this volume). Thus, deportation of a family member is one of multiple separations that these families have faced.

Participants in the United States described the ways in which migration—a byproduct of poverty, racism, and armed conflict—and deportation—a direct effect of U.S. policies—separate families. Some observed the brutal irony of overcoming separation from loved ones for years because of migration north only to face the threat of separation again due to deportation. As Diana, who faces a deportation order for herself and her 9-year-old daughter, described: "Well, as a wife, I think that he [husband] will be here alone, that we fought so hard to be together and now, well, we have to separate." The fear of separation from loved ones due to deportation is exacerbated by previous separations resulting from multiple migrations. During a KYR workshop, Julian, one of the 18 interviewees in the project, described family separation as the most difficult aspect of migration:

> The most painful thing in the U.S. is the separation of the family because no person has the right to separate a family . . . and the children suffer because they say, "What is the reason? Why are they doing this to us?" . . . "Us" as indigenous people, as Maya. Sometimes with anger I say, "We are here because of all the wars in our countries . . . the U.S. has sent the arms to our country which the military has used to kill the indigenous people. . . . and that is the reason we are here." . . . I see in the U.S. there are laws but the U.S. is not following their own laws, they are violating the laws of the U.S.

Notable in Julian's comments on family separation is his attribution of responsibility for these tears in the family fabric to the Guatemalan and U.S. governments, the latter of which he accuses of violating its own laws through financing the Guatemalan military. Additionally, he highlights how families are twice marginalized: once, as they become transnational because of repression in the country of origin, and again as they become mixed-status and face threats of separation from U.S.-born children. To further illustrate how the threats of detention and deportation transcend borders, we present analyses of surveys and interviews with deportees who have returned to Guatemala and children and youth "left behind."

Migration, Detention, and Deportation: Multiple Views from Guatemala

Patterns of migration and profiles of migrants. To estimate the impact of migration, detention, and deportation on one local community in

Guatemala, we engaged in a series of community collaborations and action research activities in Zacualpa and its surrounding villages. In 2008, a team from the CHRIJ interviewed approximately 100 family members from Zacualpa and five of its villages who responded to an invitation from the social program of the local Catholic parish to participate in interviews with U.S. human rights activist researchers. Based on this work and the interests of the recently formed Migration and Migrant Rights office in Zacualpa, in 2011 we initiated a collaborative community survey and administered questionnaires in three of the five villages in which we had conducted interviews, as well as in the town, Urban Area (Área Urbana, see table 7.1). Each home in the four surveyed communities was visited by a local research assistant who was a community member trained in data collection. Research team members in the United States and Guatemala developed the survey instrument. Sections included (1) Demographic information: family composition and gender, level of education, language, and ethnic group for head of household and all additional household members; (2) Economic information: material possessions owned by the family (such as a cell phone, radio, etc.) and information on the quality of the family's home (including type of plumbing, materials used on the walls, roof, and floors, etc.); (3) Migration information: Presence of migrant in the family, years of migration, amount paid for migration, level of remaining debt, and U.S. state destination for migrant; and (4) Effects of migration information: Remittances and the effects of migration on children living in the household.

Across all villages, the migrants were primarily male, ranging from a low of 74.8% of the migrants from the Urban Area, and a high of 86.2% of the migrants from San Antonio Sinaché I (herewith referred to as San Antonio). The vast majority of migrants were unauthorized in the United States—92% from Tablón did not have legal status, 88.5% from San Antonio, 76.4% from Arriquín, and at least 79.1% from the Urban Area (although about 10% of the Urban Area respondents did not answer the question on legal status). As argued above, the lack of documented status in the United States puts these migrants at high risk of detention and deportation and can cause pervasive stress in their daily lives. Members of sending families are deeply aware of these threats and concerned about their sons and fathers as well as about the economic insecurities facing them locally.

TABLE 7.1. Basic Description of Villages Included in Survey

	Tablón	Arriquín	San Antonio Sinaché I	Urban Area
Number of Families	137	62	303	549
Number of People	915	352	1,907	2,708
Average Household Size	6.68 people	5.66 people	6.29 people	4.93 people
Family Ethnicity	100% K'iche'	61.3% K'iche', 35.5% Ladino, 3.2% Mestizo	100% K'iche'	63% K'iche' 35.5% Ladino 0.2% Mam 0.5% Mestizo 0.8% no response
Total N and Percentage of Population under 18	454 (49.6%)	131 (37.2%)	927 (48.6%)	1,067 (39.4%)
Total N and Percentage of Adults Age 18 and Up Who Migrated to U.S.	112 (24.3%)	53 (24.3%)	128 (13.1%)	230 (14%)
Total N and Percentage of All Migrants Who Are Male	96 (81.4%)	47 (85.5%)	112 (86.2%)	172 (74.8%)
Total N and Percentage of Families with a Family Member Who Migrated to U.S.	59 (43.1%)	29 (47%)	92 (30.4%)	145 (26.4%)
Number of Deportees from the U.S.	7	1	17	24
N and Percentage of Population Who Were in Home Village at Time of the Survey	772 (84.4%)	295 (83.8%)	1,713 (89.8%)	2,505 (92.5%)
N and Percentage of Heads of Household Without Formal Education	91 (66.4%)	28 (45.2%)	228 (75.2%)	197 (35.9%)

Note: There was a small amount of missing data for some items; each individual percentage is based on available data only. One migrant in San Antonio did not have an age listed, but was assumed to be an adult.

In June 2012, the Pew Research Center reported that migration from Mexico to the United States had slowed, suggesting that after four decades of migration from Mexico into the United States, the net migration flow had stopped and may have reversed (meaning slightly more Mexicans in the United States were returning to Mexico than the number of Mexicans coming to the United States) (Passel, Cohn, and Gonzales-Barrera 2012). Our data did not reveal the same pattern for Guatemalans migrating out of Zacualpa. In fact, 81% of all migrants across all three villages and the Urban Area surveyed came to the United States between 2000 and 2012.

Moreover, the data give us a better understanding of who migrates and of the indebtedness of families in countries of origin due to financing migration. In all three villages and the urban area, adult migrants had higher levels of education than adult non-migrants, and this difference was statistically significant in all three villages but not in the urban area. The greatest difference was in Arriquín, where 96.2% of adults who migrated had some formal education, whereas only 62.4% of adults who did not migrate had some formal education. This finding suggests that those with the most education and therefore the most human capital are the ones who are leaving the community. Interview data suggest that among the most prominent reasons for migration is an inability to find jobs with a track of upward mobility. Thus, rather than investing their knowledge into improving the local community, migrants bring this human capital to the United States.

The average cost of migration in the town as well as the three villages was approximately Q36,000, whereas the most commonly reported cost was Q40,000. Using January 2014 conversion rates, this latter amount is about $5,000 USD. Each family was also asked to report how the migrants financed their trip. Overwhelmingly across all three villages and the urban area, loans with accruing interest were the most frequently used method of paying for the journey. Other common methods of financing migration included taking out mortgages using land or homes as collateral, personal resources, and loans that did not accrue interest.

Although national statistics within Guatemala and in the United States confirm continued high levels of remittances despite downturns in the U.S. economy, our local collaborations suggest that the families in this village continue to live in poverty (see Lykes et al. 2013, for details). For example, in the three smaller villages, between 24.2% and 57.4% of households had no sanitation (plumbing) service, and less than 15% of households in Tablón and San Antonio had a refrigerator to keep food fresh.

The relationship between poverty, migration, and deportation. In the Guatemalan community-based interviews with key informants and families, we heard repeated stories of extreme poverty which had prompted family migration to the southern coast of Guatemala to work on plantations, only to return after a four-month season with scarcely enough money to pay for children's schooling the following year. Participants described experiences of living separated from a family member in the United States and also recounted unsolicited stories about children and spouses' forced migrations. Many described family members being killed or disappeared during the war. During the massacres of the 1980s, some fled to the capital, others hid out in the local town, and still others fled to Mexico, with a small number reaching the United States and Canada. The stories confirm U.S.-based migrants' narratives, adding further detail about the horrors of the war and its multiple legacies. Roberto described forced recruitment into civilian patrols and migration:

> During the war there was a lot of migration . . . that time was unbelievable, I patrolled, I was 18 years old and there are others who were 12 or 13 years old and were obligated to join the patrols [PACs], if we didn't do it they [the military] would kill us. Here in Zacualpa it was horrible. . . . Twice a week I had to do it [patrol].

Manuela chronicled her experiences in her village and the neighboring town during the war:

> I was washing in the river when I heard a bomb and people running. We went running when the war started . . . it was August 15th . . . we went running to the town because my husband was working there . . . My sister was pregnant, but she wasn't afraid so she stayed on one of the plantations . . . and ended up in the hands of the soldiers . . . they tied her up saying "look at the faces of the guerrillas" . . . they stood her up, they killed her baby, they cut him into pieces then piled them up and poured gasoline on him.

As argued above, these histories frame how participants in the PAR processes experience the current atmosphere for unauthorized migrants in the United States.

In addition to confirming the stories of terror we heard from unauthorized migrants in the United States, interview participants in Guatemala recounted surprising levels of indebtedness, as confirmed in the survey results, with many families reporting interest rates of 10% calculated monthly, resulting in the doubling of indebtedness in a single year when they were unable to make payments. In one household, including three generations of women whose spouses had either been killed in the armed conflict or had migrated to the United States, a grandmother stated that their home—which had been secured through a local widows' rights organization as reparations for her husband having been assassinated during the armed conflict—had been repossessed by the bank for the family's failure to pay back interest and principal on the nearly $15,000 USD that had been borrowed to pay for three of her children's migrations to the United States. She, her children, and grandchildren had been told to leave the property by the end of the year. Although evictions numbered less than a half-dozen among the approximately 100 families we interviewed in 2008, many described similar levels of indebtedness and indicated that as remittances decreased due to un-/underemployment or detention in the United States, they were unable to pay loans that were often secured by land or homes. And when family members in the United States are deported, the family's economic prospects are decimated, again, particularly if they are in debt. Thus, policies affecting migrants in the United States have severe consequences for family members abroad.

Psychosocial effects of migration and deportation on those "left behind" and their families. Guatemalan participants whom we interviewed in Guatemala described similar psychological effects of migration, detention, and deportation as those narrated in U.S.-based migrant communities. Many children and youth in Zacualpa make sense of their parents' migration largely through understanding it as a way in which parents care for them. Kate, interviewed in 2008, reported that her father had left when she was only weeks old but stated that she spoke to him weekly on the phone and recognized that his job in the United States allows her to attend school in the nearby town. Similarly, children reported that,

"They [migrant parents] are not criminals, because they are going to search for a better life for their family members."

Still, despite acknowledging the importance of remittances in sustaining their family and giving them access to schooling, some children and youth described life without their mother as one of sadness and longing. For example, although she understood why her mother migrated to the United States after her father deserted the family, leaving them destitute, Julia noted her own and her brothers' longing to join their mother in the United States. Julia reflected upon their situation:

> . . . [I] have been thinking, and always I am saying, that I would like to go with my mother; but she is not able to [earn] money for me to come there, so I'm not going. My [older] sister would like to go also but my mother tells my sister [that] my brothers are too young; they are little and there is no one that can care for them. And so that's what she tells us. She tells us "I'm going to return soon, I'm coming when I find work and make money, and I'm going to return to my house, when I'm able to pay my debt I am going to be able to return to you all."

Migrant parents' promises to return to children left behind are complicated, not only by indebtedness and underemployment, but also by having U.S.-born children with linguistic/cultural familiarity and increased opportunities and privileges in the United States.

Among families surveyed (Lykes et al. 2013), many youth under age 18 lived with families that had experienced the migration of one or more family members. One-quarter to one-half of children in all four areas surveyed had experienced the migration of a household member. Experiencing the loss of at least the physical presence of a family member had become an increasingly normative experience for children, and schools and other organizations working with youths were slowly becoming aware of this prevalence.

To better understand some of how youth were responding to these realities, our research team facilitated participatory workshops in a Guatemalan school in the town center whose students came from the villages and the town (Lykes and Sibley 2013). Thirty-three Mayan students who had at least one parent in the United States described repeatedly asking a mother or father when she or he would be "coming home," only to be told that finances, debt, and/or reduced employment opportunities in the United States prevented parents from returning. Other children and youth referred to telephone conversations with their mothers or fathers, describing a sense of loss and sadness at their parent's absence but also their understanding that parents migrated due to the extreme poverty locally. One young girl, Vivian, remarked that: ". . . The children feel sad, but they [the parents] leave out of necessity, because of the poverty they leave. . . . they leave because there is a great need." Although these youth rarely described their own emotions, many, like Valeria, recounted younger siblings' tears upon viewing a photograph of a mother or hearing her voice on the phone: "One day I saw my sister crying and looking at a photo of my mother . . . She calls us every week . . . one day she calls, the next day she doesn't . . . She speaks to everyone, even the smallest ones. Not anymore—they have become accustomed to it—but at first they cried."

Mayan youth participating in educational workshops and interviews were very well informed about life in the United States. They revealed knowledge about discrimination against unauthorized migrants, low wages, racism, and the weakening economy—all of which they saw as constraining their parents' capacity to care for them from afar. Some described parents' experiences of racism and discriminatory treatment in the workplace and in local communities (see Lykes and Sibley 2013, for a fuller description of youth "left behind," and Hershberg and Lykes 2012, for stories from girls within these samples living in mixed-status and transnational families). Others spoke of U.S.-based parents' loss of one or more jobs, and/or parents' being fearful of leaving the home or of socializing outside of the house due to "*la migra*," i.e., ICE. Yet, despite this knowledge, most youth reported dreaming of heading north, and according to the community survey in Zacualpa, increasing numbers of youth between the ages of 18 and 25 are risking everything in hopes of improving their life options and/or supporting their families in Guatemala.

Adults in Zacualpa also reported pain and loss due to multiple separations common to transnational and mixed-status families. Augusto, a deportee interviewed in 2008, described the pain of being unable to return from the United States in order to attend his mother's funeral (his father had been killed during the armed conflict) because he lacked documents to travel—only to be "sentenced home" through deportation a short two months later.

> Our father died on August 7, 1982 during one of the massacres by the military; he was assassinated. And our mother died December 11, 2007 . . . seven months to this day . . . and sadly we were not here, since my sister Juana and I were in the U.S. It was a very difficult moment . . . we couldn't come because we were undocumented and wouldn't be able to return . . . we had made the sacrifice of not coming to my mother's burial, just so that in two months we'd be forced to come anyway and not find her here anymore. So it is a—or to say that in a psychological sense—these become traumas that little by little you will recover from.

His loss was exacerbated further when his wife gave birth to their first child in Maine after he had been deported back to Zacualpa, multiplying the separations among family members living across borders with different statuses.

Implications and Pending Challenges

Our data confirm that current threats to unauthorized migrants and their families "left behind" posed by U.S. immigration policies and their enforcement are experienced and narrated historically and transnationally by the Salvadorans and Guatemalans in mixed-status and transnational families with whom we are collaborating in the United States and in Zacualpa. Few in the United States are aware of the history of U.S. involvement in the armed conflicts in Central America (see González 2000/2011), yet our research suggests that such understanding is crucial to framing our participants' experiences of and meaning-making about contemporary immigration policies and enforcements. Additionally important to understand is that children on both sides of the U.S. border are being raised in families fractured by U.S. policies and practices. Migrants separated from their family members due to forced recruitment, massacres, disappearances, or migrations when they were children are today prevented from traveling to their countries of origin and live with daily fear of separation from U.S.-born children. Children in the United States and abroad are being separated from parents due to forced migration (rooted in poverty, racism, and violence), detention, and deportation. Children on both sides of the border hear their parents referred to as "illegal" or "criminals." They hear stories and witness evidence of unemployment, racism, and/or discriminatory U.S. policies vis-à-vis immigrants. Yet many develop a critical moral compass through which they defend their parents' choices. Moreover, despite knowledge of workplace raids, violence on the journey north, and indebtedness for those who chose to leave home, youth report dreams of traveling north or being resigned that the only option for realizing their goals is through crossing the border without authorization.

Impacting the lives of unauthorized migrants and children living in mixed-status and transnational families requires significant policy reform that enacts purportedly American values, including family integrity, human rights, protection of the vulnerable, and the best interest of children. Based on these participatory and action research processes and outcomes—and our relationships of pragmatic solidarity—we argue that such policies should benefit children and parents in countries of origin and in the United States. Children should have opportunities to reunite with their families in the United States or receive adequate resources that enable them to improve their quality of life and life options within their country of origin. U.S. citizen children should be allowed to petition for their parents to become U.S. citizens now, rather than having to wait until they are 21 years old (see Thronson, this volume). If parents are detained and threatened with deportation, children's interests should be represented in such hearings.

Interdisciplinary and transnational partnerships among activists, academics and migrants, and participatory and action research methods offer the potential for understanding the deep historical rootedness of contemporary experiences in the words of those most directly impacted and the potential to collaboratively design more systemic responses for individuals and families on both sides of the border. The PAR process described herein is one methodological resource for developing a response in that direction.

NOTE

1 Mainstream media frequently refers to this population as "illegal aliens." Recent criticisms by academics, activists, and journalists (see, e.g., http://www.nahj.org/nahjnews/articles/2006/March/immigrationcoverage.shtml) challenge this dis-

criminatory labeling of the foreign-born who have entered the United States without inspection or "overstayed the expiration date of a visa or other status" (http://www.nolo.com/dictionary/undocumented-immigrant-term.html). Although many don't meet the technical definition of immigrant (a person who leaves one country to settle permanently in another), they are also not temporary migrants. Recognizing these complexities, we use the term "unauthorized migrant" when speaking of the population with whom we are working, but defer to current government use of immigrant in describing U.S. policy and laws as well as government statistics.

REFERENCES

abUSED: The Postville Raid (documentary). 2010. Directed by Luis Argueta. New York: Maya Media.

Andrade-Eekhoff, Katherine A., and Claudia Marina Silva-Avalos. 2003. *Globalization of the Periphery: The Challenges of Transnational Migration for Local Development in Central America.* El Salvador: FLASCO.

Bacon, David, and Bill Ong Hing. 2010. "The Rise and Fall of Employer Sanctions." *Fordham Urban Law Journal.* Accessed December 11, 2011. http://works.bepress.com/billhing/11.

Barrett, Alice N., Judith L. Gibbons, and Ana Victoria Peláez Ponce. 2014. "'Now I Can Help Someone': Social Remittances Among Returned Migrants in Highland Guatemala."*International Perspectives in Psychology: Research Practice Consultation* 3:1–18. doi: 10.1037/ipp0000010.

Baum, Jonathan, Rosha Jones, and Catherine Barry. 2010. *In the Child's Best Interest?: The Consequences of Losing a Lawful Immigrant Parent to Deportation.* Berkeley: University of California Berkeley School of Law.

Betancur, Belisario, Reinaldo Figueredo Planchart, and Thomas Buergenthal. 1993. *From Madness to Hope: The 12-year War in El Salvador: Report of the Commission on the Truth for El Salvador.* Accessed May 4, 2014. http://www.usip.org/files/file/ElSalvador-Report.pdf.

Brabeck, Kalina, M. Brinton Lykes, and Rachel Hershberg. 2011. "Framing Immigration to and Deportation from the United States: Central American Immigrants Make Meaning of Their Experiences." *Community, Work, & Family* 13:275–296. doi:10.1080/13668803.2010.520840.

Capps, Randolph, Rosa Maria Castaneda, Ajay Chaudry, and Robert Santos. 2007. *Paying the Price: The Impact of Immigration Raids on America's Children.* Washington, DC: National Council of La Raza.

Carmack, Robert M., ed. 1988. *Harvest of Violence: The Maya Indians and the Guatemalan Crisis.* Norman: University of Oklahoma Press.

Chamarbagwala, Rubiana, and Hilcias E. Morán. 2011. "The Human Capital Consequences of Civil War: Evidence from Guatemala." *Journal of Development Economics* 94:41–61. doi: 10.1016/j.jdeveco.2010.01.005.

Chaudry, Ajay, Randolph Capps, Juan Pedroza, Rosa Maria Castaneda, Robert Santos, and Molly Scott. 2010. *Facing our Future: Children in the Aftermath of Immigration*

Enforcement. Washington, DC: Urban Institute. Accessed October 22, 2014. http://www.urban.org/publications/412020.html.

Cohen, Salomon. 2006. *CAFTA: What Could It Mean for Migration?* Accessed December 11, 2011. http://www.migrationinformation.org/USfocus/print.cfm?ID=388.

Comisión para el Esclarecimiento Histórico (Commission for Historical Clarification) (CEH). 1999. *Guatemala: Memory of Silence [Memoria del Silencio]. Report of the Commission for Historical Clarification, Conclusions and Recommendations*. Accessed May 4, 2014. http://shr.aaas.org/guatemala/ceh/report/english/toc.html.

Commission for Historical Clarification. 2011. "Acts of Genocide." In *The Guatemala Reader: History, Culture, Politics*, edited by Greg Grandin, Deborah T. Levenson, and Elizabeth Oglesby, 386–394. Durham, NC: Duke University Press.

Davis, Shelton H. 1988. *Land Rights and Indigenous People: The Role of the Inter-American Commission on Human Rights*. Cambridge, MA: Cultural Survival.

De Genova, Nicholas P. 2002. "Migrant 'Illegality' and Deportability in Everyday Life." *Annual Review of Anthropology* 31:419–445. doi: 10.1146/annurev.anthro.31.040402.085432.

Department of Homeland Security Office of Immigration Statistics. 2012a. "Table 39: Aliens Removed or Returned: Fiscal Years 1892 to 2012." Accessed March 29, 2012. http://www.dhs.gov/yearbook-immigration-statistics-2012-enforcement-actions.

Department of Homeland Security Office of Immigration Statistics. 2012b. *2012 Yearbook of Immigration Statistics*. Accessed May 4, 2014. http://www.dhs.gov/files/statistics/publications/yearbook.shtm.

Department of Homeland Security. 2013. *ERO Annual Report, FY 2013 ICE Immigration Removals*. Accessed May 4, 2014. http://www.ice.gov/doclib/about/offices/ero/pdf/2013-ice-immigration-removals.pdf.

Department of Homeland Security, Office of Immigration Statistics. 2013. *Estimates of the Unauthorized Immigrant Population Residing in the United States: January 2012*. Accessed September 21, 2013. http://www.dhs.gov/sites/default/files/publications/ois_ill_pe_2012_2.pdf.

Dreby, Joanna. 2007. "Children and Power in Mexican Transnational Families." *Journal of Marriage and Family* 69:1050–1064. doi: 10.1111/j.1741-3737.2007.00430.x.

Dreby, Joanna. 2010. *Divided by Borders: Mexican Migrants and their Children*. Berkeley: University of California Press.

Dreby, Joanna, and Linday Stutz. 2012. "Making Something of the Sacrifice: Gender, Migration, and Mexican Children's Educational Aspirations." *Global Networks* 12:71–90. doi:10.1111/j.1471-0374.2011.00337.x.

Fals Borda, Orlando. 1985. *Knowledge and People's Power: Lessons with Peasants in Nicaragua, Mexico, and Colombia*. New Delhi: Indian Social Institute.

Fals Borda, Orlando. 1998. *People's Participation: Challenges Ahead*. New York: Apex Press/Intermediate Technology Publications.

Fals Borda, Orlando. 2000. "People's Space Times in Global Processes: The Response of the Local." *Journal of World-Systems Research* 6:624–634.

Farmer, Paul. 2003. *Pathologies of Power; Health, Human Rights, and the New War on the Poor* Berkeley: University of California Press.

Foley, Eise. 2011. "Secure Communities Agreements Canceled, Participation Still Required." *Huffington Post*. Accessed October 4, 2014. http://www.huffingtonpost.com/2011/08/05/secure-communities-update-department-of-homeland-security_n_919651.html.

Frank, Reanne, and Elizabeth Wildsmith. 2005. "The Grass Widows of Mexico: Migration and Union Dissolution in a Binational Context." *Social Forces* 83:919–948. doi: 10.1353/sof.2005.0031.

Friedland, Joan, Lisa Johnson-Firth, and Michele Garnett-McKenzie. 2009. "State and Local Enforcement of Immigration Law and Community Responses to Find a Better Way." In Rizwan Hassan, editor-in-chief, *Immigration & Nationality Law Handbook 2009–2010* (pp. 1115–1130). Washington, DC: American Immigration Lawyers Association.

González, Juan. 2000/2011. *Harvest of Empire: A History of Latinos in America*. New York: Penguin Books.

Grandin, Greg, Deborah T. Levenson, and Elizabeth Oglesby. 2011. *The Guatemala Reader: History, Culture, Politics*. Durham, NC: Duke University Press.

Hagan, Jacqueline, Karl Eschbach, and Nestor Rodriguez. 2008. "U.S. Deportation Policy, Family Separation, and Circular Migration." *International Migration Review* 42:64–88. doi: 10.1111/j.1747-7379.2007.00114.x.

Hamilton, Nora, and Norma Stoltz Chinchilla. 1991. "Central American Migration: A Framework for Analysis." *Latin American Research Review* 26:75–110.

Hershberg, Rachel M., and M. Brinton Lykes. 2012. "Redefining Family: Transnational Girls Narrate Experiences of Parental Migration, Detention, and Deportation." *FQS: Forum Qualitative Sozialforschung/Forum: Qualitative Social Research*. 14. Accessed October 22, 2014. http://nbn-resolving.de/urn:nbn:de:0114-fqs130157.

Internal Displacement Monitoring Centre & Norwegian Refugee Council. 2011. *Internal Displacement: Global Overview of Trends and Developments in 2010*. Accessed May 4, 2014. http://www.internal-displacement.org/assets/publications/2011/2011-global-overview-2010-global-en.pdf.

Lykes, M. Brinton, and Jessica Chicco. 2011. "Políticas y Prácticas de Deportación en la Administración de Obama: 'Entre Más Cambian las Cosas Más se Quedan Igual.'" ["Deportation Policies and Practices in the Obama Administration: 'The More Things Change the More they Stay the Same'"]. *Encuentro* 90:1–18.

Lykes, M. Brinton, Erin McDonald, and Cesar Boc. 2012. "The Post-Deportation Human Rights Project: Participatory Action Research with Maya Transnational Families." *Practicing Anthropology* 34:22–26.

Lykes, M. Brinton, and Erin Sibley. 2013. "Exploring Meaning Making with Adolescents 'Left Behind' by Migration." *Educational Action Research* 21:565–581. doi: 10.1080/09650792.2013. 832346. [Spanish translation available from first author]

Lykes, M. Brinton, Erin Sibley, Ana Maria Alvárez, Jose Daniel Chich Gonzáles, and Megan Thomas. 2013. *Documenting Migration among the Maya K'iche' of Guate-*

mala: *Community-Based Surveys of Family Costs and Benefits of Heading North.* Chestnut Hill, MA: Center for Human Rights and International Justice.

Maguire, Patricia. 1987/2000. *Doing Participatory Research: A Feminist Approach.* Amherst, MA: Center for International Education, University of Massachusetts/Amherst. (Fourth printing, 2000).

Melville, Margarita V., and M. Brinton Lykes. 1992. "Guatemalan Indian Children and the Sociocultural Effects of Government-Sponsored Terrorism." *Social Science and Medicine* 34:533–548.

Migration and Human Rights Project, Center for Human Rights and International Justice Boston College. 2012. *2011–2012 Annual Report.* Chestnut Hill, MA. Accessed October 22, 2014. http://www.bc.edu/content/dam/files/centers/humanrights/pdf/PDHRP-AnnReport-FINAL.pdf.

Migration and Human Rights Project, Center for Human Rights and International Justice Boston College. 2013. *2012–2013 Annual Report.* Chestnut Hill, MA. Accessed October 22, 2014. http://www.bc.edu/content/dam/files/centers/humanrights/pdf/MHRP2013-EN.pdf.

National Conference of State Legislatures (NCSL). 2014. *2013 Immigration Report.* Accessed October 4, 2014. www.ncsl.org/research/immigration/2013-immigration-report.aspx.

National Day Laborers Organization (NDLON) and Center for Constitutional Rights (CCR). 2010. *Briefing Guide to Secure Communities.* Accessed May 4, 2014. http://ccrjustice.org/files/Secure%20Communities%20Fact%20Sheet%20Briefing%20guide%208-2-2010%20Production.pdf.

New York University School of Law Immigrant Rights Clinic. 2012. *Insecure Communities, Devastated Families: New Data on Immigrant Detention and Deportation Practices in New York City.* Accessed May 4, 2014. http://www.familiesforfreedom.org/sites/default/files/resources/NYC%20FOIA%20Report%202012%20FINAL_1.pdf.

Passel, Jeffrey, D'Vera Cohn, and Ana Gonzalez Barrera. 2012. *Net Migration from Mexico Falls to Zero—and Perhaps Less.* Washington, DC: Pew Research Center. Accessed May 4, 2014. http://www.pewhispanic.org/files/2012/04/Mexican-migrants-report_final.pdf.

Passel, Jeffrey, D'Vera Cohn, Jens Manuel Krogstad, and Ana Gonzales-Barrera. 2014. *As Growth Stalls, Unauthorized Immigrant Population Becomes More Settled.* Washington, DC: Pew Research Center. Accessed October 2, 2014. http://www.pewhispanic.org/files/2014/09/2014-09-03_Unauthorized-Final.pdf

Passel, Jeffrey, and Paul Taylor. 2010. *Unauthorized Immigrants and Their US-Born Children.* Washington, DC: Pew Research Center. Accessed October 22, 2014. http://www.pewhispanic.org/2010/08/11/unauthorized-immigrants-and-their-us-born-children/.

Post-Deportation Human Rights Project, Center for Human Rights and International Justice Boston College. 2009. *2008–2009 annual report: Keeping families connected/Manteniendo a las familias conectadas.* Chestnut Hill, MA. Accessed October 22,

2014. http://www.bc.edu/content/dam/files/centers/humanrights/pdf/PDHRPAnnualReport.pdf.

Post-Deportation Human Rights Project, Center for Human Rights and International Justice Boston College. 2010. *2009–2010 annual report: Keeping families connected/ Manteniendo a las familias conectadas*. Chestnut Hill, MA. Accessed October 22, 2014. http://www.bc.edu/content/dam/files/centers/humanrights/pdf/PDHRPAnnualReportV4.pdf.

Post-Deportation Human Rights Project, Center for Human Rights and International Justice Boston College. 2011. *2010–2011 annual report*. Chestnut Hill, MA. Accessed October 22, 2014. http://www.bc.edu/content/dam/files/centers/humanrights/pdf/PDHRP_Report_2011_Eng.pdf.

Reason, Peter, and Hillary Bradbury. 2008. *The SAGE Handbook of Action Research: Participatory Inquiry and Practice*. London: SAGE.

Remijnse, Simone. 2002. "Remembering Civil Patrols in Joyabaj, Guatemala." *Bulletin of Latin American Research* 20:454–469. doi: 10.1111/1470-9856.00025.

Salvadó, Luis Raul. 1988. *The Other Refugees: A Study of Nonrecognized Guatemalan Refugees in Chiapas, Mexico*. Washington, DC: CMP/CIPRA, Georgetown University.

Schlesinger, Stephen C., and Stephen Kinzer. 1999. *Bitter Fruit: The Story of the American Coup in Guatemala*. Cambridge, MA: Harvard University Press.

Schmalzbauer, Leah. 2004. "Searching for Wages and Mothering from Afar: The Case of Honduran Transnational Families." *Journal of Marriage and Family* 66:1317–1331. doi:10.1111/j.0022-2445.2004.00095.x.

Schmalzbauer, Leah. 2005. "Transamerican Dreamers: The Relationship of Honduran Transmigrants to the American Dream and Consumer Society." *Berkeley Journal of Sociology* 49: 3–31. http://www.jstor.org/stable/41035600.

Slevin, Peter. 2010. "Record Numbers Being Deported; Rise Is Part of Obama's Efforts to Remake Immigration Laws." *Washington Post*, July 26, 2010. p. A01. Accessed October 22, 2014. http://www.washingtonpost.com/wp-dyn/content/article/2010/07/25/AR2010072501790.html.

Smith, James. 2006. *Guatemala: Economic Migrants Replace Political Refugees*. Migration Policy Institute. Accessed December 10, 2011. http://www.migrationinformation.org/feature/display.cfm?ID=392.

Stewart, Iain. 2012. "El Quiché. The Western Highlands." In *The Rough Guide to Guatemala*, edited by Iain Stewart and Matthew Park, 94–116. London: Rough Guides Ltd.

Stone, Hannah. 2011. "Guatemala Anti-Drug Operations Force Refugees into Mexico." *InSight Organized Crime in the Americas*. Accessed December 10, 2011. http://www.insightcrime.org/news-briefs/guatemala-anti-drug-operations-force-refugees-into-mexico.

UNICEF and IOM Guatemala. 2011. *Encuesta Sobre Remesas 2010, Protección de La Niñez y Adolescencia* [*Survey on 2010 Remittances, Child and Adolescent Protection*.] Accessed December 10, 2011. http://www.iom.int/jahia/webdav/shared/

shared/mainsite/media/docs/reports/Guatemala-2010-migrant-remittance-survey.pdf.
Washington Office on Latin American (WOLA). 2003. *What Is CAFTA and Why Is It Important?* Accessed December 11, 2011. http://www.wola.org/publications/what_is_cafta_and_why_is_it_important.
Wessler, Seth Freed et al. 2011. *Shattered Families: The Perilous Intersection of Immigration Enforcement and the Child Welfare System.* New York: Applied Research Center.
Wessler, Seth Freed. 2012. "Nearly 250K Deportations of Parents of U.S. Citizens in Just Over Two Years." *Color Lines News for Action.* Accessed October 4, 2014. http://www.colorlines.com/archives/2012/12/us_deports_more_than_200k_parents.html.
Zentgraf, Kristine M., and Norma Stoltz Chinchilla. 2012. "Transnational Family Separation: A Framework for Analysis." *Journal of Ethnic and Migration Studies* 38:345–366. doi: 10.1080/1369183X.2011.646431.

8

Unwelcome Returns

The Alienation of the New American Diaspora in Salvadoran Society

KATIE DINGEMAN-CERDA AND RUBÉN G. RUMBAUT

When interviewed in El Salvador in 2011, two years after his deportation, Andrés Meranda[1] reported that he considered the United States his home. He had lived in Texas since the age of six after being reunited there with his immigrant parents. Despite his undocumented status, he did well in school and maintained a group of friends who shielded him from the gangs that were prevalent in his neighborhood. During his junior year of high school, Andrés received legal permanent resident status through his father. Later that year, however, he was found in possession of a controlled substance and was sent to juvenile hall. Once released, Andrés decided not to finish high school. He instead established a successful auto-body business and had three children, whom he dedicated his life to raising with the mother of the youngest two. Since issues of race and illegality purportedly never affected his life, Andrés did not understand that he could one day be separated from the family and career he established in the nation he understood to be his own.

Twenty years after his arrival in the United States, Andrés was deported for a felony offense he said he did not commit, but for which he accepted a plea bargain. He wanted to fight for cancellation of removal, but he could not afford legal aid and was afraid he would wait in detention for years while the case was pending. By signing an order of removal, he agreed to be returned to El Salvador, the country of his birth and citizenship, but a place he did not know. Andrés could only recall two faint memories of his life prior to migration. He was unable to recount any details about the civil war that plagued El Salvador when he was a child. He did not know the name of the Salvadoran president.

He had no direct familial or other social ties to the nation. "I don't know anything about this country," he stated.

Andrés was alienated in El Salvador. When he first arrived he had no place to live, so he stayed with another deportee he met at the airport. His aunt was eventually located and she accepted Andrés into her home. However, after about a month she asked him to find a new place to live because she was afraid that his tattoos—which depict the names of his three children on his neck—would attract gangs and police to her neighborhood. Faced with homelessness, Andrés considered re-migrating to the United States. When he heard that his stepbrother had been murdered in Texas, he fled El Salvador by foot. After a difficult journey through Mexico, Andrés was apprehended, detained, and deported from the United States a second time.

After his arrival back in El Salvador, Andrés was stopped-and-frisked at least 35 times by Salvadoran police, who erroneously assumed he was involved in gangs. It took him seven months to secure a job. Unable to support himself, Andrés grew financially dependent on remittances from family in the United States —the same people for whom he had once been a proud breadwinner. Though he was aware that his tattoos associated him with local gangs, Andrés refused to have them removed. The inscriptions represented the children he was forced to leave behind and who were gradually un-knowing him. Their branded names were his way of embodying their presence in his absence. They served as a reminder of the life to which he hoped to return and a family he dreamed of rebuilding.

Andrés eventually obtained employment as a customer service agent in a foreign-owned call center that hired him for his bilingual skills. Other deportees worked at the same call center, but Andrés resisted establishing friendships with them. Under the impression that "nobody can be trusted" in his country-of-citizenship, he minimized his physical presence in El Salvador. When not working he preferred to incarcerate himself in his apartment. He said, "I don't even think, I just stay in my room, listen to music, and draw."

Andrés represents one member of the *new American diaspora* that has emerged as a result of restrictive U.S. immigration enforcement policies in recent decades. According to Daniel Kanstroom (2012, p. xi), this diaspora "consists of a forcibly uprooted population of people with deep, cohesive, social and cultural connections" to the United States. As Andrés' story highlights, it is a population consisting mainly of individuals who emigrated from their countries-of-citizenship as children or otherwise spent a substantial amount of time in the United States. Despite their noncitizen status, they become *de facto* members of U.S. society. As a result of their participation in school, the workforce, and establishment of families and social support networks, they integrate into their cultural repertoires many ideas, behaviors, and practices associated with U.S. society. When asked post-removal, they tend to identify themselves as full or hybrid "Americans."

Nascent research examines the consequences of removal on the livelihoods of members of the new American diaspora (Brotherton and Barrios 2011; Coutin 2010b; Dingeman-Cerda and Coutin 2012; Golash-Boza 2013). This research demonstrates that this population often experiences removal as a form of banishment from the lives and families they constructed in the United States. Like many child migrants (Rumbaut 2002), they generally do not retain strong transnational ties and often lack significant memories, maintain imperfect knowledge, and sometimes lose the ability to converse in the language of their countries of citizenship. When returned to their so-called homelands, they are forced to navigate social worlds with which they have little to no familiarity, while often being subjected to stigmatization and criminalization. They undergo this process of alienation while also being estranged, sometimes permanently, from the social and economic ties they maintain to the United States (Brotherton and Barrios 2011; Dingeman-Cerda and Coutin 2012; Golash-Boza 2013; Hagan, Rodríguez, and Castro 2011; Miller 2008).

Another lesser understood consequence of mass deportation from the United States is the potential transformation of societies to which large rates of deportees are returned. Research dealing with the influence of return migrants on their native countries has hitherto focused almost exclusively on the behaviors and influence of *voluntary* return migrants. But forcibly returned migrants also carry potentially influential "social remittances" with them to their countries-of-citizenship. Such "ideas, behaviors, identities, and social capital" learned in their former host countries have the potential to diffuse through interpersonal interactions, producing ripple effects that can alter local and national contexts of return (Levitt 1998, p. 927). The question remains, however, whether the social remittances carried by deportees can be successfully diffused in a context that systematically marginalizes their social existence.

This chapter draws upon the case of deportation to El Salvador. It seeks to understand whether and the ways in which deported members of the new American diaspora impact Salvadoran society through the diffusion of social remittances. It draws primarily from life-history interviews conducted between 2008 and 2013 with 47 Salvadoran deportees identified as members of the new American diaspora.[2] These individuals tended to migrate to the United States as children during the 1980s at the height of the Salvadoran civil war (1980–1992). They were returned over a decade later for both immigration violations and criminal convictions. Because they were primarily socialized in the United States, they viewed it as the site of their national belonging. Prior to deportation they retained few ties to, and memories of, El Salvador. Most had no intentions of ever returning to the country of their birth. Attesting to their general lack of cultural affiliation with El Salvador, two participants could not speak Spanish, several retained Mexican accents absorbed from the Latino communities in which they grew up, and one thought he was a Mexican until he learned otherwise while in removal proceedings. As a result of the psycho-cultural and social connections they maintained to the United States, after removal members of this population overwhelmingly described themselves as more "American" than "Salvadoran."

This chapter's findings are consistent with past research demonstrating that deportees with strong ties to the United States constitute unwelcome foreign elements in El Salvador (see also Coutin 2007; Dingeman and Rumbaut 2010). They experience an antipathetic societal reception that subjects them to social and economic marginalization. The alienation they experience in their country of citizenship stunts their ability to diffuse the social remittances they acquired during their tenure in the United States. Their tarnished social status robs them of their potential and inhibits collective action that could improve their situation. This leaves individuals like Andrés, introduced at the beginning of this chapter, in a position where they feel they must resign themselves to existing precariously in El Salvador, while dreaming, usually in vain, of reclaiming their former U.S.-based lives.

The population as a whole is not, however, completely devoid of agency. The new American diaspora finds creative ways to hide their identities and survive post-removal. With limited social capital and opportunity structures, some of them are compelled or forced to join gangs in which they spread "negative" social remittances from the United States. Most, however, work to distance themselves from gang culture by changing their personal style, removing their tattoos, and limiting their physical presence in high-risk areas. They maintain transnational ties to the United States and seek out employment in foreign call centers that accept their labor. Though they appear unable to use their social remittances to positively affect Salvadoran social life, their narratives offer numerous feasible suggestions on how to improve the treatment of deportees and other marginalized populations in the country. If offered adequate opportunities for advancement, their presence in Salvadoran society could be seen as a boon rather than a problem.

Salvadoran Migration and Removal

El Salvador was chosen as a strategic research site, owing to its history of neocolonial political and economic ties to the United States. Contemporary migratory linkages between the countries derive from the brutal civil war that took place in El Salvador between 1980 and 1992. The war was largely funded by the Reagan administration, claimed over 75,000 lives, and sent somewhere between 25 and 35 percent of the population on a migratory trail to the United States (PNUD 2005). In the postwar period, remarkably high levels of emigration are sustained by persistent domestic economic inequality fueled largely by continued U.S. economic penetration, as well as gang violence, environmental disasters, and the constant "pull" toward economic opportunity and political refuge in the United States (Gammage 2007). Despite the small size of El Salvador, a remarkable 1.5 million foreign-born Salvadorans now live in the United States. The population constitutes the third largest Hispanic, sixth largest foreign-born, and second largest undocumented population in the United States (Hoefer, Rytina, and Baker 2012; Brown and Patten 2014).

Cold War concerns led the U.S. federal government initially to deny refugee status to Salvadoran entrants in the 1980s. Pressure from activists and the Salvadoran state eventually led to piecemeal protections, including political asylum, temporary protected status, deferred enforced departure, and cancellation of removal (Mountz, Wright, Miyares, and Bailey 2002). Despite these efforts, Salvadorans now constitute one of the most deportable migrant populations in the United States: 46 percent of the foreign-born population is undocumented and another 25 percent hold temporary or partial statuses that lack pathways to citizenship (Brick, Challinor, and Rosenblum 2011; Brown and Patten 2014). Thus, among Salvadoran-born migrants, 71 percent are noncitizens and subject to removal if they commit deportable offenses. The overall state of "liminal legality" that has been argued to characterize the population limits their life chances, makes them vulnerable to economic exploitation and human rights abuses, and forces them to lead lives haunted by the specter of U.S. immigration control (Menjívar 2006).

Most, though certainly not all, Salvadoran immigrants are consigned to poor urban centers with high levels of racial and ethnic tensions. Salvadorans are disproportionally employed in service, manufacturing, and construction industries characterized by instability and low wages (Brown and Patten 2014). They tend to live in states with high costs-of-living and reside in overcrowded households in poor and working-class neighborhoods (Hamilton and Chinchilla 2001). The vast majority of the Salvadoran foreign-born and native-born population avoids gang life in the United States. But the vulnerable states of "multiple marginality" in which many live has contributed to the formation of Latino street gangs such as the infamous Mara Salvatrucha 13 (MS-13) and 18th Street gangs (Vigil 2002). The politicization of these gangs has stigmatized the entire Salvadoran population, leading to a heightened state of deportability (Chacón 2007).

Salvadorans now constitute one of the most highly deported populations from the United States by percentage of total removals. Out of 391,953 in FY 2011, 4.4 percent (17,308) of deportations were to El Salvador. This made them the fourth most-deported group, behind only Mexicans at 75 percent (293,966), Guatemalans at 7.7 percent (30,313), and Hondurans at 5.6 percent (21,963) (OIS 2012). Despite the politicization of Salvadoran gang members, the vast majority of Salvadoran deportations have been the result of immigration violations, not criminal convictions (OIS 2012). In 2011, Salvadorans deported for "criminal convictions" suddenly constituted 49 percent of removals to the country.

Though data are not available on the types of crimes resulting in removal to El Salvador in 2011, cross-national data from 1997 to 2007 show that most "criminals" deported over that period were removed for minor, nonviolent offenses (HRW 2009). All available evidence indicates that this trend of criminalizing immigration has continued, suggesting that the majority of deportees currently being deported to El Salvador are far from the hardened, violent criminals they are often portrayed to be.

Regardless of reason for removal, the context to which deportees return in El Salvador impedes the successful integration of the new American diaspora. Progressive efforts have been made since the moderate-leftist Mauricio Funes was elected to the presidency in 2009 (see Arnson et al. 2011; Mills 2012; Seelke 2013; Shifter and Schwartz 2012). But the country still continues to struggle with high degrees of poverty, unemployment, and street crime. In the postwar years the neo-liberal model of economic development followed by the Salvadoran state has done little to improve socioeconomic inequalities (Velásquez Carrillo 2010). Deportees are thus returning to a highly stratified society with limited occupational choices.

They are also returning to a repressive political environment. Until the historic gang truce was negotiated in Salvadoran prisons in 2012, the government relied upon a zero-tolerance approach to gang violence (Zilberg 2011). Heavy-handed strategies exacerbated violence and contributed to the criminalization and insecurity of the new American diaspora (Dingeman-Cerda and Rumbaut 2010; Zilberg 2011). The institutional context of return could conceivably mitigate such a harsh climate for deportees returning from the United States. But neither the Salvadoran nor the U.S. government have sufficiently invested in deportee reinsertion. The onus for post-deportation integration rests almost entirely on deportees and their families, constraining their ability to contribute to Salvadoran society in positive, progressive ways.

What Deportees Carry

Deportees carry the remnants of their acculturation into U.S. society with them as they navigate El Salvador post-removal. These "social remittances" are never carbon copies of some mythologized U.S. culture, but are hybridized and creolized versions of cultural ideas and practices from sites in which deportees were once embedded in the United States (Levitt 1998). Social remittances are constantly being defined, redefined, and reformulated through deportees' engagement with family and friends left behind in the United States, and through their daily interactions in El Salvador. The remittances they carry can be viewed as either "positive" or "negative" (Levitt and Lamba-Nieves 2010, 2011). They can contribute to progressive social change or disrupt native cultures, weaken families, encourage delinquent behaviors among disenfranchised youth, and contribute to mythologies supporting high rates of emigration in El Salvador (ibid.).

Objectively identifying social remittances garnered in the United States can be a difficult task because in the era of globalization, cultural beliefs, ideas, and practices are rapidly exchanged across national contexts through multiple modes of diffusion. However, members of the new American diaspora rhetorically revealed their subjectively defined social remittances in part through descriptions of themselves as visibly culturally different from the local Salvadoran population. They maintained identities and tastes garnered in the United States, including food and music preferences, leisure activities and holiday traditions, and beliefs about acceptable standards of living, environmental practices, government policies, and courtship rituals. They also claimed to embody the United States through the presence of tattoos, a casual or "baggy" style of attire, use of English and Mexican slang, and subtle ways of walking and gesturing they defined as "Americanized" and thus qualitatively distinct from non-migrants As Luis Aguilar, 31, stated:

> After so much time in the U.S. your customs become American. The way you dress, you don't dress like people here. This is the way you dress in the United States (points to his khaki shorts, t-shirt, and diamond-like earrings). This is the way I used to dress in New York City. Now, I don't even walk around. People look at you different, like this guy is not from here.

Deportees' less readily apparent social remittances often surfaced as recommendations for social change in El Salvador based on ideologies, values, and beliefs they claimed to have learned in the United States. The narrative of Pablo Día, 47, is instructive. Pablo spent 30 years in the United States prior to his removal to El Salvador in 2008. Like many deportees, he underwent a dramatic "reverse culture shock" upon return, describing himself as "a new puppy in the house that doesn't know where to go or what to do." Disillusioned with his treatment in Salvadoran society, he romanticized the United States as an efficient, wealthy, and clean society completely lacking political and economic corruption. Frustrated by the dearth of jobs and high levels of inequality in El Salvador, he protested that the Salvadoran government "really steps on the poor people. They step on their face, on their throat, so they don't have much air to breathe."

Demonstrating his internalization of the "American Dream," Pablo argued that the United States was more socioeconomically "advanced" than El Salvador and that "everyone can make it there." Drawing from political debates in the United States, he recommended that the Salvadoran state work to create more jobs, increase the minimum wage, reduce corruption among politicians and the police, develop national infrastructure, and place restrictions on smog output.

Freddy Mendoza, 28, was another individual whose comparisons of Salvadoran society with the United States during a period of reverse culture shock led recommendations for social change. Freddy migrated to the United States at age 5, grew up speaking English only, and adorned his body with several visible tattoos. Though he had no gang history in El Salvador, he was treated like a gang member after his first deportation in 2002. He was harassed by police, beat up by gangsters, rejected by employers, and treated with suspicion by locals who feared him. He re-migrated to the United States shortly after his deportation but was removed again in 2008 after being apprehended for illegal reentry. After the second deportation, he learned to cover his identity by "acting like a tourist." He wore long-sleeved shirts and sunglasses, lived off his parents' credit cards and remittances from the United States, ate in chain restaurants like Burger King and Pizza Hut, hired a cab driver in lieu of taking the bus, and sought employment in a foreign-owned call center looking for bilingual employees. Despite these efforts he still reported feeling like he did not belong in El Salvador. A self-purported "typical American" who felt he could express his identity in the United States, he believed that El Salvador could benefit from "freedom of tattoos, freedom of speech, and freedom of dressing the way you wanna dress."

There are many elements of Salvadoran society that members of the new American diaspora appreciate, and the recommendations made by deportees like Pablo and Freddy are not unique to deportees. Their narratives still suggest that deportees are not just passive pawns of the contemporary U.S. deportation machinery. They are also "cultural carriers" whose linguistic capacities, personal styles, preferences for food, transportation, and employment, and ideas for improved public policy are understood as remnants of their acculturation in the United States. Such ideas and behaviors, if diffused and enacted, could be transformative for Salvadoran society. However, the spoiled reputation of the new American diaspora denies them the power to be as positively influential as they might otherwise be.

Unwelcome Interventions

The United States has a long history of political, economic, and cultural intervention in El Salvador. Salvadoran elites have historically invited U.S. presence into the country and, in spite of public resistance surrounding many U.S. interventions, Salvadorans still retain the most positive view of the United States of any nation in Latin America (Pew Research Center 2013). Some interventions remain nearly universally unwelcome. Members of the new American diaspora almost unanimously reported feeling like undesirable and potentially threatening outsiders in Salvadoran society. Owing to the conflation between their identities and those of local gang members and other criminal delinquents, most are systematically alienated upon return.

Feelings of marginalization are rooted in the history of gangs and their enforcement in El Salvador. When members of the new American diaspora returned in the mid-1990s, they knew little of the country, had few social ties, and encountered limited economic opportunities (Cruz 2009; Zilberg 2011). Many took to the streets, where they encountered local gangsters who admired their style and mannerisms (Zilberg 2011). Though they only accounted for 10 percent of the total gang population (Cruz and Portillo Peña 1998), deportees attained elevated status and were able to diffuse negative social remittances. They transmitted "the use of tattoos, the utilization of gang signs to communicate and . . . the norms, values, and knowledge about how to behave, about who is the enemy, and about who is friend" (Cruz 2009:4). Local gangs became more involved in extortions, robberies, assaults, cocaine and meth sales, rapes, and murders under deportee leadership (Cruz and Portillo Peña 1998). Rates of homicide escalated accordingly and El Salvador became the most murderous country in the Western Hemisphere, at least until 2008, when it was surpassed by Honduras (UNODC 2012).

Postwar material conditions and the Salvadoran state's repressive response were as much, if not more, responsible for the intensification of gang violence in El Salvador (Cruz 2009). When the deportees returned in the 1990s, there was an abundance of disenfranchised youth who attended weak schools, confronted violence in their families and neighborhoods, had access to war weapons, and engaged in relatively low-level street crimes (Cruz 2009). When the gang crisis exploded in the 1900s, police, security agents, and vigilantes began a social cleansing campaign against any and all suspected gang members (Seelke 2014). From 2003 to 2012, the repressive *Mano Dura* (heavy hand) and *Super Mano Dura* (super heavy hand) programs criminalized gang membership, resulting in the incarceration of tens of thousands of tattooed people. This approach caused oppositional gang identities to harden and gangsters to hide and remove tattoos, change their style of attire, and reduce their use of hand signals (Seelke 2014). Control over loosely affiliated cliques also consolidated inside prisons, helping MS-13 evolve into the increasingly cartel-like organization it is perceived to be today (Cruz 2010).

Regardless of the state's and the media's role in exasperating the transnational gang problem, the often sensationalized narrative of deportee-induced gang expansion continues to stigmatize deported members of the new American diaspora. They already arrive ashamed because they were not able to remain in the United States with their families, but soon encounter a much more devastating sense of alienation. Markers of their history in the United States, especially the presence of tattoos, make them the targets of police and security agents, who survey their mobility, stop and search them, and detain them without evidence of gang affiliation. As Miguel Rivera, 37, a former gang member in the United States who successfully avoided gangs in El Salvador in part by working in a formerly existing program to reinsert deportees, explained:

When the United States started to deport [Salvadorans en masse in the 1990s], the government of El Salvador convinced the people that we—those of us who came deported—were criminals, were rapists, and that we hadn't changed, and that we came to make the country worse; to ruin it. That we are still coming with this mentality to grab a child, teach him how to be in a gang, how to make a gang, use drugs, or rape our women. So, the government started to poison the minds of the people, of all of the people in general. So they look at us like criminal people. They don't look at me like I am a human. Instead they look at me like a criminal.

This pervasive stereotype leads to the criminalization of the new American diaspora in El Salvador. They are subjected to state surveillance and harassment and sometimes violent beatings from police officers. They are also systematically denied the economic opportunities they need to establish sustainable livelihoods in El Salvador, not only because of the general lack of jobs but because employers deny them available positions for which they are qualified without offering them interviews, especially after they see tattoos or learn of individuals' deportee status. Members of the new American diaspora are shunned by the public, who give them dirty looks, avoid them in the streets, and refuse to sit next to them on public buses. Perhaps most problematic, however, are the threats and physical harm sometimes inflicted on them by local gang members trying to mark their territory or recruit deported persons. As Giovanni, 31, an individual who went to the United States at age 5 and was removed 16 years later, explained:

> They real racist about the tattoos here. Look, me, I didn't want to adjust my tattoos and my way of dressing. You know, (in the U.S.) you don't have to be a gangster or be bad to wear some jewelry or a basketball jersey and show off your tattoos. You do that here, you walk two blocks, and the third block, you are dead. Or the cops got you all wrapped up and they gonna take you downtown. And the people look at you like, "Oh, you gangsta! Watch out!" And you might not even be one, but just because you a little baggy, watch out! Or they call the cops and you might not even be doing *nothin'*! That happened to me a lot. It still happens to me. *Man*, with all the shit I've been through down here, I would be Rodney King up there!

Coping Mechanisms

Despite their spoiled identities and alienation, deported members of the new American diaspora find creative ways to maneuver through Salvadoran society. Evidence from our interviews suggests that most deportees actively resist association with local gangs. This is the case even if deportees had been involved in gangs in the United States, especially if they have sources of financial and social support in El Salvador or abroad in the United States. The population accepts housing and job references from family members, removes and covers their tattoos, alters their personal style, monitors their geographic mobility, improves their Spanish skills, employs Salvadoran slang, and attends local church services. They also seek out "little pockets" of the United States in El Salvador, like fast food restaurants, foreign-owned call centers, and informal friendship networks of other deportees who spent a lot of time in the United States. (Coutin 2007). Engaging in such spaces sometimes helps them construct legitimate livelihoods while also shielding them from outside threats. Taken together, these coping mechanisms demonstrate the resilience of the new American diaspora in the face of a hostile societal reception.

The case of Luis Aguilar remains illustrative. For the first few months after his arrival in El Salvador, Luis avoided social interaction with locals. This was especially true after he was harassed by police officers and threatened by gang members in his neighborhood. He preferred to stay in his aunt's home as much as possible—a space in which he could "just be" himself. While this strategy offered him protection, he also said that "it was hell. I felt like I was still in jail." After three months of self-imposed incarceration, he learned that if he exchanged his preferred shorts and t-shirt for long pants and a button-up shirt he could venture outside of the house and travel to other parts of the country. Luis regularly visited distant relatives in the more rural department of Usulután. Such excursions provided him respite from seemingly constant harassment he experienced from police in San Salvador. They also gave him hope that though he may not thrive he could at least survive as a deportee.

Like Luis, most members of the new American diaspora found that the key to blending into Salvadoran society was to alter their appearance. If this strategy was insufficient to break the association between them and gangs, some monitored physical mobility. Over time they learned the "hot" areas of San Salvador where gang activity was prevalent. They avoided riding buses or otherwise passing through those zones. Some monitored their mobility more carefully, preferring to stay in their homes as much as possible or only visiting well-guarded, wealthy, or tourist areas, like commercial malls, dining establishments, or the beach. Others turned to Christianity as a way to avert recruitment from gangsters or interrogations from police officers. They found that the language and symbols of Christianity powerfully demonstrated that they accepted culpability for their past and were humbly working toward a better future. It also offered them a source of solidarity and a framework to make sense of their traumas and work toward acceptance of their realities.

While often effective in reducing social stigma, none of these coping mechanisms guaranteed deportees employment. As a result, members of the new American diaspora frequently remained dependent upon remittances from family members living abroad. Most of them, however, wished to become financially independent. A few of them eventually found and accepted low-wage employment in the local labor market—working, for example, as a bellhop or a car mechanic. Others worked in the informal labor market selling gum or toiletries on public buses, peddling in markets and on the streets, and babysitting for family members in exchange for housing. Some occasionally provided tattoos to "middle class kids," for whom tattoos are gradually becoming more acceptable in El Salvador, perhaps in part due to the increasing numbers of people sporting them since deportations to the country began on a large scale. Still others capitalized on the human and cultural capital they obtained in the United States by securing and maintaining employment as bilingual customer service agents in foreign-owned call centers.

Call centers provide the new American diaspora a space in which they may earn sustainable wages and develop social capital. Employers at call centers reportedly do not regularly discriminate on the basis of tattoos alone. They also provide an average of $450 in salary per month—four times what most other deportees interviewed for this study earned. In call centers, deportees encounter other individuals who spent substantial time in the United States. While some avoid developing friendships with fellow deportees, others get together with each other after work to share life experiences. Informal friendship cliques of deportees reportedly hold barbeques after work and on weekends. They also often watch American football games, enjoy Budweiser beer, and share stories of lives past and present. Carlos Pérez, 30, commented on how call centers facilitate such interactions for the new American diaspora:

> So it's pretty nice. We continue with whatever you grew up with over there in the U.S., especially those that have been a long time over there, like living. You come back here and you meet people that were over there. Sometimes you see people talking in English. That's 'cause they were over there and, you know, they likely work in a call center. They just probably talk. Like with my friends, I talk English and Spanish. It depends on the scene and all that. But I mean, we continue all that, you know, with the culture, with the habits that we were doing over there.

Social support of this kind reinforces a sense of psycho-cultural belonging in El Salvador. It can be difficult, however, to find employment in call centers. For deportees unable to secure such positions, call centers represent an "unfulfilled promise" of economic sustainability.[3] Faced with limited alternatives, some deportees do eventually turn toward gang life. Gangs provide such individuals a sense of family when such ties are absent, a source of income when no alternate options exist, and a means to reclaim the power they feel they lost through removal. This was certainly the case for Ernie Martínez, 36, who was a deeply entrenched but low-level member of MS-13 in the United States. Ernie remembered how, when he first arrived in El Salvador in 1992, "kids would be like 'Oh wow, you're over *here*! You've got *Nikes*! You've got *Levis*!'" Far from being social remittances that would alienate him, in the gang context these symbols granted him power. Local youth deferred to Ernie and he quickly claimed control over the clique.

Though the gang trajectory does exist, a far more common coping strategy is dreaming or planning to return to the United States. When asked what percentage of deportees try to go back post-removal, most deportees responded that between 80 and 90 percent make at least one re-migration attempt. This sample was biased toward individuals that stayed in El Salvador, at least initially. Still, 9 of the 47 interviewees (19 percent) tried to go back to the United States at least once. Though he was an original founder of MS-13 who held substantial power in Salvadoran gangs, even Ernie Martínez tried to go back to the United States five times. Pablo Día described the motivation behind such re-migration decisions. He said, "They feel so bad, so bad, because they don't have no family here that can receive them—to feed them. And they say . . . 'I feel that I have more power, I feel more strong to be leaving, to be going.'" Though he was beginning to adjust to El Salvador, Pablo planned to return to the United States within a year of his interview. He further explained:

> My plan is by next year in January to leave from here . . . If God gives me the last opportunity and gets me to the house up there, I can be with my kids and my mother. That's the only one dream I had in my head. Just get up there and work two jobs and make my money and have my kids with me and be with my kids, enjoying my life with my kids. See my kids grow up, raise my kids, educate my kids . . . That's my dream. And I ask God, give me my opportunity that I deserve. He knows what kind of man I am, and I deserve a second chance in his hands.

Members of the new American diaspora with and without gang histories want to return to the United States for numerous personalized reasons. Most wish to leave because they are unable to establish in El Salvador the sense of belonging they more successfully crafted in the United States. They want to escape stigmatization, poor economic prospects, and threats to their personhood. They hope to reclaim the sense of agency they once held in the United States prior to it being stripped of them via the process of removal and post-deportation integration. Perhaps most importantly, they want to reunite with those they were forced to leave behind in the United States. Merely surviving in El Salvador (even when sustainable employment and solidarity with other deportees is available) cannot replace the children, spouses, parents, and friends from whom they were banished when they were deported.

Conclusion: Limits and Potential of the New American Diaspora

The logic of the deportation machinery that has emerged in the United States in recent decades considers deportees to be collateral damage in an important state effort to control the size and characteristics of the U.S. foreign-born population (De Genova and Peutz 2010). Deportable persons represent undesirables who have either unlawfully transgressed national borders or violated the implicit contract of territorial personhood allowing their continued presence in the United States (Motomura 2006). When deportees return to their countries-of-citizenship, it is sometimes assumed that they will easily reinsert themselves due to their shared national origins with the local population. However, as this chapter shows, deported persons with deep psycho-cultural, economic, and social ties to the United States regularly experience a "reverse culture shock" upon return (Peutz 2006). They often face antipathetic contexts of return that interact with their migration and criminal histories to limit and constrain their life chances.

When members of the new American diaspora return to El Salvador as deportees, they often experience a reactive nativism emanating from the Salvadoran state and society who view them as unwelcome products of the worst elements of U.S. society. They are treated as undesirable foreign elements that threaten the security and the cultural integrity of El Salvador. Though legally Salvadoran, they believe they are identifiable as visibly and culturally different from locals. Potential employers, police and security agents, and average citizens often erroneously associate them with gang members or delinquents. The new American diaspora is systematically denied the opportunities they need not only to contribute positively to Salvadoran society, but to develop self-sufficient livelihoods.

Though there are numerous constraints on their post-deportation existence in El Salvador, Salvadoran deportees are far from passive pawns of the U.S. deportation regime and the context to which they return. They have the potential to transmit "little pieces" of the United States to El Salvador. Members of the new American diaspora carry "social remittances"—remnants and legacies of their acculturated experiences in the United States—on their bodies and in their minds. They have the potential to impact Salvadoran culture through how they visually represent themselves and move through the world. Their narratives also highlight numerous suggestions garnered through their comparisons of El Salvador with the United States on how to improve Salvadoran society. While they may subtly influence Salvadoran culture in the long term, the tarnished social status they maintain in the country appears to be inhibiting their ability to become involved in collective action around the social problems they identify.

The new American diaspora—if we can even accurately call them a "diaspora" in the Salvadoran context—is a population who live highly alienated post-deportation lives. The unwelcome reception extended to them by the Salvadoran state and society inhibits their personal and collective potential. Some individuals are able to sustain themselves economically and have even fostered the development of social capital through their friendships with other deportees. Ultimately, however, the limited opportunity structures available for their socioeconomic mobility forces them into a position in which they are, as one deported person put it, "too busy just trying to survive." A remarkably resilient population, deportees still find creative ways to reduce stigma and survive economically in El Salvador. But even with these efforts, the new American diaspora remains a highly vulnerable population. As Pablo Día stated when asked if there exists any emergent collective action among deportees in the country:

> I don't think there is nothing like that. Nothing. Not even. It's just like Pac-Man, when he got hit, he melts. [Deportation] melts the personality, their mind, and their feelings, you hear? The same moment, the same feeling, the same situation that they have is, "I just won't make it here." They [are] kind of like ashamed, like embarrassed. They feel like low. They feel like nobody, you hear me? They feel like a piece of trash. They feel like nobody, nothing.

The narratives of the American diaspora clearly show that their agency has been repressed through the process of removal and reintegration into El Salvador. Even if they were to collectively voice opposition to their treatment or to other social problems, many believe they would not be taken seriously by the Salvadoran government. They still agree that the United States should handle deportation more humanely and that El Salvador needs to better facilitate deportee insertion. Though most agreed that an amnesty or pathway to citizenship for undocumented people in the United States would be beneficial, they focused their critiques on current deportation law and how it is implemented. For example, they consistently argued that in removal proceedings the United States should take into greater consideration migrants' long-standing ties and positive contributions to the country. They also advocated for free legal aid to detainees, the expansion of judicial discretion in cancellation of removal hearings, and the institution of a visa for some deportees to return to the United States to legally visit the children and spouses left behind.

The new American diaspora also reported recommendations to improve the treatment of deportees in El Salvador. They agreed that, at a bare minimum, the stigma of deportees who grew up or spent significant time in the United States should be eliminated. The majority of them are not the hardened gangster-criminals they are often portrayed to be, but average persons trying to do the best they can for themselves and their families. They also believe that their outcomes in El Salvador would be greatly improved if efforts were made by the Salvadoran state—perhaps with funding from the United States—to improve the institutional context of return. As Ramón, 28, suggested, El Salvador should "create a program from different deportees," that might look something like the assistance provided to refugee populations in the United States. Such a program would not only provide assistance at the airport, but would offer transitional housing, training for and assistance in locating jobs, referrals for healthcare and mental health services, and proactive, preventive efforts to reduce the pull some deportees feel toward gangs.

Efforts such as these will situate the new American diaspora in a much better position to construct sustainable post-deportation lives and make more positive contributions to Salvadoran society. As the position of deportees in El Salvador improves, they will begin to realize their societal potential beyond the status of low-wage earners, participants in informal labor markets, and gang members contributing to widespread state insecurity. As they begin to feel like they belong legally *and* socially in El Salvador, their desires to re-emigrate clandestinely to the United States would likely begin to decline. When treated like valuable additions to Salvadoran society, they would become more empowered to contribute their unique perspectives (informed by their time abroad) to the political process in El Salvador. Allowing them the space to flourish in these ways will allow the new American diaspora not only to construct more meaningful post-deportation lives, but to make more positive contributions to Salvadoran society.

NOTES

1 Pseudonyms are used throughout this chapter to protect the identities of study participants.
2 These 47 participants emerged from a larger sample of 100 life-history interviews conducted with deportees in El Salvador over the same period of time. 86 of the interviews were conducted by Dingeman-Cerda and Cristy Alaya between 2008 and 2013. 14 were conducted by Susan Bibler Coutin in focus groups, with Katie Dingeman-Cerda serving as a research assistant. Of the 100 interviews, 96 were conducted in El Salvador and four were conducted in Los Angeles. Consistent with the observation that deportation is a gendered phenomenon, 96 of the 100 interviewees were male (see Golash-Boza and Hondagneu-Sotelo 2013). Participants were identified through a combined referral, snowballing, and purposive sampling method designed to capture maximum variation in post-removal experiences. Once theoretical saturation was obtained, interviews were transcribed and coded by Katie Dingeman-Cerda, Danny Gascón, and Carlos Batres, with the assistance of a team of undergraduate research assistants.
3 Thank you to M. Brinton Lykes for this observation.

REFERENCES

Arnson, Cynthia J. Adam Drolet, H. E. Hugo Martínez, Rep. Jim McGovern, Cristina Eguizábal, Ricardo Córdova Macías, Federico Hernández, José Miguel Cruz, William Pleitéz, and Luis Membreño. 2011. *The Administration of President Mauricio Funes: A One-Year Assessment.* Accessed October 8, 2014. Washington, DC: Woodrow Wilson International Center for Scholars. http://www.wilsoncenter.org/sites/default/files/Funes_One_Year.pdf.

Baker-Cristales, Beth. 2004. *Salvadoran Migration to Southern California: Redefining El Hermano Lejano.* Gainsville: University Press of Florida.

Brabeck, K., Lykes, M. Brinton, and Hershberg, Rachel, 2011. "Framing Immigration to and Deportation from the United States: Guatemalan And Salvadoran Families Make Meaning of their Experiences." *Community, Work and Family* 14(3):275–296. doi.org/10.1080/13668803.2010.520840.

Brabeck, Kalina and Qingwen Xu. 2010. "The Impact of Detention and Deportation on Latino Immigrant Children and Families: A Quantitative Exploration." *Hispanic Journal of Behavioral Sciences* 32(3):341–361. doi: 10.1177/0739986310374053.

Brick, Kate, A. E. Challinor, and Marc R. Rosenblum. 2011. *Mexican and Central American Immigrants in the United States.* Accessed October 8, 2014. Washington, DC: Migration Policy Institute. http://www.migrationpolicy.org/research/mexican-and-central-american-immigrants-united-states.

Brotherton, David C. and Luis Barrios. 2011. *Banished to the Homeland: Dominican Deportees and their Stories of Exile.* New York: Columbia University Press.

Brown, Anna and Eileen Patten. 2014. *Statistical Portrait of the Foreign-Born Population in the United States, 2012.* Accessed October 7, 2014. Washing-

ton, DC: Pew Research Center. http://www.pewhispanic.org/2014/04/29/statistical-portrait-of-hispanics-in-the-united-states-2012/.
Capps, Randolph, Rosa Maria Castaneda, Ajay Chaudry, and Robert Santos. 2007. *Paying the Price: The Impact of Immigration Raids on American's Children*. Report. Accessed October 8, 2014. Washington, DC: Urban Institute. http://www.urban.org/uploadedPDF/411566_immigration_raids.pdf.
Chacón, Jennifer. 2007. "Whose Community Shield? Examining the Removal of the 'Criminal Street Gang Member.'" *University of Chicago Legal Forum* 317–357.
Coutin, Susan Bibler. 2007. *Nations of Emigrants: Shifting Boundaries of Citizenship in El Salvador and the United States*. Ithaca, NY: Cornell University Press.
Coutin, Susan Bibler. 2010a. "Confined Within: National Territories as Zones of Confinement." *Political Geography* 29(4):200–208. doi:10.1016/j.polgeo.2010.03.005.
Coutin, Susan Bibler. 2010b. "Exiled by Law: Deportation and the Inviability of Life." In Nathalie Peutz and Nicholas De Genova, eds., *The Deportation Regime: Sovereignty, Space, and the Freedom of Movement* (pp. 351–370). Durham, NC: Duke University Press.
Cruz, José Miguel. 2009. "Global Gangs in El Salvador: Maras and the Politics of Violence." Paper presented at the Global Gangs Workshop, Centre on Conflict, Development, and Peacebuilding, Geneva. Accessed October 1, 2014. http://graduateinstitute.ch/files/live/sites/iheid/files/sites/ccdp/shared/5039/Cruz-global-gangs-in-el-salvador.pdf.
Cruz, José Miguel. 2010. "Central American Maras: From Youth Street Gangs to Transnational Protection Rackets." *Global Crime* 11(4):379–398. doi: 10.1080.17440572.2010.519518.
Cruz, José Miguel and Nelson Portillo Peña. 1998. *Solidaridad y violencia en las pandillas de Gran San Salvador: Mas allá de la vida loca*. San Salvador, El Salvador: UCA Editores.
De Genova, Nicholas. 2002. "Migrant 'Illegality' and Deportability in Everyday Life." *Annual Review of Anthropology* 31:419–447. doi: 10.1146/annurev.anthro.31.040402.085432.
De Genova, Nicholas and Nathalie Peutz. 2010. *The Deportation Regime: Sovereignty, Space, and the Freedom of Movement*. Durham, NC: Duke University Press.
Dingeman-Cerda, M. K. and Susan Bibler Coutin. 2012. "The Ruptures of Return: Deportation's Confounding Effects." In Marjorie Zatz, Charis Kubrin, and Ramiro Martínez, eds., *Punishing Immigrants: Policy, Politics, and Injustice*. (pp. 113–137). New York: New York University Press.
Dingeman, M. K. and Rubén G. Rumbaut. 2010. "The Immigrant-Crime Nexus and Post-Deportation Experiences: En/Countering Stereotypes in Southern California and El Salvador." *La Verne Law Review* 31(2):363–402.
Dreby, Joanna. 2012. "The Burden of Deportation on Children in Mexican Immigrant Families." *Journal of Marriage and Family* 74(4):829–845. doi: 10.1111/j.1741-3737.2012.00989.x.
Gammage, Sarah. 2007. *El Salvador; Despite End to Civil War, Migration Continues*. Accessed October 8, 2014. Washington, DC: Migration Information Source. http://

www.migrationpolicy.org/article/el-salvador-despite-end-civil-war-emigration-continues.

Golash-Boza, Tanya. 2013. "Forced Transnationalism: Transnational Coping Strategies and Gendered Stigma among Jamaican Deportees." *Global Networks* 14(1):63–79. doi: 10.1111/glob.12013.

Golash-Boza, Tanya and Pierrette Hondagneu-Sotelo. 2013. "Latino Immigrant Men and the Deportation Crisis: A Gendered Racial Removal Program." *Latino Studies* 11(3):271–292. doi:10.1057/lst.2013.14.

Guarnizo, Luis, Alejandro Portes, and William Haller. 2003. "Assimilation and Transnationalism: Determinants of Transnational Political Action among Contemporary Migrants." *American Journal of Sociology* 108(6):1211–1248. http://www.jstor.org/stable/10.1086/375195.

Hagan, Jacqueline, Brianna Castro, and Nestor Rodríguez. 2010. "The Effects of U.S. Deportation Policies on Immigrant Families and Communities: Cross-Border Perspectives." *North Carolina Law Review* 88:1799–1823.

Hagan, Jacqueline, Nestor Rodríguez, and Brianna Castro. 2011. "Social Effects of Mass Deportations by the United States Government, 2000–2010." *Ethnic and Racial Studies* 34(8):1374–1391. doi: 10.1080/01419870.2011.575233.

Hamilton, Nora and Norma Stoltz Chinchilla. 2001. *Seeking Community in a Global City: Guatemalans and Salvadorans in Los Angeles.* Philadelphia, PA: Temple University Press.

Hoefer, Michael, Nancy Rytina, and Bryan C. Baker. 2012. *Estimates of the Unauthorized Immigrant Population Residing in the United States: January 2011.* Accessed October 8, 2014. U.S. Department of Homeland Security: *Office of Immigration Statistics.* https://www.dhs.gov/sites/default/files/publications/ois_ill_pe_2011.pdf.

Human Rights Watch (HRW). 2009. *Forced Apart (By the Numbers): Noncitizens Deported for Mostly Nonviolent Offenses.* New York, NY.

Kanstroom, Daniel. 2012. *Aftermath: Deportation Law and the New American Diaspora.* New York: Oxford University Press.

Levitt, Peggy. 1998. "Social Remittances: A Local-Level, Migration-Driven Form of Cultural Diffusion." *International Migration Review* 32(124):926–949.

Levitt, Peggy and Deepak Lamba-Nieves. 2010. *It's Not Just about the Economy Stupid: Social Remittances Revisited.* Accessed October 8, 2014. Washington, DC: Migration Information Source. http://www.migrationpolicy.org/article/its-not-just-about-economy-stupid-social-remittances-revisited.

Levitt, Peggy and Deepak Lamba-Nieves. 2011. "Social Remittances Reconsidered." *Journal of Ethnic and Migration Studies* 37(1):1–22.

Menjívar, Cecilia. 2006. "Liminal Legality: Salvadoran and Guatemalan Immigrants' Lives in the United States." *American Journal of Sociology* 4:999–1037. doi: 10.1086/499509.

Miller, O. Alexander. 2008. *Migration Can Fall Apart: Life Stories from Voluntary and Deportee Return Migrants* Lanham, MD: University Press of America.

Mills, Frederick B. 2012. *Education Reform Gets High Marks in El Salvador*. Washington, DC: Council on Hemispheric Affairs. Accessed October 1, 2014. http://www.coha.org/education-reform-gets-high-marks-in-el-salvador/.

Motomura, Hiroshi. 2006. *Americans in Waiting: The Lost Story of Immigration and Citizenship in the United States*. New York: Oxford University Press.

Mountz, Alison, Richard Wright, Ines Miyares, and Adrian J. Bailey. 2002. "Lives in Limbo: Temporary Protected Status and Immigrant Identities." *Global Networks* 4:335–356. doi: 10.1111/1471-0374.00044.

Negroponte, Diana Villiers. 2012. *Seeking Peace in El Salvador: The Struggle to Reconstruct a Nation at the End of the Civil War*. New York: Palgrave Macmillan.

Office of Immigration Statistics (OIS). 2012. *Yearbook of Immigration Statistics*. Accessed October 8, 2014. Washington, DC: Department of Homeland Security. https://www.dhs.gov/sites/default/files/publications/ois_yb_2012.pdf.

Peutz, Nathalie. 2006. "Embarking on an Anthropology of Removal." *Current Anthropology* 47:217–241. http://www.jstor.org/stable/10.1086/498949.

Pew Research Center. 2013. *America's Global Image Remains More Positive than China's: But Many See China Becoming World's Leading Power*. Accessed October 1, 2014. http://www.pewglobal.org/2013/07/18/americas-global-image-remains-more-positive-than-chinas/.

PNUD. 2005. *Informe sobre Desarrollo Humano de El Salvador 2005: Una Mirada al Nuevos Nosotros, Impacto de las Migraciones*. San Salvador, El Salvador: UN Development Program. Accessed October 10, 2014. http://www.sv.undp.org/content/el_salvador/es/home/library/hiv_aids/informe-sobre-desarrollo-humano-el-salvador-2005.html.

Rodríguez, Nestor and Jacqueline Hagan. 2004. "Fractured Families and Communities: Effects of Immigration Reform in Texas, Mexico, and El Salvador." *Journal of Latino Studies* 2(3):328–351.

Rumbaut, Rubén G. 2002. "Severed or Sustained Attachments? Language, Identity, and Imagined Communities in the Post-Immigrant Generation." In Peggy Levitt and Mary C. Waters, eds., *The Changing Face of Home: The Transnational Lives of the Second Generation*, (pp. 43–95). New York: Russell Sage Foundation.

Seelke, Clare Ribando. 2013. "El Salvador; Political and Economic Conditions and U.S. Relations." Washington, DC: Congressional Research Service. April 5, 2013. Accessed October 1, 2014. http://www.fas.org/sgp/crs/row/RS21655.pdf.

Seelke, Clare Ribando. 2014. *Gangs in Central America*. February 20, 2014. Accessed October 1, 2014. http://www.fas.org/sgp/crs/row/RL34112.pdf.

Shifter, Michael and Rachel Schwartz. 2012. "Democracy in Transition; El Salvador's Unfinished Transition." *World Politics Review*. Accessed January 8, 2014. http://www.worldpoliticsreview.com/articles/12369/democracy-in-progress-el-salvadors-unfinished-transition.

UNODC. 2012. *Intentional Homicide, Count and Rate per 100,000 Population (1995–2011)*. United Nations Office on Drugs and Crime. Accessed October 13, 2014. https://data.un.org/Data.aspx?d=UNODC&f=tableCode%3A1.

Velásquez Carrillo, Carlos. 2010. "The Neoliberal Oligarchic Consolidation in El Salvador: Origins, Impacts, and Challenges for the FMLN." Paper presented at the NALACS 2010 Annual Conference. "Latin America and the Caribbean: Beyond Neoliberalism?" University of Groningen, Netherlands, November 18–19, 2010.

Vigil, James Diego. 2002. *A Rainbow of Gangs: Cultures in the Mega-City*. Austin: University of Texas Press.

Zilberg, Elana. 2011. *Space of Detention; The Making of a Transnational Gang Crisis between Los Angeles and San Salvador*. Durham: University of North Carolina Press.

ABOUT THE EDITORS

Daniel Kanstroom, JD, LLM, is Professor of Law, Thomas F. Carney Distinguished Scholar, Director of the International Human Rights Program at Boston College Law School, and Associate Director of the Center for Human Rights and International Justice at Boston College. He teaches Immigration and Refugee Law, International Human Rights Law, Constitutional Law, and Administrative Law. He founded the Law School's Immigration Clinic and co-founded the Post-Deportation Human Rights Project, which seeks to conceptualize a new field of law while representing U.S. deportees abroad. He has published widely in the fields of U.S. immigration law, human rights, criminal law, and European citizenship law. His most recent edited book, with sociologist Cecilia Menjívar, is *Constructing Immigrant "Illegality": Critiques, Experiences, and Responses* (2013). His prior books include: *Aftermath: Deportation Law and the New American Diaspora* (2012) and *Deportation Nation: Outsiders in American History* (2007). His articles have appeared in such venues as the *Harvard Law Review*, the *Yale Journal of International Law*, the *UCLA Law Review*, and the French *Gazette du Palais*. He was a member of the national Immigration Commission of the American Bar Association.

M. Brinton Lykes, PhD, is Professor of Community-Cultural Psychology and Associate Director of the Center for Human Rights and International Justice at Boston College. She works with survivors of war and gross violations of human rights, using cultural resources, the creative arts, and participatory action research methodologies to analyze the causes and document the effects of violence and develop programs that aspire to rethread social relations and transform social inequalities underlying structural injustices. Her current participatory and action research focuses on (1) sexual violence against women in contexts of armed conflict and post-conflict transitions, and their struggles for truth, justice, healing, and reparations; and (2) migration and post-deportation human rights violations and their effects on women and children, with a particular focus on transnational identities and mixed-status families. Professor Lykes has published extensively in refereed journals and edited volumes, co-edited three books and co-authored two others. In 2012 she received the Ignacio Martín-Baró Lifetime Peace Practitioner Award from the Society for the Study of Peace, Conflict and Violence, of the American Psychological Association, in 2013 she was awarded the American Psychological Association's International Humanitarian Award, and in 2014, the Florence L. Denmark and Mary E. Reuder Award for Outstanding International Contributions to the Psychology of Women and Gender from the American Psychological Association's Division of International Psychology. Her website is www2.bc.edu/~lykes.

ABOUT THE CONTRIBUTORS

Luis Argueta is a Guatemalan-American director and producer. *The Silence of Neto*, a coming-of-age film set in 1954 Cold-War Guatemala, is the first internationally recognized and awarded Guatemalan film. *The Guardian* listed Mr. Argueta as one of Guatemala's National Living Icons, alongside Nobel Laureate Rigoberta Menchu and Singer/Songwriter Ricardo Arjona. *abUsed: The Postville Raid* is Argueta's first documentary film in his *Immigration Trilogy*. The second documentary film, *ABRAZOS*, follows the journey of 14 U.S. citizen children from Minnesota to Guatemala to meet their grandparents—and in some instances their siblings—for the first time. Luis Argueta's films can now be viewed online at www.luisarguetaa.com.

Maurice Belanger is an expert in the field of immigration policy. Until recently, Maurice was Director of Public Information for the National Immigration Forum, where he served for 25 years as an analyst and writer in various capacities. He produced a news bulletin on immigration law and policy, incorporating political context and background to help readers understand current developments. The bulletin and short papers analyzing policy developments and trends in immigration helped make immigration policy accessible to readers. Prior to his work at the Forum, Maurice worked for the American Civil Liberties Union. He has a degree from Cornell University.

Kalina M. Brabeck, PhD, is a licensed psychologist with twelve years of experience in clinical work and research with Latino immigrant families. She is an Associate Professor and Department Chair in the Department of Counseling, Educational Leadership and School Psychology at Rhode Island College. She has been an affiliated member of the Center for Human Rights and International Justice at Boston College and a co-investigator with the Migration and Human Rights Project since 2007.

She is currently a Foundation for Child Development Young Scholar, conducting mixed-methods research on the influence of immigrant parent legal vulnerability on developmental outcomes for U.S.-born children.

Jessica Chicco, JD, was Human Rights Fellow at the Center for Human Rights and International Justice at Boston College, 2010–2015. As part of the Center's Migration and Human Rights Project, Ms. Chicco's work included interdisciplinary collaborations with community-based immigrant organizations in the greater Boston area. As the supervising attorney for the Center's Post-Deportation Human Rights Project, Ms. Chicco worked with and on behalf of deported individuals, and successfully reunited deportees with their families in the United States. She has also worked alongside Professor Daniel Kanstroom on the drafting of a *Declaration on the Rights of Expelled and Deported Persons*.

Elaine P. Congress, DSW, LCSW, is Professor and Associate Dean at Fordham University Graduate School of Social Service, as well as cofounder and Educational Director of the Fordham Center for Nonprofit Leaders. At the UN, Dr. Congress represents the International Federation of Social Workers and serves on the NGO Committee on Migration. She heads the Publications Council for the Council on Social Work Education and has published extensively in the area of cultural diversity and immigrants. She is the author/editor of seven books, including *Social Work with Immigrants and Refuges: Legal Issues, Clinical Skills*, and *Advocacy and Multicultural Perspectives in Working with Families*.

Katie Dingeman-Cerda, PhD, is a Visiting Assistant Professor in the Department of Sociology & Criminology at the University of Denver. Her research examines the subjective experience and unintended consequences of the modern deportation regime. Her research is funded by the National Science Foundation, UC Berkeley Center for Human Rights, and UC Irvine Center for Law, Society, and Culture. Her publications appear in the *La Verne Law Review* and in an edited volume, *Punishing Immigrants: Policy, Politics, and Injustice* (NYU Press, 2012). Prior to academia, she was a social worker for refugee families and unaccompanied minors in immigration detention. She serves as an expert witness for Central American and Caribbean migrants in removal proceedings.

Cristina Hunter, PhD, has worked on multiple research projects related to the experiences of Latino migrants in the United States, including transnational research with the Center for Human Rights and International Justice at Boston College; the NICHD-funded Kindergarten Language Study/Intervention with Spanish-speaking young children; and developmental and longitudinal projects with minority families at the Center for Research for Culture Development and Education at New York University. She is currently the Associate Director of Research Initiatives at the Barbara and Patrick Roche Center for Catholic Education at Boston College.

Yliana Johansen-Méndez, JD, worked for the Center for Human Rights and International Justice's Migration and Human Rights Project (MHRP), formerly the Post-Deportation Human Rights Project, while completing her JD at Boston College Law School. She collaborated on an interdisciplinary project designing and evaluating participatory Know Your Rights workshops with New England migrant organizations and worked in Zacualpa, Quiché, Guatemala. She is currently serving as Attorney Advisor for the U.S. Department of Justice's Executive Office for Immigration Review. Previously, she was an Equal Justice Works Fellow at Kids In Need of Defense in Los Angeles.

Maryanne Loughry, AM, PhD, is a Sister of Mercy and the Associate Director, Jesuit Refugee Service Australia. Dr. Loughry has been associated with the Jesuit Refugee Service (JRS) since 1986. She has worked in Indochinese refugee camps in the Philippines (1988) and the Vietnamese Detention Centres in Hong Kong (1990, 1992–93) as a psychologist and trainer. Dr. Loughry is a Research Professor at Boston College, at the Centre for Human Rights and International Justice and the Graduate School of Social Work. She is a research associate of the Refugee Studies Centre, University of Oxford, where she was the Pedro Arrupe tutor (1997–2004). In 2010, Dr. Loughry was awarded the Order of Australia (AM) for service to refugees and displaced persons.

Judge Dana Leigh Marks is President of the National Association of Immigrant Judges (NAIJ). She has served as either President or Vice President of NAIJ since July 1999. Judge Marks has been an Immigration Judge in San Francisco since January 1987. Prior to her appointment as an Immigration Judge she was an attorney in private practice for ten years, specializing in immigration law. She served as lead counsel in the landmark case of *INS v. Cardoza-Fonseca*, 480 U.S. 421 (1987), which established that persons applying for asylum need only prove a reasonable possibility of future persecution. She has testified before Congress, lectured, and published numerous articles on the urgent need to restructure U.S. Immigration Courts.

Ali Noorani has more than a decade of successful leadership in public policy advocacy, nonprofit management, and coalition organizing, across a wide range of issues. He continues this mission as Executive Director of the National Immigration Forum, advocating for the value of immigrants and immigration to the nation. Under Noorani's leadership since 2008, the Forum plays a leadership role and works closely with business, law enforcement, faith and immigrant leadership across the country to ensure that New Americans have the skills, opportunities, and status they need to reach their fullest potential.

Brittney Nystrom is Director for Advocacy at Lutheran Immigration and Refugee Service in Washington, DC and is the organization's lead campaign strategist to ensure it achieves its key advocacy priority objectives. Nystrom is a recognized expert on immigration and refugee issues, has testified before the U.S. House of Representatives and the Inter-American Commission on Human Rights, and is a volunteer case screener for the Board of Immigration Appeals Pro Bono Project. Previously, she served as Director of Policy and Legal Affairs at the National Immigration Forum, Legal Director at the Capital Area Immigrants' Rights Coalition ("CAIR Coalition"), and an associate with Fried Frank LLP. Nystrom holds degrees from the University of Notre Dame and Northwestern University School of Law. She is admitted to the bar in Washington, DC, and Illinois.

Katherine Porterfield, PhD, is a clinical psychologist at the Bellevue/NYU Program for Survivors of Torture, where she provides care to individuals and families who have survived torture and refugee trauma. Dr. Porterfield has served as an expert in criminal and human rights cases involving torture and war trauma and has consulted on international cases involving human rights violations. She has trained medical and legal professionals in the consequences of war trauma and torture. Dr. Porterfield chaired the American Psychological Association's *Task Force on the Psychosocial Effects of War on Children and Families Who Are Refugees From Armed Conflict Residing in the United States.*

Rubén G. Rumbaut, PhD, is Distinguished Professor of Sociology at the University of California, Irvine. Over the past three decades he has directed seminal empirical studies of immigrants and refugees in the United States, including the landmark *Children of Immigrants Longitudinal Study* (with Alejandro Portes). Among other books, he is the co-author of *Immigrant America: A Portrait*, and *Legacies: The Story of the Immigrant Second Generation*, which won the American Sociological Association's top award for Distinguished Scholarship. He is the founding chair of the International Migration Section of the American Sociological Association and an elected member of the National Academy of Education and of the American Academy of Arts and Sciences.

Dora B. Schriro is the Commissioner of the Connecticut Department of Emergency Services and Public Protection, a state agency focused on public safety and service. Dr. Schriro served as Senior Advisor to Department of Homeland Security Secretary Napolitano and was the first Director of the Immigration and Customs Enforcement Office of Detention Policy and Planning. During her tenure at DHS, she authored *A Report on the Preliminary Assessment of ICE Detention Policies and Practices: A Recommended Course of Action for Systems Reforms*, DHS's template for improving the nation's immigration detention system. She teaches and publishes in the areas of correction and immigration innovation and systems reform. Dr. Schriro currently serves as a commissioner on the boards of the Women's Refugee Commission and the American Bar Association's Commission on Immigration.

Erin Sibley, PhD, received her EdM in Human Development and Psychology at the Harvard Graduate School of Education, and received her PhD in Applied Developmental and Educational Psychology at Boston College. She is currently a research associate at the Center for Optimized

Student Support at Boston College. Her primary research interests are the academic achievement of immigrant children and educational involvement among immigrant families.

Judge Denise Noonan Slavin is the Executive Vice President of the National Association of Immigrant Judges (NAIJ). She has served as either President or Vice President of NAIJ since July 1999. She was appointed as an Immigration Judge in March 1995, and since then served at the court in Miami, Florida until April 2015, when she transferred to the Baltimore Immigration Court. She was a trial attorney for legacy INS and the Office of Special Investigations in the Criminal Division of DOJ. She previously served as an Investigator for the Maryland Commission on Human Relations, and as a Social Worker for the Department of Social Services in Baltimore City.

David B. Thronson is Associate Dean for Academic Affairs and Professor of Law at the Michigan State University College of Law, where he is co-founder of the Immigration Law Clinic. His research explores the intersection of family and immigration law, with a particular focus on children. As a Skadden Fellow, Thronson founded the immigration project at the Door's Legal Services Center, and as a Gibbons Fellow in Public Interest and Constitutional Law he litigated a wide variety of civil rights issues related to immigration and to access to education.

INDEX

Page numbers in italics refer to illustrations

ABA. *See* American Bar Association
ABRAZOS, xx–xxi, xxvii, 253
Abuse, xvii, 150, 171; child abuse, 151, 153–54, 156, 161, 164n1; domestic, 162; government, 4; human rights, 232; labor, xviii; substance, 169, 227. *See also* Racism; Trauma; Violence
abUsed: The Postville Raid, xiv; educating on both sides of border, xxii–xxiii; educator collaborations, xxi–xxii; Guatemala National Theater premiere, *xiv*, xxiii; as immigration deterrent, xxiv–xxv; PBS premiere, xxii–xxiii; purpose, xxvii; screenings, xxii; Spanish-language versions, xxiii; study guide, xxi; for work with undocumented migrants, xxiii
ACA. *See* American Correctional Association
Accountability, 65–66, 80–82, 119, 133
Acculturation, 13, 163, 177, 179, 233, 236, 243. *See also* Assimilation; Psychocultural belonging
Adjudication priorities, 93–94
Adjustment of status, 44
Administrative Procedure Act, 91, 110n4
AEDPA. *See* Anti-terrorism Effective Death Penalty Act
Aggravated felonies, 7, 104, 126, 159, 198
Agriprocessors, Inc., Postville, IA, xi–xii, xv; arrests, xxvi; deportations, xvii;
ICE actions, xxii; understanding, xvi; violence, xx
AJA. *See* American Jail Association
Alienation, 228–30, 237, 239
Aliens: children of deportable, 51n4; criminal, 11, 17, 85n37; discharge planning, 79; DO for, 80; due process and, 52n17, 61–62; families and, 43; healthcare for, 78; ICE detaining, 57, 60–61, 66–67, 70–75, 77, 84n29; illegal, 9, 13, 25n5, 219n1; incarceration and, 60; national security and, 126; noncriminal, 67; protections for, 81; removable, 85n38; restrictive supervision, 75; services for, 79; special populations, 80. *See also* Immigrants; Noncitizens; Unauthorized migrants; Undocumented migrants
AMA. *See* American Medical Association
American Action Network, 130
American Bar Association (ABA), 65, 108; Civil Immigration Detention Standards, 65; Model Rules of Professional Conduct, 152–54, 161
American Correctional Association (ACA), 66
American Declaration of the Rights and Duties of Man, 64
American Dream, xvii, 235
American Immigration Lawyers Association, 108
American Jail Association (AJA), 66

259

American Medical Association (AMA), 66
American Psychological Association (APA), 179, 257
Americans for a Conservative Direction, 130
Amnesty International, 171
Anti-terrorism Effective Death Penalty Act (AEDPA), 15, 196
Applied Research Center (ARC), 19, 125, 148, 197
Arbenz, Jacobo, 200
ARC. *See* Applied Research Center
Arizona immigration enforcement legislation, 119–20, 131
Arrival and Departure Information System, 122
Article I Court proposal, 108–9
Assimilation, 13, 171. *See also* Acculturation; Bicultural identity
Asylum: to Guatemalans, 201; Immigration Judges and, 89; mental health workers and, 181; PTSD in asylum seekers, 176–77
Attica prison riot, 59
Attorneys: American Immigration Lawyers Association, 108; community lawyering, 164; immigration, 22; Immigration Judges treated as, 92, 96

Bail, 5, 11
Banishment, 90, 229
Baptists, xxii, 130, xxviiin6
Barbour, Haley, 130–32
Beneficiaries, 41–44, 52n16, 199
Berks Family Residential Facility, 74
BIA. *See* Board of Immigration Appeals
Bibles, Badges and Business for Immigration Reform, 131
Bicultural identity, 160
Big Brothers, 160
Bipartisan Policy Center, 131–32

Board of Immigration Appeals (BIA), 96, 99, 105, 107
Border control, 10–12
Border Patrol: agent increase, 133; budget, 117; DHS and, 117; emergency funding, 118–19; INS and, 117
Border security, 117–18, 123, 126, 132–34
Border Security, Economic Opportunity and Immigration Modernization Act, 132–34
Border surge amendment, 133
Border violence, 118–19
Bush, George W. administration, 15, 196–97

CAFTA. *See* Central American Free Trade Agreement
Call centers, 240–41
Camayd-Freixas, Erik, xi
Cambodia: repatriation agreement, 158; violence, 177
Capacity, 68–69
Case completion goals, 92–97
Catch and release, 70
Catch and remove, 70
CBO. *See* Congressional Budget Office
CBP. *See* Customs and Border Protection
CBT. *See* Cognitive behavioral therapy
CEH. *See* Commission for Historical Clarification
Center for Human Rights & International Justice (CHRIJ), 193–94, 202–3, 211
Center for Public Policy Priorities, 171
Central American Free Trade Agreement (CAFTA), 194
Central Index System, 123
Central Intelligence Agency (CIA), 200
Centrist network, 131
Chamber of Commerce, US, 129
CHC. *See* Congressional Hispanic Caucus
Chicago Appleseed Fund for Justice, 99, 108
Child abuse, 151, 153–54, 156, 161, 162, 164n1

INDEX | 261

Child Protective Services, 172
Children: asymmetric treatment of, 44; complicated reunification, 173; cultural identity, 171; *de facto* deportees, 16; of deportable aliens, 51n4; deportation effects, 23; detention effects, 23; emotional well-being, academic performance, health status, 170; in foster care, 125, 148, 197; hardship and, 45; ICAN, 181; ICE and, 10, 171; INA defining child, 42–43; left behind, 37, 156, 168, 193, 196, 199–202, 210, 215–18, 245; of Mayan undocumented workers, 217; mental health and, 180–81; migration effects, 23; in mixed-status families, 23, 48, 148, 155, 193; numbers in immigrant families, 46; parent-child relationship, 35, 43, 49, 51n7; raids and, 39–41; right to reunite with parents, 219; social benefits for, 47–48; social isolation, 40; special immigrant juvenile status, 162; of transnational families, 168; of unauthorized migrants, 46–47, 170–71; undocumented, 48, 132, 227; of undocumented migrants, 14, 19, 125
Child welfare system, 49, 161, 163, 173
CHRIJ. *See* Center for Human Rights & International Justice
Christianity, 240
CIA. *See* Central Intelligence Agency
Cisneros, Henry, 132
Civil Immigration Detention Standards, 65
Clinician bias, 178
Clinton administration, 15, 196
Cognitive behavioral therapy (CBT), 180, 181
Cold War, 231
Coleman, Norm, 130
Collaborations: educator, xxi–xxii; goal-setting, 179; interdisciplinary, 151–54, 157, 164, 254; with NGOs, 10, 16, 202, 211, 213, 254

Commission for Historical Clarification (CEH), 201
Commitment, 68, 70–73
Community lawyering, 164
Competency, 69–70
Congressional Budget Office (CBO), 133
Congressional Hispanic Caucus (CHC), xii
Constitution, US, 34, 107
Consular Consolidated Database, 122
Consular Lookout and Support System, 122
Contempt authority rules, 102–3
Conundrum of confidentiality, 161
Corbin, James R., 161
Corker, Bob, 133
Corrections: ACA, 66; case law, 79, 81; courts and, 58–60; facilities, 76–77; hands-off, hands-on, one-hand-on eras, 58–59; improving, 65; standards, 66, 73, 84n32; systems, 68, 71. *See also* Incarceration
Counsel, right to, 11
Countries-of-citizenship, 228–30, 243
Courts: corrections and, 58–60; detention history and, 60–62; DHS functioning in, 102; family, 49, 161; IACHR, 63; intervention waning, 71. *See also* Attorneys; Immigration Courts; Immigration Judges; Supreme Court, US
Crime control, 12
Criminal aliens, 11, 17, 85n37
Cultural carriers, 236
Custody law, 37; mixed-status families and, 48–49
Customs and Border Protection (CBP), 10

DACA. *See* Deferred Action for Childhood Arrivals
De facto deportees, xx, 16, 148, 197, 229
Deferred Action for Childhood Arrivals (DACA), xviii, 9, 128
Democratic Party, 113, 128

Department of Homeland Security (DHS), 89; Border Patrol and, 117; contempt authority rules and, 102–3; databases, 122–23, 198; detention facilities, 65; detention standards, 66; function in court, 102; immigration issues, 90; investigative branch, 171; recommendations for ICE, 71–72; representatives, 98–99; on undocumented persons, xxviin2; workplace resources, 101

Department of Justice (DOJ): Bureau of Prisons, 65–66; criminal violations and, 60; Government Performance and Results Act compliance, 96–97; Immigration Courts and, 90, 92, 101; Immigration Judges and, 105; implementing authority, 102; Legal Orientation program, 79; mission statement, 110n5; setting case completion goals, 97

Department of Labor, US, 115

Departure bar, 105

Deportable migrants, 18, 51n4, 232

Deportation: Bush, George W., administration and, 15; Clinton administration and, 15, 196; as death sentence, 90; defined, 10; effects on children, 23; extended border control, 10–12; failing families before, 41–45; fast-track, 104, 156; goals, 12; Guatemala migrant view of, 210–18; harshness of system example, 6–9; Immigration law, families and, 35–41; impact on community, 174; increasing numbers, 14–15, 148; lack of rights, 11; lawful residents and, 13–16; mental health and, 176–78; mental health workers and, 181; nation of, 2–4; nature and limits of law, 8–9; Obama administration and, 15, 121, 127, 197; overview, 10–17; post-entry social control, 10–11; psychological consequences, 205; questions and issues, 1–2; record-breaking numbers, 113; Salvadoran migrants, 24; Supreme Court on, 5–6; transnational families and, 172–74; trauma exposure, 174–75; unauthorized migrants and, 172; wrongful, 5–6. *See also* Detention; Removal

Deportation delirium: comparing 1920s and current eras, 4–5; when to speak of, 4

Deportees: *de facto*, xx, 16, 148, 197, 229; length of residence, 13; PAR with, 17–24

Deportees, legal and social work response: biopsychosocial assessments, 159–60; community lawyering, 164; confidentiality responsibilities, 153–54; conundrum of confidentiality and, 161; deferred action status, 157; definition of client, 152–53; deportation numbers, 148–49; ethical standards, 147, 152; humanitarian parole, 163; human rights approach, 152; integrative approach to immigrants and families, 154–63; interdisciplinary collaboration challenges, 151–54; legal case assessments, 149–50; overview, 147; professional lines intersecting model, 154–57; social work case assessments, 150–51; social workers as legal team members model, 157–63; task delineations, 153; three-stage approach, 151

Depression, 177, 180

Detention, 2; accountability, 80–82; alternate forms, 75; capacity, 68–69; commitment, 70–73; competency, 69–70; corrections and US courts history, 58–60; criminal incarceration difference, 57; DHS standards, 66; discipline, 71; due-process protection, 61–62; effects on children, 23; as exceptional measure, 63; facilities, 60–61, 65; government standards, 64–65; Guatemala migrant view of,

210–18; health-care system, 77–78; history and US courts, 60–62; human rights standards for immigrants, 62–64; ICE and, 57–58; immigration enforcement and, 20; management, 76–77; mandatory, 159; mental health and, 171–72, 176–78; mental health workers and, 181; not for punishment, 60; overview, 57–58; population management, 73–76; professional standards, 64–67; programs management, 78–79; psychological consequences, 205; record-breaking numbers, 113; special populations, 79–80; strengths and opportunities for improvement, 67–73; summary and suggestions, 73–82; transnational families and, 172–74; unauthorized migrants in, 171–72. *See also* Incarceration

Detention officer (DO), 80

DHS. *See* Department of Homeland Security

Discrimination, 23, 151–52, 170, 174–75, 217. *See also* Racism; Stigma

Displacement, 169, 175, 206

DO. *See* Detention officer

DOJ. *See* Department of Justice

Domestic violence, 16, 151, 175

Dow, Mark, 20

DREAMers, 127–28, 132. *See also* DACA

Driver's licenses, xviii

Due process, 52n17, 61–64

EGP. *See* Guerrilla Army of the Poor

Enforcement Integrated Database, 122–23

English-as-a-Second Language classes, 79. *See also* English for Speakers of Other Languages

English for Speakers of Other Languages, 16

EOIR. *See* Executive Office for Immigration Review

Equitable tolling, 106

Evangelical Immigration Table, 129–30

Even-handed sanctions authority, 101–3

Evidence: evidence-based treatments, 180; illegally seized, 11; practice-based, 179–80; secret, 197

Exceptional and extremely unusual hardship, 36–38, 89–90

Executive Office for Immigration Review (EOIR), 92, 94

Expedited removal, 11, 104

Ex post facto laws, 11

Faith-based groups, xxii

Falla, Ricardo, 203

Families: aliens and, 43; integrity, 35; legal and social work integrative approach, 154–63; mental health and, 180–81; nontraditional, 48; nuclear, 38–39; separation, 5, 14, 37, 40, 50, 116, 208–10; Supreme Court on, 34–35; therapy techniques, 181; UDHR on, 51n1. *See also* Immigration law, families and; Left behind families; Mixed-status families; Transnational families

Family-based immigration system, 116

Family courts, 49, 161

Family law, 37, 49

Family-sponsored immigration, 43–44, 52n14

Fast-track deportation, 104, 156

Federal Bar Association, 108

Federal poverty level (FPL), 169

Film: educating beyond classroom, xxii; raising awareness through educator collaborations, xxi–xxii; synthesizing complex issues, xxii

Forced migration, 22, 214, 218–19

Forensic: contexts, 181; mistakes, 5

Foster care, 125, 148, 197

FPL. *See* Federal poverty level

Funes, Mauricio, 233

FWD.us, 129

Gallardo, Beatriz, *xvi*
Gangs, 228; 18th St., 232; Latino, 232; MS-13, 232, 237, 241–42; new American diaspora and, 242; Salvadoran migrants and, 232, 236–41; zero-tolerance, 233
GAO. *See* Government Accountability Office
Globalization, 1, 234
Goldman, Emma, 4
Government: abuse, 4; bias allegations, 99–100, 109; detention standards, 64–65. *See also* Department of Homeland Security; Department of Justice; Immigration Courts; Immigration Judges; Immigration law, families and; Supreme Court, US
Government Accountability Office (GAO), 119
Government Performance and Results Act, 93, 96–97
Gowdy, Trey, 134
Green card holders, 158
Grief, 177, 181
Guatemalan migrants, 232; Anglo-Guatemalan gap, xvi; asylum and, 201; EGP and, 200; family separations, 210; impact on left-behind families, 215–18; mixed-status families, 218; PAR workshops, 204; patterns and profiles, 210–14; poverty and, 207–8, 214–15; racism and, 207–8; second war and, 207; state-sponsored violence and, 206–7; transnational families, 194–95, 218; undocumented workers, xii, 154–57, 199–200; views on detention and deportation, 210–18; workplace raids and, 207, 219. *See also* Mayan undocumented workers
Guerrilla Army of the Poor (EGP), 200
Gutiérrez, Luis V., xii

Hands-off corrections, 58–59
Hands-on corrections, 58–59
Hardship: children and, 45; exceptional and extremely unusual, 36–38, 89–90
Hashmi v. Attorney General of the United States, 95–96
Health-care system, 72, 75, 77–78
Heavy hand (*Mano Dura*), 237
Hoeven, John, 133
Honduran migrants, 201, 232
Hoover, J. Edgar, 4
Human capital, 213. *See also* Social capital
Humanitarian openness, 4
Humanitarian parole, 163
Human rights, xv, 219; abuse, 232; IBHR, 62; Inter-American Commission on Human Rights, 63–64, 162; international, 1; in legal and social work response, 152; MHRP, 16; Special Rapporteur on the Human Rights of Migrant Workers, 63; standards for immigrants, 62–64; violations, 175; worker's, xv. *See also* Universal Declaration of Human Rights
Human Rights Watch, 12, 148
Human Subjects Review Board, 205
Hybrid Americans, 229

IBHR. *See* International Bill of Human Rights
ICAN. *See* Immigrant Children's Affirmative Network
ICCPR. *See* International Covenant on Civil and Political Rights
ICE. *See* Immigration and Customs Enforcement
IDENT, 122
Identity: bicultural, 160; cultural identity of children, 171. *See also* Acculturation
IFSW. *See* International Federation of Social Workers
Illegal Immigrant Reform and Immigrant Responsibility Act (IIRIRA), 15, 103, 105–6, 196
IMF. *See* International Monetary Fund

Immigrant Children's Affirmative Network (ICAN), 181
Immigrant Rights Clinic, 197
Immigrants: bicultural identity and, 160; children in families, 46; human rights standards for, 62–64; ICE categories, 126; legal and social work integrative approach, 154–63; United States as nation of, 2–3. *See also* Migrants
Immigration: *abUsed: The Postville Raid* as deterrent, xxiv–xxv; American Immigration Lawyers Association, 108; Arizona enforcement legislation, 119–20; attorneys, 22; BIA, 96, 99, 105, 107; Border Security, Economic Opportunity and Immigration Modernization Act, 132–34; broken system, 125–26; Civil Immigration Detention Standards, 65; criminalizing, 233; DHS issues, 90; enforcement, 20; EOIR, 92, 94; Evangelical Immigration Table, 129–30; family-based system, 116; family-sponsored, 43–44, 52n14; National Immigration Forum, 130–31; offenders, 120; USCIS, 128. *See also* Migration
Immigration Act of 1990, 114
Immigration and Customs Enforcement (ICE), xi–xii; accountability operating principles, 80–82; admissions and releases, 66; Agriprocessors, Inc. actions, xxii; aliens detained by, 57, 60–61, 66–67, 70–75, 77, 84n29; ankle bracelets, xxvi; audits, 72; bed census, 71–72, 83n7; budget for 2004-2013, *119*, 120; from catch and release to catch and remove, 70; categories of immigrants and, 126; children and, 10, 171; custody warrant, 61; delegation by, 81; detainees as criminals, 67; detention and, 57–58; detention facilities, 60–61, 67; detention management, 76–77; DHS recommendations for, 71–72; discharge planning, 79; health-care system and, 72, 75, 77–78; impact of polices, 194; INA empowering, 60; lack of tracking, 69; management tools, 71; needs assessment, 72; Office of Enforcement and Removal Operations, 197; online locator, 73; performance-based standards, 75, 83n10; population management, 73–76; programs management, 78–79; prosecutorial discretion, 126–27; required services, 79; risk assessment, 73, 75; second war with, 18, 207; workplace raids, 155, 171, 172–73
Immigration and National Act (INA), 35–36, 41; defining child, 42–43; ICE empowered by, 60
Immigration and Naturalization Service (INS), 92; Border Patrol and, 117; contempt authority, 102–3; Immigration Courts and, 108; Immigration Judges and, 98
Immigration Courts, 2; adjudication priorities, 93–94; appearances before, 156; Article I Court proposal, 108–9; co-locations, 98–99; departure bar, 105; DOJ and, 90, 92, 101; INS and, 108; noncitizens before, 89; public perception of, 99; revisiting findings, 159; uniqueness, 91
Immigration Judges, 6–7, 11, 159; asylum and, 89; case completion goals, 92–97; conflicts with law enforcement agency, 97–101; Congress and immigration reform, 107–9; DOJ and, 105; even-handed sanctions authority, 101–3; government bias allegations, 99–100, 109; impartiality, 99, 102; INS and, 98; law clerks, 108; limitation of powers, 12; mission, 91; NAIJ, 103, 110; overview, 89–92; pending cases, 89; performance evaluations, 96, 99–100; post-deportation matters, 103–7; requirements, 91; treated as attorneys, 92, 96; unclear authority, 106; workload, 91

Immigration law, families and: asymmetric treatment of adults and children, 44; cross-border difficulties, 49; enforcement and deportation, 35–41; failing families before deportation, 41–45; family law and, 49; family-sponsored immigration, 43–44, 52n14; harsh realities of, 46–48; legal institutions and systems, 48–50; loss and separation, 36; nontraditional families and, 38; ongoing impacts, 45–50; overview, 33–34; post-deportation consequences, 41, 45; privileged narratives, 34–45; proving exceptional and extremely unusual hardship, 36–38; raids and, 39–41; wasted resources, 50. *See also* Deportees, legal and social work response

Immigration reform, xviii, 21, 92; Bibles, Badges and Business for Immigration Reform, 131; Border Security, Economic Opportunity and Immigration Modernization Act, 132–34; broken immigration system, *114*; change during 2012 election, 128–29; Congress and, 107–9; current broken immigration system, 116–21; enforcement consequences and collateral damage, 123–25; expanded intelligence sharing and, 121–23; Latinos and, 127–29; Operation Streamline, 124–25; overview, 113–17; priorities in absence of reform, 125–28; Republican Party and, 130; SAFE Act and, 134; speaking out on, 129–32

INA. *See* Immigration and National Act

Incarceration: aliens and, 60; of civil prisoners, 63; criminal, 57; pre-trial and sentenced inmates, 64; strengths and opportunities for improvement, 67–73

INS. *See* Immigration and Naturalization Service

Integrated Automated Fingerprint Identification System, 122

Intelligence sharing, 121–23

Inter-American Commission on Human Rights, 63–64, 162

Inter-American Court of Human Rights (IACHR), 63

International Bill of Human Rights (IBHR), 62

International Covenant on Civil and Political Rights (ICCPR), 8, 62–64

International Covenant on Economic, Social and Cultural Rights, 62

International Federation of Social Workers (IFSW), 152

International Monetary Fund (IMF), 194–95

Iowa Work Force Development, xix

Irregular migrants, 63

Johnson, Kevin, 39

Judulang v. Holder, 91

Jury trial, 11

Kennedy, John F., 3

Knowledge integration model, 16

Know Your Rights (KYR), xxiii, 16, 23, 204, 210

Labor, 115; abuse, xviii; child labor violations, xix, xx; rights, xviii. *See also* Workers

Latinos, 113, 180, 230; gangs, 232; immigration reform and, 127–29; National Latino Evangelical Coalition, 130

Laws: case law, 79, 81; custody, 37, 48–49; ex post facto, 11; family law, 37, 49; rule of law, 1, 14; three strikes, 60. *See also* Immigration law, families and; *specific laws and acts*

Lawyers. *See* Attorneys

Left behind families, xii, xv, 19, 23, 37, 168; children of, 193, 196, 199–202; of Guatemala migrants, 215–18; parent promises to children, 216–17. *See also* Transnational families

Legal Permanent Resident (LPR), 168
Lethal force, 78
LPR. *See* Legal Permanent Resident

Mandatory detention, 159
Mano Dura (heavy hand), 237
Mara Salvatrucha 13 (MS-13), 232, 237, 241–42
Massey, Douglas, 125
Mayan undocumented workers, xii, 154–57, 199; children of, 217; Mayan genocide and, 201; racism and, 217
Memoranda of Agreement (MOAs), 198
Mental health: children and, 180–81; clinical assessment, 178; clinician bias and, 178; collaborative goal-setting for, 179; deportation and, 176–78; detention and, 171–72, 176–78; evidence-based treatments, 180; families and, 180–81; family therapy techniques, 181; practice-based evidence and, 179–80; services, 178; therapeutic relationships, 178–79; trauma and, 175; treatment of symptoms, 179–80; unauthorized migrants and, 169–74; workers in forensic contexts, 181–82
Mexican border, 202
Mexican migrants, 125, 213, 232
MHRP. *See* Migration and Human Rights Project
Migrants: community-based work with, 21; decisions to leave home, 21, xxviin4; deportable, 18, 51n4, 232; Honduran, 232; irregular, 63; lives of, 21; Mexico, 125, 213, 232; PAR with, 17–24; psychosocial interventions, 22; voluntary return, xv, 148, 229; well-being, 183; workers, 12, 63. *See also* Guatemalan migrants; Immigrants; Push and/or pull factors; Salvadoran migrants; Unauthorized migrants; Undocumented migrants

Migration: alternatives models, xxv; effects on children, 23; forced, 218–19; Guatemalan migrants, 218, 232; Salvadoran migrants, 231–33; stressors, 177; trauma exposure, 174–75
Migration and Human Rights Project (MHRP), 16
Miller, Thomas H., *xix*
Miller, Tom, *xix*
Mixed-status families, 14, 15, 23, 193–96; challenges, 209, 217–18; characteristics, 168–69; children in, 148; custody law and, 48–49; decisions to make, 168–69; Guatemala migrants, 218; legal challenges, 155–56; PAR and, 202–5, 208–10; population, 45, 46, 48; Salvadoran migrants, 218. *See also* Transnational families
MOAs. *See* Memoranda of Agreement
Model Rules of Professional Conduct, 152–54, 161
Montt, Efraín Ríos, 200
Morton, John, 126
MS-13. *See* Mara Salvatrucha 13

NAFTA. *See* North American Free Trade Agreement
NAIJ. *See* National Association of Immigration Judges
Napolitano, Janet, 123–24, 127–28
NASW. *See* National Association of Social Workers Code of Ethics
National Association of Immigration Judges (NAIJ), 103, 110, 110n1
National Association of Social Workers Code of Ethics (NASW), 151–52
National Association of Women Judges (NAWJ), 108
National Immigration Forum, 130–31
National Latino Evangelical Coalition, 130
National security, 12, 90, 126, 197
Nativism, 3, 243

Naturalization, 7, 157, 158. *See also* Immigration and Naturalization Service
NAWJ. *See* National Association of Women Judges
New American diaspora, 24; call centers and, 240–41; criminalization of, 238; gangs and, 242; insecurity of, 233; limits and potential, 242–45; Salvadoran migrants, 228–31, 236, 239–40, 242–45; stigma, 237
Nixon administration, 121
Nken v. Holder, 107
Noncitizens, 46–48, 52n16; immigration cases, 197; legal advice for, 90; removal, 105–6; status, 229
Nontraditional families, 38
Norquist, Grover, 130
North American Free Trade Agreement (NAFTA), 194
Nuclear families, 38–39
Nutrition program, xx

OAS. *See* Organization of American States
Obama administration: Border Patrol emergency funding, 118–19; broken immigration system and, 125–26; DACA, xviii, 9, 128; deportation and, 15, 121, 127, 197; extended border control and, 10–11; federal and local initiatives, 198–99; increased border enforcement and, 119–20; raids and, 198; unauthorized migrants and, 5; undocumented migrants and, 5, 128
Office of Professional Responsibility (OPR), 100
One-hand-on corrections, 58–59
Operation Streamline, 124–25
OPR. *See* Office of Professional Responsibility
Organization of American States (OAS), 63–64
Organizing for Action, 132
Other mothers, 168

Padilla v. Kentucky, 5–6, 12, 24n2, 90
Palmer, Mitchell, 4
PAR. *See* Participatory action research
Parent-child relationship, 35, 43, 49, 51n7
Participatory action research (PAR), *195*; community surveys, 211, *212*, 213–14; contributing to change, 18; Guatemala migrant view of detention and deportation, 210–18; implications and challenges, 218–19; life project, 17; with migrants and deportees, 17–24; mixed-status families and, 193, 202–5, 208; narration of experiences, 205–10; overview, 193–96; processes, 204–5; strategies and reflexive practices, 17; transnational families and, 193, 199–205; unauthorized migrants, 196–99, 202–5; workshops, 204
Partnership for a New American Economy, 129
Permanent residents, 158–59
Personal Responsibility and Work Opportunity Reconciliation Act (PRWORA), 15
Person in environment, 150
Play therapy, 161
Population management, 73–76
Post, Louis, 4
Post-entry social control, 10–13
Posttraumatic Stress Disorder (PTSD), 176–77, 180
Postville Solidarity march, *xv*
Poverty, 23; FPL, 169; Guatemala migrants and, 207–8, 214–15; Salvadoran migrants and, 207; unauthorized migrants, 170; undocumented migrants and, 47
Practice-based evidence, 179–80
Preston, Julia, xi
Price, David, 118
Prisoner Litigation Reform Act, 60, 84n34
Prison Rape Elimination Act, 65, 66, 77, 84n28

Prosecutorial discretion, 111n8, 126–28
PRWORA. *See* Personal Responsibility and Work Opportunity Reconciliation Act
Psycho-cultural belonging, 241
Psychosocial: biopsychosocial assessments, 159–60; effects, 23, 195, 215–18, 257; evaluation, 158; interventions, 22; mental health and, 167; services, 6; theory, 164, 167; well-being, 183
PTSD. *See* Posttraumatic Stress Disorder
Public assistance, 47
Push and/or pull factors, 151, 194, 199, 202, 231

Racism, 23, 175, 179, 201, 203; Guatemalan migrants and, 207–8; Mayan undocumented workers and, 217; racial profiling, 134, 170; racist, 238
Raids: children and, 39–41; Guatemalan migrants and, 207, 219; ICE workplace, 155, 171, 172–73; Obama administration and, 198; silent, 198. *See also abUsed: The Postville Raid*
Rakoff, Jed, 107
Reagan administration, 231
Reentry, 44; re-migration, 228, 241–42, 245; ten-year bar, 116
Refugees, 174, 180, 231–32
Reinstatement of removal, 11
Religious Land Use and Institutionalized Persons Act, 60, 77
Removal, 10, 24n1; as banishment, 229; cancellation of, 36–37, 51n3, 227, 245; expedited, 11, 104; fiscal years 1997-2011, *121*; of noncitizens, 105–6; Office of Enforcement and Removal Operations, 197; of parents, 36; reinstatement of, 11; Salvadoran migrants, 231–33
Rendell, Edward, 132
Republican Party, 113, 127, 128; immigration reform and, 130
Resiliency, 176, 179, 180

Restrictionist sentiment, 3–4, 120
Retroactivity, 6–7
Returnee Integration Support Center (RISC), 160
Reverse culture shock, 235, 243
Rice, Condoleezza, 132
Rights: of children to reunite with parents, 219; to counsel, 11; ICCPR, 8, 62–64; Immigrant Rights Clinic, 197; International Covenant on Economic, Social and Cultural Rights, 62; KYR, 204, 210; labor, xviii; lack of in deportation, 11; violations, xxvi. *See also* Human rights; Know Your Rights
RISC. *See* Returnee Integration Support Center
Rubio, Marco, 127
Rule of law, 1, 14

SAFE Act. *See* Strengthen and Fortify Enforcement Act
Saint Bridget's Catholic Church, xi–xii
Salvadoran migrants, 199, 203; Christianity and, 240; coping mechanisms, 239–42; criminalizing immigration, 233; deportable status, 232; deportations, 24; family separations, 208–9; gangs and, 232, 236–41; migration and removal, 231–33; mixed-status families, 218; new American diaspora, 228–31, 236, 239–40, 242–45; overview, 227–31; poverty and, 207; refugee status, 231–32; reintegration, 244; re-migration, 241–42, 245; social remittances from US, 233–36, 243; stigma, 232; tattoos and, 228, 231, 235–40; transnational families, 218; unwelcome interventions for, 236–38; violence threats and, 206
SC. *See* Secure Communities
School absenteeism, 40
School desegregation, 59
Second war, 18, 207
Secret evidence, 197

Secure Communities (SC), 12–13, 198
Selective prosecution, 11
Senate Bill 744, 92, 109
Sending countries, xvii, xviii, 196, 199, 206
Sentenced home, 218
Separation, 150; family, 5, 14, 37, 40, 50, 116, 208–10; forced, 51n6, 174; immigration law and, 36
Silent raids, 198
Smart entry enforcement, 11
Smith, Lamar, 100
Social capital, 229, 231, 240, 244; human or cultural capital, 240
Social remittances, 229–30, 233–36, 243; positive or negative, 234, 236
Social services, 2, 148–49, 156–57, 168, 170, 174
Social support, 241
Social work: person in environment and, 150; perspective and emphasis, 21–23. *See also* Deportees, legal and social work response
Soros Foundation, xxiii
Southern Baptist Convention, 130, xxviiin6
Special immigrant juvenile status, 162
Special populations, 79–80
State compacts, 131
State Department, US, 122–23
Status: adjustment of, 44; child health, 170; deferred action, 157; deportable, 232; noncitizens, 229; refugee, 231–32; special immigrant juvenile, 162; unauthorized migrants, 169–71, 183n1. *See also* Mixed-status families
Stigma, 229; eliminating, 245; escaping, 242; new American diaspora, 237; reducing social, 240, 244; Salvadoran migrants, 232. *See also* Discrimination; Racism
Strengthen and Fortify Enforcement Act (SAFE Act), 134

Student and Exchange Visitor Information System, 122
Substance abuse, 169, 227
Super heavy hand (*Super Mano Dura*), 237
Super Mano Dura (Super heavy hand), 237
Supreme Court, US, 12, 107; on aggravated felony, 159; on banishment, 90; on deportation, 5–6; on due process, 61–62; on families, 34–35. *See also specific cases*

Tattoos, 228, 231, 235–40
TECS, 122
Terrorism, 90; AEDPA, 15, 196; Terrorist Screening Database, 122; war on terror, 117. *See also* Uniting and Strengthening America by Providing Appropriate Tools Required to Intercept and Obstruct Terrorism Act
Three strikes laws, 60
Tolstoy, Leo, 33
Tombs jail riot, 59
Tough on crime era, 60
Transnational families, xxi, 23; challenges and left-behind children, 168, 209; country conditions and events, 167; deportation and, 172–74; detention and, 172–74; Guatemala migrants, 194–95, 218; kidnapping and murder, 173; other mothers and, 168; PAR with, 193, 199–205, 208–10; realities of, 1; Salvadoran migrants, 218; in shadows, 2. *See also* Left behind families
Trauma: avoidance symptoms, 182; exposure during deportation, 174–75; mental health and, 175; migration and, 174–75; PTSD, 176–77, 180; traumatic grief, 181
Truth-in-sentencing, 59–60

UDHR. *See* Universal Declaration of Human Rights
UN. *See* United Nations
Unauthorized migrants, 52n15; challenges facing, xvii; characteristics, 169;

children of, 46–47, 170–71; deportation and, 172; in detention, 171–72; fear of, xxvii; fear of police, xix, 175; mental health and, 169–74; Obama administration and, 5; PAR and, 196–99, 202–5; poverty, 170; protective factors, 176; in shadows, 199; status, 169–71, 183n1. *See also* Undocumented migrants

Undocumented migrants, xxviin2; *abUsed: The Postville Raid* for working with, xxiii; challenges and labor rights, xviii; children in foster care, 125; children of, 14, 19; death of, 125; defending, 22; fear of, xxvii; future, 9; Guatemalan undocumented workers, xii, 154–57, 199–200; numbers, 116; Obama administration and, 5, 128; other worker visas and, 115; poverty and, 47; rights violations, xxvi; survival challenges, 2; unclear future, 9; workers, xi–xii. *See also* Unauthorized migrants

United Fruit Company, 200

United Nations (UN): General Assembly, 62; Special Rapporteur on the Human Rights of Migrant Workers, 63

Uniting and Strengthening America by Providing Appropriate Tools Required to Intercept and Obstruct Terrorism Act (USA PATRIOT Act), 15, 196–97

Universal Declaration of Human Rights (UDHR), 8; adoption of, 62; on families, 51n1

USA PATRIOT ACT. *See* Uniting and Strengthening America by Providing Appropriate Tools Required to Intercept and Obstruct Terrorism Act

USCIS. *See* US Citizenship and Immigration Services

US Citizenship and Immigration Services (USCIS), 128

US-VISIT, 122

The U-Turn, xix–xx

U visas, xviii–xix, xxiii, 181

VAWA. *See* Violence Against Women Act

Vincent, Peter, 126

Violence: at Agriprocessors, Inc., Postville, IA, xx; border, 118–19; Cambodia, 177; domestic, 16, 151, 175; Guatemala migrants and, 206–7; lethal force, 78; threats to Salvadoran migrants, 206

Violence Against Women Act (VAWA), xviii, 181–82

Visas: eligibility, 44; for family-based immigration, 116; for foreign professionals, 114–15; other worker, 115; petitioning for, 41–42; review process, 122; temporary, 115; U visas, xviii–xix, xxiii, 181; visitor, 155, 163

Voluntary return migrants, xv, 148, 229

Wages, xvii–xviii, 16, 50, 200, 232, 240

War on terror, 117

Washington, George, 4

West, Arvin, 133

Workers: IFSW, 152; mental health, 181–82; migrant, 12, 63; other worker visas, 115; in temporary work programs, xviii. *See also* Labor; Mayan undocumented workers

World Bank, 195

World Channel America Reframed Program, xxiii

Xenophobia, 175, 179. *See also* Discrimination; Racism

Zadvydas v. Davis, 57, 60, 61, 64, 85n38

Zero-tolerance policies, 60, 233

Zuckerberg, Mark, 129